CELEBRATING THE FOURTH

CELEBRATING THE FOURTH

Independence Day

and the Rites of Nationalism

in the Early Republic

LEN TRAVERS

UNIVERSITY OF MASSACHUSETTS PRESS
Amherst

This book is published with the support and cooperation of the Massachusetts
Historical Society and the University of Massachusetts Boston.

Copyright © 1997 by
The University of Massachusetts Press
All rights reserved
Printed in the United States of America
LC 96-18431
ISBN 1-55849-060-4
Designed by Sally Ann Nichols
Printed and bound by Braun-Brumfield, Inc.
Library of Congress Cataloging-in-Publication Data

    Travers, Len, 1952—
       Celebrating the fourth : Independence Day and the rites
    of Nationalism in the Early Republic / Len Travers.
        p. cm.
       Includes bibliographical references and index.
       ISBN 1-55849-060-4 (alk. paper)
       1. Fourth of July celebrations—History. I. Title.
    E286.A184   1997
    394.2'634—dc20   96-18431
                                             CIP

British Library Cataloguing in Publication data are available.

To Mom and Dad, who had faith in their prodigal son.
And to Carolyn.

CONTENTS

ACKNOWLEDGMENTS

It is an unfortunate fact that few people read acknowledgment pages, and that's a pity. By the time an author gets to the stage of writing this part of a manuscript, he has a sharpened sense of indebtedness to a raft of people whose names do not appear on the cover, but whose contribution to the finished work was nevertheless vital. It is a last chance for the author to pay the properly humble respects to the advisers, friends, colleagues, librarians, and archivists who saved him so much work or embarrassment, and he would like the world to know their worth.

Alan Taylor deserves most of the credit for encouraging the growth of what began as a seminar paper, and none of the blame that may accrue for what it has become. With patient exhortation and much red ink, he prodded me to rethink, revise, rewrite, and publish, and has almost cured me of my abuse of the passive voice. Without his continual encouragement and cajoling (like nagging, but in a positive way), this study might not have expanded far beyond the limits of its original geographic and conceptual bounds. His conscientious attention to his students' professional welfare brought me opportunities to present earlier versions of this study at the Salem Conference, and to the Boston Area Early American History Seminar, which in turn brought my work to the attention of Paul Wright, of the University of Massachusetts Press. The result you have before you.

At Professor Taylor's urging, I submitted the revised seminar paper for inclusion in the Ninth Salem Conference schedule. Barbara Ward's acceptance of that paper brought my topic much-needed exposure and criticism from colleagues. The Essex Institute later published the paper in its journal.

In each of the cities singled out in these pages for study, I received open-handed aid and advice. My sincere thanks goes to the staffs of the Massachusetts Historical Society, the Mugar Library at Boston University, and the Boston Public Library; the American Antiquarian Society in Worcester; The Library Company and the Historical Society of Pennsylvania in Philadelphia; and the Library Company of Charleston, the South Carolina Historical Society, and the College of Charleston, for their patient and professional help. Gathering Philadelphia material was immeasurably aided by a fellowship from the Philadelphia Center for Early American Studies at the University of Pennsylvania, and from Wayne Bodle's helpful advice. In Charleston, C. Patton Hash was my guide through the collections in the Charleston Historical Society. Conrad Wright, my boss at the Massachusetts Historical Society, generously extended me the time needed for rewrites.

Several readers of the manuscript provided extremely helpful advice and much-appreciated encouragement: Robert St. George, Richard Fox, Shirley Wajda, Marilyn Halter, Anita Tien, Paul Wright, Matthew Dennis, and fellow musketeers Martha MacNamara and Nancy Lee Nelson. Following their leads enriched the study, alerted me to alternative interpretations, and saved me from more than a few outright gaffes.

I save the best for last. Carolyn Freeman Travers has provided unflinching support (in every sense) for this project since its inception. She gave me a second opinion when I asked for it, solitude when I needed it, and confidence when I lacked it. I am proudest of all to acknowledge her love and friendship.

INTRODUCTION

> The culture of a people is an ensemble of texts,
> themselves ensembles, which the anthropologist
> strains to read over the shoulders of those to whom
> they more properly belong.
>
> CLIFFORD GEERTZ, *MYTH, SYMBOL, AND CULTURE*

Charles William Janson arrived in Boston on July 3, 1793, in no very good mood. This was the Englishman's first trip to the United States, and his initial impressions were far from positive. He was unaccustomed to the midsummer heat and may have suffered a mild heat stroke from the exertion of getting his baggage ashore. Arriving at his lodgings in "a most profuse perspiration," he threw himself upon the bed, "from which I had no inclination to rise." He could eat no supper, taking only large quantities of weak punch and tea. Even sleep eluded him, for the night was still and brought no relief from the oppressive warmth and humidity, nor from the hordes of mosquitoes that plagued him until dawn.

Compounding Janson's misery were his landlady's three daughters. No sooner, it seemed to him, had he fallen asleep when one of them, "a pert virgin," rapped on his door and brightly demanded that he rise and join the festivities. Outside, church bells rang and cannon from nearby Fort Hill fired salutes; only Janson's utter exhaustion could have allowed him to sleep through the din. Struggling to collect his thoughts, he recalled that this day was July 4—the Americans' In-

1

dependence Day—and that he had arrived just in time for it. The realization and the young lady's interruption were equally unwelcome. Janson attempted to beg off, protesting his incapacity and pleading for more tea. His tormentor was not to be put off, however. Despite Janson's appeals, "nothing could be obtained, without a promise of rising." Yielding to this extortion, he rose and dressed himself for what already promised to be another hot day. At the breakfast table the three sisters besieged Janson with questions, "adding a torrent of empty compliments and insipid jokes," to which he responded as well as his desperately frayed nerves would allow him. In the course of the conversation it dawned on Janson that the scheming sisters intended to dragoon him into escorting them about the town during the celebrations, "to make of me as their gallant." Nothing could have pleased him less. In his present condition, Janson found the girls' buoyant cheerfulness and Yankee familiarity especially insufferable. Pleading a promise to call upon a fellow traveler that morning, Janson somewhat ungraciously detached himself from his ardent hosts.

After mutual commiserations with his friend, who had spent an equally unpleasant night, the two Britons reluctantly decided it would be "good policy to appear in public" on this day, "that on no account should we give cause of offense" to the people of Boston. Shielding themselves from the merciless sun with parasols ("an indispensable article in America"), they joined the crowd gathering at the Mall, a fashionable promenade on the edge of Boston Common, to watch the militia companies perform. The marching, wheeling, and volley firing received mixed reviews from the Englishmen, but the Bostonians cheered and applauded their fellow townsmen enthusiastically. The visitors then followed a large procession to hear the town-sponsored oration. The meeting house selected for the auditorium was terribly crowded, and Janson and his friend were barely able to squeeze inside the doors. Forced to stand in the stultifying closeness at the rear of the building, they could barely hear the orator, but what they heard was objectionable enough. The address "was abundantly interlarded with invective against England for her oppression before, and cruelties during the revolutionary war. I could not see the policy of this method of proceeding."[1]

Charles Janson was introduced to American political culture in much the same way that one is taught the skill of swimming by being thrown into a pond. Nevertheless, his account of that whirlwind experience gives modern readers a rare glimpse of how the celebration of Independence Day in the early republic appeared to an outsider (albeit a rather grumpy one). His account of the events is simple and descriptive, and without the rhetorical hyperbole of his American contemporaries. Janson's irascible candor does confirm the broad participation cited in Boston's newspaper accounts, however. He alerts his readers to the "great number of citizens of both sexes" that obviously looked forward to the day, and to the spectrum of social orders that he saw involved, from "gentlemen" and "ladies" to his own "boarding-house misses."[2] Additionally, he details many of the public forms of expression that, by 1793, had already become traditionalized in American cities for observing "America's birth-day." But Janson's account also reminds the reader of the insurmountable barrier between the observer of a foreign culture and the culture itself. While Janson could record what he saw and heard, he could not so easily (and to his credit, did not try to) relate what his subjects felt and thought about what they were doing. Janson and his companion were outsiders, and they knew it, and had to be content with drawing tentative conclusions from the evidence of their senses.

Students of the past face similar difficulties. They scrutinize records from the past and from them reconstruct events, but the *experience* of past peoples, what they felt and thought about what they did, can usually only be approached obliquely. Nevertheless, the events that Janson observed on July 4 in Boston two centuries ago are vital clues to understanding American political culture in the post-Revolutionary era. The activities he witnessed constituted a "performance of culture" expressing the beliefs, values, and prevailing social assumptions of the people around him. With the help of Janson and his contemporaries, it is possible to reconstruct much of what Americans said and did on that annual festival. Those actions, as I shall argue, reflected and affected what they felt and thought about themselves as a people, and also what they wanted other people to feel and think about them.[3]

Independence Day was by far the noisiest, most popular, and most important public ritual to emerge in the early American republic. After a decade of fitful starts, the Fourth of July succeeded in becoming "the American Jubilee," a "truly American Festival," overshadowing and even eclipsing local or regional patriotic observances. In 1815, at the close of a second war against Britain, a newspaper correspondent boasted that the nation's entire population of "eight millions of people united in one festive celebration of the National Birth Day."[4] That claim was exaggerated, as we shall see, but certainly July 4 inspired huge numbers of Americans, high and low, to suspend their normal activities in order to participate in the martial displays, parades, public and private dinners, formal orations and fireworks that were part and parcel of a proper observance of July 4. Solemn ceremony mingled with civic abandon as citizens glorified the mythic past, hyperbolized the contemporary, and breathlessly imagined America's future.

The mere fact that Americans elected to set aside a day for an annual commemoration of the Revolution is not in itself surprising. The impulse to identify and to celebrate pivotal events in the history of a people is overpowering and universal.[5] The purpose of this study is not simply to trace the history of a holiday, but to understand the role of Independence Day in the formation and communication of national identity and national consciousness in the early republic.

Public ritual has always had a vital place in American societies and politics.[6] It may be, as David Proctor asserts in his study of late twentieth-century American rhetoric, that the political culture of the United States is a *distinctly* symbolic process, "a chimera of traditions, ritual, and ceremonies that create and energize fundamental national symbols."[7] There is no need, however, to assert a distinctly American predisposition to act out political culture. Lynn Hunt has ably argued that the exercise of political power, as with religious power, has always required symbolic practices, and indeed may be impossible without them. Even in supposedly "unmagical" and "demystified" govern- ments such as democracies, governing "cannot take place without stories, signs, and symbols that convey and reaffirm the legitimacy of governing in thousands of unspoken ways." Reduced to the bare es- sentials, according to Hunt, political legitimacy is nothing more or less than a "general agreement on signs and symbols."[8]

Because ritual is traditionally associated with religious activities, and because modern Americans like to think of themselves as having separated religion from politics long ago, students of history are often unaware of the vital role that ritual has played in American society and politics, and continues to do today.[9] American political culture is the product of a national mythos formulated during the Revolution and crafted by many hands since then. The intensity with which

Americans ritualize that mythos may have diminished over time, but the mythos itself has immense power still.[10] The challenge facing Americans today is to appreciate the unconsciously accepted place of private and especially public ritual in their past and present.

In his introductory work in ritual studies, anthropologist Ronald Grimes referred to a "bewilderment" factor that handicaps the modern student of ritual. We moderns, he maintains, live in times so "ritually poverty-stricken" that we have lost all sense of ritual: "ritual itself has become foreign to us."[11] I disagree. Americans are less self-consciously ritualistic than their ancestors, perhaps, but they are still enthusiastically committed to flag-waving, marching, ribbon-wearing, dressing their windows, bedecking their cars with bumper stickers, and wearing apparel emblazoned with popular slogans or the logos of their favorite sports teams. Americans still invoke long-dead statesmen to support modern political agendas, and invariably use the American flag as a backdrop while doing so. In contrast to Grimes, I argue that any "bewilderment" modern Americans may feel about ritualization arises because their rituals, personal and political, are so ubiquitous and so commonplace as to be virtually invisible; taken for granted. It is far easier to perceive the messages embedded in public ritual, and their functions, at a distance, just as anthropologists study distant peoples first, in order to understand their own. This study crosses time rather than distance to examine the ritual practices surrounding Independence Day in late eighteenth- and early nineteenth-century America.[12]

Previous discussions of Independence Day as a mirror for political culture have concentrated upon July 4 orations.[13] Merle Curti believed that the rhetoric contained in these popular and conveniently printed public speeches "epitomized the whole pattern of American patriotic thought and feeling."[14] More than thirty years later, Kurt Ritter and James Andrews elaborated Curti's argument, maintaining that orations, poetry, and newspaper editorials were legitimate materials for discovering the thoughts of "inarticulate" Americans. Together, claim Ritter and Andrews, these sources constitute a "faithful guide to the convictions of a society," because the authors presumably "know [their] audience."[15] Referring strictly to orations, Robert Hay declared: "this type of literature, written as it was by lawyers, clergymen, college professors, politicians, editors, and ordinary citizens, reflects the opinion of a wide cross section of the public."[16]

Again, I cannot agree. For reasons that will appear in the chapters that follow, Independence Day orations provide evidence that must be used cautiously. Their texts were always prepared for specific audiences, bound by conventions of the discourse, and subject to the writers' political perspectives. Additionally, my own surveys of these public addresses indicate that few, if any, "ordinary citizens" actually performed the task, at least in the seaport cities studied here. Indeed, it is expressly *because* these orations were consistently delivered by lawyers, clergymen, college professors, and politicians that I question their validity as representative of popular belief. Certainly orations were important events on Independence Day, but they constituted only one rite among many. Most July 4 celebrants participated in less didactic activities, such as civil and military processions, dinner parties, fireworks displays, sporting events, and serious drinking bouts. I consider all of these activities in the context of American political culture.

I shall argue that the annual observance of Independence Day served four important functions in the young nation. First, and most obvious, the Fourth of July fixed a specific, pivotal moment in the past from which to date a national existence, and against which to assess the republic's progress. As the Revolution receded into memory, the celebration of the Fourth of July mystically reconnected postwar Americans to an increasingly legendary past.[17] Every year on the official anniversary of the Declaration of Independence, citizens of the new republic ritually acted out their understanding of the American Revolution, its fruits, and of their relation to them.

Second, Independence Day endorsed and cultivated a mythos of national identity and national interests that transcended local and regional concerns, stressing historical and moral origins which Americans assumedly held in common. However various the motivations and outlooks of the newly independent states, Independence Day proclaimed an essential unity and collective destiny born of an overwhelming, shared experience.

Third, the Fourth of July provided an opportunity for Americans to reexamine their comprehensions of the past at regular intervals, and to alter those perceptions to accommodate new understandings, or even to broach wholly new interpretations. In this way, Independence Day rituals allowed Americans the flexibility to redefine the significance of their collective past (and thus of their collective present) as needed. This flexibility often bred serious tensions among the celebrants, but was at the same time crucial for the survival of Independence Day as an annual occasion of self-discovery.

Fourth, and perhaps most important, the ritualized celebrations of the Fourth of July helped to mask disturbing ambiguities and contradictions in the new republic, overlaying real social and political conflict with a conceptual veneer of shared ideology and elemental harmony. In the post-Revolutionary years, Americans with political and social axes to grind continually shaped and reshaped their comprehensions of the Revolution's ideals, goals and achievements, often in competition with one another. Even in the midst of disruptive debates over fundamental republican issues, and while political groups used the holiday to do battle with their opponents, other Americans employed the rituals, rhetoric, and symbolism of Independence Day to minimize the conflicts and to assert the idealized (but dubious) unity of the American people.

The nature and development of American nationalism in the early republic, of a patriotism superior to more ancient, established regional loyalties, is a thorny issue. The half-century that followed 1776 was characterized, in Gordon Wood's words, by a "search for an American identity."[18] The War of Independence from Britain did not of itself bring a sense of confident nationalism to the former colonies. Many Americans, perhaps most, saw the Continental Congress, and the Articles of Confederation that they produced, as mere expedients, temporary measures that could be discarded once the crisis of separation had passed. They spent far more energy hammering out the states' constitutions than they did debating an overall federal authority.[19] Although there were some nationalistic sentiments at the beginning of the War for Independence, "few in 1776 conceived of the thirteen states becoming a single republic, one community with one pervasive public interest."[20] Such a possibility was simply beyond the experience, and perhaps even beyond the imagination, of most Americans. The Revolutionary experience taught some the benefits of intercolonial cooperation and limited regulation, but for most citizens that did not necessarily translate into political and social homogenization. Just as often, intensified intercolonial contact resulted in unhappy experiences and confirmed ill will, as "mutual suspicion and fascination jostled for preeminence in the hearts of patriots." The nationalism that came out of the Revolutionary War experience was more a by-product of that experience, "an unexpected, impromptu, artificial, and therefore extremely fragile creation."[21]

The fragility and ambiguity that characterized American nationalism faced continued stress even in peace. As independence extended the possible applications of "life, liberty, and the pursuit of happiness," Americans entered an era of uncertainty. What would their new republic, the first of its kind in modern times, be like? On the one hand, Enlightenment-era understandings of republicanism, founded on the histories of ancient Greece and Rome, emphasized the willing subordination of virtuous citizens to community interests and government by a selfless elite. But the Revolution unleashed popular egalitarian impulses that challenged classical models. In a "world turned upside down," traditionally unfranchised people—propertyless white men, women, and blacks—saw opportunities for entry into the political and economic arenas. Political innovators advocated an end to elite domination of politics and welcomed the complete unfettering of the individual's impulse for self-improvement. Instead of self-denial, republican virtue began to signify an aggressive self-centeredness and self-reliance, characterized by a person's "capacity to look out for himself and his dependents."[22] This new, "liberal" interpretation of republicanism rationalized a concurrent rise in the spirit of capitalist self-aggrandizement in the new republic. The classical/Enlightenment ideals of republicanism persisted, but the new materialism inherent in the liberal republican model transformed American political culture in only a few decades: "in place of a classical republic led by a disinterested, enlightened elite, Americans got a democratic marketplace of equally competing individuals with interests to promote."[23]

This rapid ideological metamorphosis had traumatic consequences. Conservative Americans espousing the classical understanding of republicanism sought to ensure and enshrine elitist politics through the federal establishment under the 1787 Constitution, accordingly assuming the term "federalist" to identify their position. Advocates of the "liberal" republican strain were first labeled "anti-federalist" by their opponents, but were later known as Democratic-Republicans, indicating their more populist stance. Federalists and

Democratic-Republicans associated into nascent political parties, a circumstance that few had envisioned or desired. The prolonged and bitter competition between these two parties aroused political passions that occasionally burst forth in serious social unrest and violence, particularly in the 1790s.[24] The conversion from the "classical republicanism" of the late eighteenth century to the "romantic democracy" of the early nineteenth was not a smooth one, and in the process provoked "a cultural crisis as severe as any in American history."[25] The resolution of that crisis in the period immediately following the War of 1812 owes much to the widespread development of a national consciousness, albeit a tenuous and conditional one.

Historians seeking the roots of "American nationalism" are first faced with the problem of naming the beast. Nationalism is not an objective, empirically definable entity, although some of its qualities may be described. It is primarily a mental construct, a belief in and, more important, an emotional response to, membership in a parent society. It subordinates local and personal interests to those of the "mother" country, "father" land, or even to a group without geopolitical borders.[26] Because of its abstract, intangible quality, and because of its very novelty in Revolutionary America, the ascendancy of pan-colonial nationalism over older, parochial concerns could not be achieved merely with new institutional forms. When John Adams asserted, many years afterward, that the Revolution had really been "in the minds of the people," he was close to describing the effervescent quality of nationalism. For the Revolution to be anything more than a war for independence by thirteen temporarily confederated colonies, the minds of the people would have to recognize a preeminent national identity of which they had not previously been aware. This did not mean (and practically speaking, could not mean) forsaking an older, more established "community of allegiance."[27] Rather, American nationalism required *expanding* the community of allegiance to include not several thousand but several million people, across a vast geographic expanse.

Creating a national community where none had existed before was a tall order; in the event, most Americans never quite realized the complete transferal of traditional loyalties envisioned by early nationalists. Fragile and variously imagined though it was, however, American nationalism was sufficiently viable to bring people in the different states to at least a grudging acceptance of their relatedness. Despite threats of secession from the West, South, and Northeast during this turbulent time, a curious attraction to the conceit of being "one people," as well as an awareness of common interests, kept the union intact. If local identities and regional concerns acted as centrifugal forces, nationalism was the countervailing gravity that kept the states in orbit about "the nation."

The celebration of Independence Day fed and reflected the idealized (if only partly realized) nationalism of the Revolution and the years immediately following. The annual rites, however, did not simply give vent to wishful thinking. In the ensuing decades, the continued observance of these rites was increasingly vital to the maintenance of a collective belief in (or myth of) a national community that superseded a myriad of regional identities and interregional antagonisms.[28] In the midst of anxious uncertainty, the observance of Independence Day assured people of a common identity and purpose. At the same time, the ritual celebrations seemed to obliterate distance and diversity, and to rein in ideological warfare by declaring a one-day truce. Throughout the period studied here, the Fourth of July served the purpose of political and social reconciliation more or less successfully. But by 1826, the nation's Jubilee year, Independence Day was clearly losing its immediacy and its power to persuade Americans of their homogeneity. In the face of rapid geographic expansion, new national concerns, and budding sectional issues, the nationalist message of July 4 became increasingly diffused, and was occasionally drowned out, as the communities of allegiance contracted again.

Just how and how effectively Independence Day spread the gospel of nationalism will make up much of the pages that follow. In defining what it meant to be American, the ceremonies and symbols surrounding Independence Day initially pointed to the past, but the holiday was not entirely backward-looking. Celebrating the Fourth of July was part of a dynamic process by which Americans not only interpreted their history, but actually shaped new ideas and legitimized them, adopting new symbols and associations into the cultural repertoire. The exuberant and creative displays of the new national flag as Independence Day decoration, for example, focused public attention on a ubiquitous and unequivocal symbol of the nation's revolutionary saga. At the same time, with its ever-changing number of stars, the flag validated at the popular level the federal notion of an infinitely expandable union of states. In this manner the ritual celebration of Independence Day not only perpetuated tradition but "traditionalized" new materials and beliefs. This creative process of "inventing tradition" is common during periods of rapid social, political, or cultural change, as the era of the early republic surely was.[29] New rites and symbols can be traditionalized in a relatively short time; in the case of annual occasions such as Independence Day, a few years will often suffice. New meanings for old forms can likewise be rapidly inculcated. In this way Americans worked the national flag, heroes of the moment, and ritual performances (like orations) into the "traditions" of Independence Day.

Not all such symbolic transformations were so easily digested. In the years following the French Revolution, Democratic-Republicans linked the principles of American independence (as they interpreted them) to a worldwide republican mission, turning their celebration of Independence Day into a republican May Day. By introducing novel significance to July 4, partisans turned the annual celebrations into political arenas in which abstract values (such as liberty, Federalism, economic liberalism) competed and took form. Private and political groups recognized the potential of public ceremony to shape public awareness, and fought to control the forms and meanings of the annual rites of nationalism. Nowhere is this more evident than in the actions of Federalists and Democratic-Republicans on the Fourth of July in the two-and-a-half decades before the end of the War of 1812. In Boston especially, these groups organized competing celebrations, to a large degree transforming the Fourth of July into an occasion for boisterous rallies for the party faithful. Even these essentially partisan musters, however, contributed elements to a "festival of national purpose."[30] In effect, I am using the celebrations of Independence Day in the early republic like a strobe light, illuminating at regular intervals the variety of ways in which Americans understood and enacted their political culture at a specific time. Cumulatively, variation in the use of rituals and symbols discloses how those understandings, and how that political culture, changed over time.

Since certain "loaded" words will come up frequently in this study, a few working definitions are in order at this point. *Culture* should be understood not as any static, persistent human construct, but rather as something dynamic, "a continuous constructing process of sense-making."[31] Likewise, then, *political culture* is an ever-active interpretive process concerning "the values, expectations, and implicit rules" that express and shape the "collective intentions and actions" of a people.[32] The reader will note that this last definition embraces the ability of political culture to adapt to changing circumstances. I recount how the symbols and rituals employed on Independence Day could thus be expressions of continuity of political culture, or of tentative changes in that culture, depending on the context.

Symbols are "marvelous syntheses" of ideas that can reduce " 'a complexity of factors' . . . including experiences, attitudes, beliefs, and values" into "a single word, act, or work."[33] Symbols may be as deceptively simple as words (such as "liberty" or "American"); nevertheless these words actually represent elaborate compounds of meaning that inform and structure experience. As commonly understood, symbols are more likely to be nonverbal and tangible entities: objects (such as flags) and culturally significant personages (such as George Washington).[34] In whatever form, symbols have the ability to encode and establish the parameters of group identity, values, motivations, and actions, especially when manipulated in ritualized performance.

Ritual is a term traditionally laden with religious associations, but social scientists accept the applicability of the term with relation to secular, nonmystical transactions as well.[35] Sally F. Moore and Barbara G. Myerhoff define ritual as "an act or actions intentionally conducted by a group of people employing one or more symbols in a repetitive, formal, precise, highly stylized fashion."[36] This definition, which I accept, implies ritual's persuasive function—appropriate to this study. Implicit also in the above definition is the social and political function of popular ceremonies such as those occurring on Independence Day. Collective ritual is an especially dramatic attempt to bring order and control to some potentially chaotic aspect of life; as such it is a positive, socially "structuring" activity.[37] When successfully performed, ritual conducted with broad participation strengthens and perpetuates a society by invoking and then reaffirming the underlying social values upon which that society rests.[38]

Ritual structuring is at its most imperative, and faces its most crucial challenge, during periods of social anxiety, such as revolution. In response to stress by disruptive forces, people turn more readily and fervently to rituals that assert group identity and group cohesion. This does not mean, however, that ritual is merely an emergency measure to which people resort only in crises. Even in periods of relative social stability, the regular performance of ritual creates and cements social bonds, integrating people into a "single nationalistic body politic, distinguishing them from other collectives."[39] The rites of Independence Day indeed helped foster an ideal of national unity in the early American republic, but one that was frequently at odds with regional identity and concerns.

The chapters that follow focus upon the celebrations in three urban centers, Boston, Philadelphia, and Charleston, South Carolina, during the half-century between 1777 and 1826. The geographic parameters of this study are somewhat dictated by the subject itself, since the earliest, most organized, and best-documented celebrations of Independence Day took place in populous towns and cities. Independence Day was largely an outgrowth of early national urban culture; in rural areas the comparatively sparse population, and especially the daily demands of farming, initially discouraged large-scale public celebrations, excepting the Sabbath, from spring planting to fall harvest. Independence Day began in the large towns and cities, where populations were exempt from the rigors of the agricultural calendar.[40]

My choice of the cities selected for study employs a familiar north-middle-south model for comparative purposes. Boston was the oldest of the three, and contained the most homogeneous population. It was also the most notorious for its restless crowds and, partly as a result, the only city studied here in which the municipal government actively attempted to manage the celebration of Independence Day. Philadelphia's more cosmopolitan population (and the largest of the three) also had a reputation for rambunctiousness, but found accommodation for differing modes of celebration by segregating them along political and social lines. Charleston, the largest urban area south of Philadelphia, stands in interesting contrast to its northern counterparts in several regards. In addition to being the southeastern seaboard's most important entrepôt, Charleston also had the flavor of a resort town. Many low-country planters fled to Charleston in the fierce summer months, to enjoy the (somewhat) healthier climate and to associate with others of their station. Noted by travelers for its urbane elegance, Charleston also contained proportionately the largest under-class of any city in the United States. Slaves made up approximately half of the city's population throughout the period studied here, and their presence affected the celebration and interpretation of Independence Day in Charleston significantly.

The time frame for this study corresponds with the growth and maturation of the "rising generation" that succeeded the Revolutionary one. Their words and actions reflect the progress of their understanding of recent American history, culminating in what they self-consciously called their "Second War for Independence," followed by the short-lived "Era of Good Feelings" and the rise of democracy's new darling, Andrew Jackson. The concluding chapter brings the story to the Jubilee year of 1826, by which time the sons and daughters of the Revolution had dramatically changed the flavor, character, and message of Independence Day from the days of its inception.

Earlier I expressed my belief that the barrier between observer and observed is ultimately insurmountable. But that does not mean it cannot be scaled. Like Charles Janson, I know that I am observing these past celebrations as an outsider. Unlike Janson, I shall attempt to find some of the meanings and significances that his subjects drew from, and infused into, their actions. If the barrier cannot be cleared, we should at least be able to get our eyes above the edge for a better look.

1

"Excellent Political Moves"

I am apt to believe that it will be celebrated by
succeeding generations as the great anniversary
festival. It ought to be commemorated, as the day of
deliverance, by solemn acts of devotion to God
almighty. It ought to be solemnized with pomp and
parade, with shows, games, sports, guns, bells,
bonfires, and illuminations, from one end of this
continent to the other, from this time forward,
forevermore.

JOHN ADAMS TO ABIGAIL ADAMS, JULY 3, 1776

In his now-famous letter to wife Abigail, John Adams was
in fact referring to July 2 (the date that Congress passed the resolution
for independence), but he was not to be disappointed in his hope for
an annual day of "pomp and parade." It is worth taking a closer look
at this excerpt from Adams's letter; in it he alerts the reader to a range
of acceptable festive categories and specific practices drawn from the
political culture of Adams and his contemporaries.

Adams subdivided the overall "festival" into two general categories of festive form and behavior. First, he felt, the date of independence should be "commemorated" by "solemn acts of devotion."
He did not elaborate, but Adams undoubtedly intended the kinds
of religious and quasi-religious services (such as sermons, orations,
processions, communal dining) that formed a central place in pre-

Revolutionary public observances. Second, he declared that the day should be "solemnized" with a variety of entertainments and public rejoicing. Adams mixed his categories somewhat ("pomp and parade," I shall argue, belong in the first category), but clearly he had in mind two distinct ritual styles drawn from Euro-American traditions.

Ceremonial rituals are highly structured affairs and demand a relatively high level of decorum: marriage ceremonies, for example, or procedures in courts of law. Ceremonial rites tend to involve definite, manageable numbers of people in a variety of interconnected roles. In the course of the ceremony the participants (and this, as we shall see, includes observers) signify their respect for the offices, causes, values, or traditions represented in the performances. Ceremony is thus a conspicuously "structuring" activity.[1]

Celebration, on the other hand, is not intentionally structuring (though often is indirectly), does not insist on habitual decorum, and sanctions exuberant releases of energy. In other words, it is play; or at least, play is at its core. In celebration, strict decorum is set aside; there is no apparent message, no desired "result," and it may seem unmotivated and spontaneous. When Adams wrote of "games, sports, guns" in connection with an annual commemoration, he was recalling a celebratory tradition in American colonial culture that was as familiar as ceremony.[2]

Americans in the late eighteenth century had experience with both ritual traditions. In the decades before independence, for example, the king's birthday and the annual observance of his accession provided opportunities for ceremonial statements, in ritual form, of royal majesty and benevolent protection on the one hand, and the people's deference and allegiance on the other. Public proclamations, formal dinners, loyal toasts and cheers, and illuminations of principal houses all signified the attachment and affection that people felt toward their sovereign. Relatedly, the king's birthday was a time for exhibiting and reinforcing the entire social hierarchy, as evidenced by the presence in the evening of the "*Gentry* of both *Sexes*" promenading through the streets "with much decency and gravity."[3] High spirits occasionally crossed the lines of propriety, but the dominant temper of these royal holidays was one of decorum and order.[4]

Exemplary of the other ritual tradition, and representative of the other extreme of the social scale, were saturnalian events such as

"Pope's Day" in Boston. During the second quarter of the eighteenth century, the artisans and laboring people of Boston increasingly came to dominate the celebration of Pope's Day, the November 5 commemoration of the abortive Gunpowder Plot in 1605. Though originally an anti-Catholic rally, and by the mid-eighteenth century still revolving nominally around that theme, Pope's Day in Boston became a occasion on which the lower orders turned the social pyramid on its head. In a dramatic example of status inversion, the "mob" ruled the streets for the day, parading large and often elaborate effigies of the Pope, the Devil, and / or the Pretender, and extorting money from the wealthier citizens to support the excessive eating and drinking that fueled the festivities. Toward late afternoon, the occasion climaxed with a violent brawl between the North End and South End gangs sporting rival "guys" (the effigies, named after gunpowder conspirator Guy Fawkes). The winners of this bone-breaking melee earned the right to take the losers' guy in tow, and the evening finished with both effigies being burned in a bonfire.[5] Pope's Day is admittedly an extreme case of celebratory behavior. But there were few official festivals in colonial America to serve as outlets for public energy; it may be, as Peter Shaw has suggested, that American colonists suffered psychologically from "festival deprivation."[6] Nevertheless, celebratory practices of a more controlled nature, such as fireworks displays, found a place even on ostensibly ceremonial occasions.

So when John Adams asserted that the anniversary of American Independence *ought* to be "commemorated" and "solemnized," he was acknowledging two established ritual traditions then current in American culture. One was orderly, socially structuring, and appealed particularly to the middle sector of society and the well-to-do; the other was more casual, temporarily chaotic, and favored by the lower orders. Adams thought, at least in 1776, that there was a place for both ritual styles in future anniversaries of independence. His own experience on the first Independence Day must have confirmed his belief.

The people of Boston marked the first full year of independence in 1777 in enthusiastic style. The cannon on Fort Hill, Castle William (aptly renamed Fort Independence), and the ships in the harbor fired a "grand salute" to announce the dawn. In the afternoon the Reverend Dr. Gordon of Roxbury preached a patriotic interpretation of 1 Kings 12:15–16 to the state Assembly, enlisting Jehovah in the American cause.[7] Afterward, from the balcony of the statehouse, Governor John Hancock proposed thirteen toasts, one for each of the states, each salutation punctuated by the crash of cannon fire in the street below. Boston's militia companies turned out for parade and drill, occasionally firing *feux de joie*—rippling volleys of musketry begun at one end of a line and proceeding to the other. In the evening, Colonel Croft's artillery company furnished more noise and pyrotechnics when they "illuminated the Park on the Common with several shells, and exhibited a number of fireworks" to the delight of the onlookers. A correspondent noted that "the cheerful Appearances of the gentlemen and Ladies in the Park, and the Pleasantness of the Evening, closed with universal Satisfaction the Joys of the Day."[8]

Three hundred miles to the south, Philadelphians similarly observed the first anniversary of independence. The navy ships and galleys in the Delaware River, all of them bedecked with streamers and with colors flying, began the commemoration at noon. As each ship warped close to the city's waterfront it delivered a thirteen-gun salute. The members of Congress then in town sat down to an elegant dinner at the prestigious City Tavern, with music provided by a Hessian regimental band captured at Trenton the previous Christmas. A "corps" of British deserters fired occasional salutes outside the hall where Congress dined. When the plates were cleared, the members drank a number of formal toasts, "all breathing independence." At four o'clock, a brigade of Carolina troops en route to join Washington's main army assembled in review on the Commons. Firing a *feu de joie* for appreciative onlookers, they were cheered as they left the city. The clamor of bells closed the day, but at night, as in Boston, the people were treated to a "grand exhibition" of fireworks that began and ended with the whoosh of thirteen rockets. As Congressman John Adams discovered, getting about at night was easier than usual. "In the evening, I was walking about the streets for a little fresh air and exercise and was surprised to find the whole city lighting up their candles at the windows. I walked most of the evening and I think it was the most splendid illumination I ever saw." Another eyewitness corroborates the extent of the spectacle: "In the evening the whole City were Illuminated with Lights at every window . . . till 12 O clock at which time the Lights were Ordered to be extinguished." Impromptu bonfires in some of the streets also helped banish the darkness in Philadelphia on this night.[9]

In Charleston, the first Independence Day was something of an anticlimax after an anniversary of more local import. On June 28, 1776, six days before Congress's acceptance of the Declaration, Charleston militia had turned back a British invasion force attempting to force the harbor entrance. At the southern tip of Sullivan's Island, the Americans had built a low, square fort (unfinished at the time of the battle) with ramparts of sand faced with palmetto tree logs. British cannonballs fired from the Royal Navy ships did not splinter or shatter the logs when they struck, but sank ineffectually into the spongy wood. June 28 became known thereafter in Charleston as "Palmetto Day." Its first observance in 1777 was marked with all the by now familiar trappings of civic ceremony, and in contrast to the first July 4 celebrations in Boston and Philadelphia, there was little left to spontaneity.

The Palmetto Society, formed by Charleston's artisans and mechanics expressly to commemorate the victory, carefully worked out the day's schedule of events. As with the more northerly towns, there were bells and cannon fire to greet the dawn. At noon the state congress gathered at the statehouse at the intersection of Meeting and Broad streets to receive and review the two volunteer companies who had defended the fort the year before. These "heroes of the 28th of June" then formally renewed their "oath of allegiance to the cause of Independence," received the cheers of their fellow townsmen, fired three volleys, and were dismissed to their homes. Next came the formal dinners. The colonel commanding the two companies treated his officers, while the Palmetto Society held an "elegant entertainment" for the state president, vice president, council, and some three hundred others. The congress, with some militia officers, remained at the statehouse and probably ate the best of all; according to a witness, they enjoyed "food . . . in abundance, and even in profusion," although, he discretely added, "without much pomp and without much etiquette." When the toasts were drunk, as in Boston, artillerists in the square outside cheered and fired thirteen-gun salutes. Sundown and a final salute from the harbor forts closed the daytime ceremonies, but the celebration went on in the center of town, where in the relative cool of the summer evening, and under a canopy of their beloved palmetto

trees, the noncommissioned officers and privates attended a collation "provided for them by the Ladies." Fireworks in several places
throughout the town and an unprecedented illumination of houses
and public buildings capped the night's activities.[10]

Topping these festivities for July 4, less than a week later, would
have been difficult, and apparently Charlestonians did not try. Instead, they simply repeated many of the elements of the June 28 celebration, with some subtle differences. When the same bells rang and
the same cannon fired the dawn salute, all the forts, batteries, and
vessels in the harbor broke out their new "American colors." After the
noontime parade and review of the militia (all companies this time),
the harbor forts coordinated a seventy-six-gun salute. The dinner at
the statehouse, with accompanying artillery salvos, proceeded much
as the June dinner had done, but in the evening there were apparently
no fireworks.[11] To any observer unaware of the date, Charleston's
Palmetto Day exercises could have passed easily for an Independence
Day celebration anywhere else. There was little to distinguish the two;
circumstances alone lent different meanings to the same forms. It is
tempting to imagine that the period of June 28 to July 4 would become
a sort of patriotic festival week in Charleston, with Palmetto Day kicking off observances climaxing on Independence Day, but such does
not appear to have been the case.

If the occasions for the celebrations in Boston, Philadelphia, and
Charleston were novel, the forms of expression were not. Before independence, fireworks and militia reviews often marked the occasions of
royal birthdays, accession days, and new royal governors in all three
towns.[12] Victories over the French during the Seven Years' War inspired days of public thanksgiving, upon which the governor and
assembly in Boston gathered to hear prayers, anthems, and sermons
appropriate to the occasion. Any of these events might be the opportunity for salutes of artillery and special public events. Adopting the
familiar in public celebration is not unusual; ritual forms are basically
conservative within given cultures, although their meanings may be
flexible. Consequently, new rites stand a better chance of acquiring
legitimacy if they are initially recognizable to the people who will
ultimately award them authority.[13] To mark the first anniversary of
independence, the people of Boston, Philadelphia, and Charleston un-

abashedly endowed customary elements of celebration with custom-made signification. As Catherine Albanese pointed out, in eighteenth-century Anglo-American culture even spontaneity had structure.[14]

This traditional framework for festive behavior explains the similarity of the celebrations in all three towns, as well as the apparent smoothness with which they transpired. Neither state nor local ordinance authorized or encouraged the observances in either of the three cities. Indeed, despite Adams's prophetic vision of the future of Independence Day the year before, he admitted that, if left to Congress, the anniversary in Philadelphia might have passed much like any other day. "The thought of taking any notice of this day [by Congress]," wrote Adams, "was not conceived until the second of this month and it was not mentioned until the third. It was too late to have a sermon, as everybody wished, so this must be deferred another year." Congress determined only to take the day off. Nevertheless, Adams relates, the dearth of official recognition of the day was compensated by elements of the armed forces and by the general public "with a festivity and ceremony becoming the occasion. . . . Considering the lateness of the design and suddenness of the execution, I was amazed at the universal joy and alacrity that was discovered, and the brilliancy and splendour of every part in this joyful exhibition."[15] Much the same could be said for Boston, where military, religious, and civil representatives, as well as the general population, pooled their energies and resources without much apparent planning and no official prompting. Charleston's Independence Day activities also appear to have been carried out with a minimum of formal planning and no radical departure from celebratory norms.

Adams may have also been surprised at the date selected for the commemoration of independence. The resolution for independence was approved by the Congress on July 2. Thus, although the Declaration itself was not adopted by that body until the fourth, the official moment of independence (the success of which was still in doubt in 1777) had occurred two days earlier. Historians are occasionally bemused by the apparent "error"; Daniel Boorstin went so far as to style the ultimate selection of July 4 "a mystery that may never be solved."[16] The solution is not nearly so enigmatic. Soon after the Declaration was approved, it was printed in newspapers and broadsides and widely distributed. General Washington ordered copies read to his troops, and public readings of the document occurred in nearly every major town in the thirteen new states. At the top of the document, for all to read or have read to them, was the heading: "In Congress July 4, 1776." In a society where the printed word carried tremendous authority, where wills, deeds, and indentures were the mainstays of everyday life and the guarantors of stability, a written document was the final word. As far as most people were concerned, the Declaration, not the vote of July 2, gave the United States its legal status.[17]

This legalistic origin of nationhood satisfied Americans who had to argue for legitimacy while simultaneously preaching rebellion.[18] Certainly July 4, 1776 held broader appeal than April 19, 1775, as "the national birth-day." That dramatic day in Lexington and Concord when the shooting war began was an obvious candidate for commemoration as a "birth-day," especially considering the allegorical shedding of blood. Thomas Paine, writing six months before the congressional resolution, considered April 19, 1775, "the commencement of hostilities," the pivotal moment when "a new era for politics [was] struck," and "a new method of thinking" came into being.[19] For Charlestonians, whose attachment to the cause of independence was initially equivocal, the resistance of June 28 may have seemed like the moment of commitment, when the sword had been drawn and the scabbard thrown away. But to avoid parochialism and promote unity, there had to be one historical moment at which all of the colonies "began to be free, having then escaped from the worse than Egyptian bondage of Great-Britain."[20] That people as far apart as those of Boston, Philadelphia, and Charleston chose to so regard July 4 indicates the broad appeal among Revolutionary Americans of a national identity in the exuberant early stage of the war.

More important than the precise event or date is the obvious need the revolutionaries felt to determine a decisive instant, one crucial event that changed everything, in the first place. All events are unique by definition, but some events become definitive ones; epic turning points or moments of high drama used by a people to identify themselves as a group or a nation.[21] For the revolutionaries, no event in their colonial past was adequate to the task of determining when their new collective identity began. Instead, they looked to the recent past and found their "myth of origins" centering on the *act* of revolution; that is, the one that took place on July 4, 1776.[22] That highly dramatic, self-conscious moment of self-determination seemed to mark the most unequivocal rejection of the colonies' former status and the assumption of a new estate. Roberto Da Matta might have been writing of the American Independence Day, instead of the Brazilian counterpart, when he observed:

> It is of fundamental importance to appreciate that Independence Day is a ceremony related to a specific historical event—it is a *historical rite*, to borrow a phrase from Lévi-Strauss. . . . [T]he time of Independence Day is a unique moment, emphasizing the final break with the colonial period and the beginning of a political "coming-of-age." It is then a historical *rite of passage* since its performance is not only intended to recreate a glorious event in the past, but also to emphasize, in a quite explicit way, the shift from the colonial world to the world of freedom and self-determination.[23]

For the American revolutionaries, the moment that Congress adopted the Declaration of Independence was a moment of metamorphosis; they were no longer the people they had been before July 4, 1776. And the commemoration of Independence Day a year later connected participants with that climactic moment, placing them within the context of a new history.

Those who did not participate fell outside of that context. Promoters of the 1777 celebration in Philadelphia expected that "all true Whigs" and "all friends to America" would participate and that "every mark of joy and festivity will be shewn by those who have a proper sense of its importance." In a city where there was such diversity of ethnic and ideological backgrounds, the revolutionaries' determination to make the Fourth of July a patriotic litmus test caused some alarm. In particular, the large Quaker population rejected public celebrations of any kind on religious grounds. Additionally, their pacifist beliefs and links with Pennsylvania's Proprietary party and Tories made them highly suspect in the eyes of the revolutionaries.[24] Anticipating trouble, the Philadelphia city council tried to head off any victimization of Quakers. They conceded that the occasion and the festivities, "when conducted with decency and good order," were "commendable," but pleaded that the celebrants "show moderation and forbearance toward those persons who, either through their religious principles, or on any other account, may not in the present join with them in those expressions of joy; and that they conduct themselves in a way that will do honor to themselves, and to the great cause in which they are engaged."[25]

Those who made themselves conspicuous by their absence during the celebration ran the risk of being stigmatized. Although the patriot newspapers subsequently claimed that "everything was conducted with the greatest order and decorum," private accounts were more candid.[26] John Adams noted with approval the intimidation inspired by the "vast concourse of people, all shouting and hurrahing in a manner which gave great joy to every friend of this country, and the utmost terror and dismay to every lurking Tory." During the illumination that evening, Adams observed a number of darkened houses that made prominent targets for patriotic indignation. "I suppose," wrote Congressman William Williams of Connecticut the day after, "and I conclude much Tory unilluminated glass will want replacing."[27] Williams was right. A Continental officer wrote the next day that the whole city was lit up, "Except Torrey Houses whose Windows Paid for their Obstinacy."[28] Quaker glass probably suffered as well, for the Friends refused to close their shops or illuminate their windows on holidays.[29]

The 1777 celebrations were models for future observances. Familiar forms were easily adapted to new meanings, and already the celebrations had taken on powerful doctrinaire overtones. Festivities combined decorous ceremonies (military displays, solemn toasts) with sanctioned disorderly behavior (bonfires, Tory window breaking). The appropriateness of it all depended upon one's point of view. William Williams deplored the time taken away from congressional matters for what he saw as needless extravagance: "Yesterday was in my opinion poorly spent in celebrating the Anniversary of the Declaration of Independence, but to avoid singularity and reflection upon my dear Colony, I thought it my duty to attend the public entertainment—a great expenditure of liquor, powder, etc., took up the Day and of candles thro the City a good part of the night."[30] A correspondent for the *Pennsylvania Evening Post*, however, considered the day a signal success: "Thus may the fourth of July, that glorious and ever memorable day, be celebrated through America, by the sons of freedom, from age to age till time shall be no more. Amen, and amen."[31]

During the remainder of the war years there was never again a Fourth of July celebration in Philadelphia like that of 1777. Within a few months of its first Independence Day, Philadelphia was occupied by British troops. When these withdrew from the city in June 1778, they left it in a considerably degraded state, physically and economically. Private houses and public buildings suffered badly from the billeting of soldiers and their animals, and trade was temporarily ruined. Congress officially observed the Fourth of July with a "grand festival" at City Tavern, and numerous cannon were fired to dispel rumors of gunpowder shortages, but the rest of Philadelphia was less able to contribute materially. Witnesses reported "a great fuss in the evening" and "great rejoicing," but illuminations were out of the question this year: candles were "too scarce and dear, for Alluminations." Congress was forced to concede the scarcity and, probably to keep order and save innocent glass, informed the public that they did not expect illuminations that night. In an ironic reversal of the previous year's situation, the members of Congress held virtually the only organized celebrations in Philadelphia. At their private dinner (which civil and military officers, and "other gentlemen" attended by invitation only), the members drank patriotic toasts accompanied by band music, but the general citizenry could not follow their example. The relatively quiet evening was appreciated by some; Elizabeth Drinker thought that the waiver on illuminations "sav'd some of our Windows."[32]

Congress tried again the next year, with little better effect. The Fourth of July falling on a Sunday, the members heard a special sermon delivered by the chaplain of the Congress, and deferred their dinner to the next day. The William Williamses of the Congress were apparently multiplying; three states voted against the resolution to observe the day at all, and the people of Philadelphia seemed no more inclined. The year 1779 was the worst of the war for Philadelphians; trade was minimal, rebuilding at a standstill, and commodities scarce. On this Independence Day, no one pretended artificial bounty to boost morale as in 1778. Extravagant salutes were out of the question this year, reported one Philadelphian, "because we cannot afford to fire cannon." Even the prospect of Tory-bashing did not bring out the mobs of two years before. The most odious loyalists and British collaborators had left town, leaving an observer to predict sullenly that "no windows will be broke on Monday."[33]

For the next two years Congress gave up the effort to observe the Fourth of July; Independence Day received only a passing reference in the 1780 and 1781 Philadelphia newspapers.[34] Nor did Philadelphians celebrate the Fourth with much enthusiasm even after the British surrender at Yorktown in the fall of 1781. Bells rang again and people found powder for their cannon, but little else distinguished the day. In 1783 the public was treated to the sight of a certain Mr. Mason's "Triumphal Car," pulled by eight white horses and displaying portraits of Generals Washington and Gates, accompanied by a music band and "a number of little boys and girls dressed in white, carrying torches." But the "Grand Exhibition" was little more than a publicity stunt: Mr. Mason was an upholsterer, and his "triumphal car" consisted of a platform surmounted by one of his sofas, around which the portraits stood.[35]

In Boston the Fourth of July was more regularly and enthusiastically observed, although here too the joyful delirium of 1777 was never quite repeated. The 1778 observances were occasioned as much by the presence in the harbor of a French fleet, the first tangible manifestation of the crucial alliance forged that year, as by patriotic sentiment.[36] The next year seemed almost a return to the Fourth's initial spontaneous zeal; the town militia presented a "mock-engagement, highly entertaining to a vast concourse of spectators," after which "near an hundred gentlemen dined under a tent erected on the Common." In the evening there were fireworks, including thirteen rockets fired simultaneously, "signifying the Thirteen Rising States." In the dark years of 1780 and 1781 the patriotic fervor flagged somewhat, but by the war's end Boston had settled into a familiar routine of bell ringing, cannon firing, parading, and feasting.[37]

For the two years following the first anniversary of independence, Charlestonians continued to celebrate both Palmetto Day and Independence Day, but evidence suggests that of the two, Palmetto Day may have garnered more local interest. A young Loyalist woman and her family left inhospitable Charleston the day before the second anniversary of the Fort Moultrie battle (perhaps the timing was intentional). In what must have appeared as a secular version of a Catholic Palm Sunday, Louisa Wells noticed "many boats were employed in carrying up Palmetto trees and boughs to celebrate, in Town, the Anniversary of the ever inglorious 28th of June 1776!"[38] Wells's observation suggests that some Charlestonians, at least, were willing to make strenuous efforts to honor June 28 with the appropriate focal symbols. Another, friendlier observer noted that there were no fewer than three "public celebrations" in the town, where no doubt the palmetto boughs cut previously and brought into the town were displayed prominently.[39] In contrast, the Independence Day activities of 1778 seem a slightly scaled-down version of the previous year's. Perhaps the future of the July 4 celebrations in Charleston was in doubt; David Ramsay delivered an oration at Saint Michael's Church that year in which he urged his listeners to perpetuate the festival as an annual observation.[40] The exhortation apparently fell on deaf ears, however: the 1779 observances were not even reported in a Charleston newspaper until two weeks later, and even then only merited a cursory paragraph.[41]

Patriotic celebrations of any kind were impossible during the last years of the war, as it was Charleston's fate to be the last of the towns studied here to be occupied by British troops. After a brief siege, the Americans surrendered Charleston to the enemy in May 1780. Not until the war was over would Charlestonians have the opportunity to express their patriotism, local or national, openly.[42]

Despite the preemptions of war and the sometimes ambivalent attitudes of Americans, Independence Day addressed a variety of needs during the years of military conflict. Initially, the observances bolstered public enthusiasm for war at a time when American arms had fallen far short of expectations and real independence was far from certain. A perceptive French observer reported that patriotic celebrations were "usual and frequent with the Americans, probably because they need to maintain their spirits at a high degree of enthusiasm."[43] The bell ringing, fireworks, and military displays that had once stirred pride in being part of the British Empire now stirred pride in making war against that empire. Militia gatherings henceforth signified not attachment to an abstract father figure, but resistance to him.[44] Hearkening to another human rite of passage, the presence of the militia on the national birthday reminded spectators that blood accompanies birth. Choreographed mock-combats on Boston Common acted out the struggle vicariously for people to whom the theater of war was far away.

Fashioning new loyalties meant purging old ones; in order for the new society to be born, faith in the old one had to be killed. Paradoxically, this was accomplished by reappropriating the very forms with which Americans had pledged loyalty to their king before the Revolution.[45] Patriotic toasts ritually absolved people of former loyalties, and even the mystical power of numbers was invoked in the liturgical drinking of thirteen toasts, thirteen-gun or seventy-six-gun salutes, or in the sight of thirteen rockets flying simultaneously to dizzying heights. The substitution of substance in the ritual liturgy was sometimes subtle, sometimes explicit, but always understood by the faithful. Familiar forms, even though charged with new meanings, gave an impression of stability and continuity in a period of tension and change.[46]

By creating a new ritual program (or rather, reprogramming old ones), the revolutionaries discovered a fairly simple means of communicating complex combinations of ideas. A wealth of messages could be packed into speeches, symbols, mock-combats, and fireworks. The new practices were also useful for distinguishing friend from foe. Philadelphians, and probably their Charleston counterparts, easily identified out-groups on Independence Day by their failure to take part in the rites of revolution. "These celebrations," wrote the French observer, "serve as excellent political moves, making not only enthusiastic citizens of the people, but ardent partisans of the new system as well. Even the followers of the Royalists and many who are indifferent to the common cause, see the example set by the others at these affairs and are gradually educated around to their beliefs."[47] Thus, during the war years, Independence Day served a number of vital functions at once. It gave Revolutionary Americans an opportunity to identify themselves as a group publicly, "educate" the uncommitted, and isolate enemies. For the faithful it fueled enthusiasm for a "new system" and rededicated them to a cause not yet won.

For Revolutionary Americans, the War for Independence was a transitional period between an older, familiar status and a new, hopeful, but uncertain one. For this reason, historians have frequently used the term "rite of passage" in association with the war years, as a kind of "initiation" to "adult" status. The metaphor has almost become trite, but may actually be more appropriate than ever in light of anthropological studies that reveal how cultural rites of passage effect powerful social alterations in their subjects. According to these studies, rites of passage exhibit three distinct phases. In the "separation" phase, the subject dissociates himself from his former condition, jettisoning the trappings that identified him with that status. In the second, or "liminal" phase (from the Latin word for "threshold") the ritual subject's status is ambiguous, indeterminate; he is neither what he was, nor has he yet achieved his new status. The "aggregation" phase completes the process; the subject is "whole," made over, and embarks upon a new stage of life.

While in the liminal phase of their passage, initiates are cut off from their past associations, and not yet accepted by those of the status to which they aspire. Often they are divested of their former belongings. They have nothing, are nothing, and have no one to turn to but one another, all equally in a social limbo. The liminal phase is a time of intense emotional bonding among initiates. Those who share this temporary condition aspire to, and achieve, if only briefly, a sense of social communion, of *un*structured oneness that Victor Turner calls *communitas*—society without structure, without hierarchy, a communion of undifferentiated individuals.[48]

Communitas is necessarily a transitory experience. All cultures assert the desirability of social order and structure (however defined). But while it lasts, *communitas* focuses group self-awareness and forges a sense of common identity whose effects last beyond the liminal moment. According to sociologists, this collective "effervescence" is the "glue" that holds society together; without it there can be no group identification or cooperation.[49] In what seems a paradox, social stability requires occasional periods of structured chaos.

In imagining the War for Independence as a rite of passage, the "separation" phase commenced on July 4 (or July 2) and the "aggregation" upon the war's conclusion; what came in between was the "liminal" phase, in which we would expect to find examples of experienced *communitas*. Some early histories of the Revolution give the impression of a widespread, sustained *communitas* extending from 1775 (or even before) to the end of the war, but scholarship in this century has suggested a far different reality.[50] Nevertheless, the revolutionaries of Boston, Philadelphia, and Charleston appear to have come fairly close to this transcendent sensibility on Independence Day in 1777 especially, and to diminishing degrees after that. In the processions, fireworks, and orations, the celebrants saw and heard "more than a picture and a poem; the audience witnessed a sacred event, and by bearing witness in common with others, each member entered into a communion with society as a whole."[51] *Communitas*, even if infrequent or of varying intensity, cultivated the social bond and common purpose that saw Americans through eight years of liminal existence.

But *communitas* is a condition associated with the indeterminate state. While the United States was in this phase (that is, before the end of hostilities), Independence Day invited Americans to experience the patriotic camaraderie of the moment. The war's end brought the survival of the annual celebration into question: What function did Independence Day perform now that the conflict was over, now that "aggregation" had been accomplished? Surely, with independence recognized by the parent country, and with the former combatants reestablishing diplomatic and mercantile connections, there could be little place or purpose for annual anti-British rallies. And what need was there to reassert the independence that was now internationally recognized as fact? The Fourth of July had outlived its original function as a rite of passage in the immediate sense. If it was to continue, as John Adams hoped, "from one end of this continent to the other, from this time forward, forevermore," it would have to acquire new significance.

2

SPIRITUAL BLOOD

> A great nation, engaged in an arduous contest for
> the establishment of her rights, has not thought it
> unworthy of her power, to excite the courage of her
> citizens, by commemorating the actions they had
> achieved; and has owed, perhaps, not a few of her
> victories, to the tribute she has offered up to the
> merits of her departed heroes.
>
> HENRY M. RUTLEDGE, *An Oration delivered in*
> *St. Philip's Church*

"EXCELLENT PURPOSES"

Far from being a foregone conclusion, the survival of Independence
Day was an open question in the early 1780s. This uncertainty was due
in large part to the functional ambiguity of the anniversary once independence had been secured. America's "liminal" phase seemed to be
over; with the end of the war the nation's rite of passage appeared to
be completed. What use could Independence Day serve now?

At half past twelve on the chilly afternoon of March 5, 1783, the
Boston town meeting at Faneuil Hall adjourned, and the members
made their way toward the Old Brick Meeting House in Cornhill.
Their route took them up State Street and past the spot, a snowball's
throw from the statehouse; where five townsmen had fallen before

British muskets thirteen years before. The blood that had once stained the cobbles under their feet and the Redcoats were of course long gone; nevertheless it must have been a solemn and reflective crowd that gathered in the Old Brick to commemorate, for the last time, the infamous Boston Massacre.

By the appointment of the selectmen the year before, the Reverend Dr. Thomas Welch delivered the required oration for this day. Fortunately, the selectmen had also had the foresight to reserve the venerable meetinghouse for the occasion, as the "large and crowded assembly" of Bostonians that gathered to hear Dr. Welch could not have been accommodated at Faneuil Hall. Taking up the accustomed theme for the day, Welch proceeded to "impress on the Minds of the Citizens the ruinous tendency of standing Armies being placed in Free and Populous Cities." At the conclusion of the lecture, which was met with enthusiastic applause, the selectmen reconvened at Faneuil Hall and voted, as they had every year since the Massacre, to confer the official thanks of the town upon the speaker and to request a copy of the speech for printing.[1]

Customarily, the meeting's next move was to proceed to the business of selecting the orator for the next year. Instead, the town clerk moved to discontinue further ceremonies of this sort. Although, he argued, the commemoration of the fifth of March had "answered excellent purposes,"

> a Signal Revolution has been effected through the Favor of Heaven . . . by the establishment of the Independence of these United States of America . . . this Memorable Event has induced many of the Inhabitants to make a Question whether in our present situation it would not be for the public benefit to exchange the present Institution for another of the same General nature—such for instance as an Anniversary for celebrating the glorious and happy Declaration of the Independence of the United States. . . .

Now that independence was a virtual reality, the clerk continued, such timely themes as the superiority of republican government, public virtue, and education were more appropriate and relevant to the needs of the new nation. Orators could recount for the generations to come the experience of the Revolution, its causes and events, its heroic personages, and the "important and timely aid" received from the French ally. The meeting chose a committee to consider the motion.[2]

From 9:15 to 10:00 that night, the bells of the town's churches tolled for the last time in official remembrance of the Massacre martyrs. Five days later the committee recommended that henceforth public observances of the day should cease. The reason for abandoning this Boston tradition, the committee admitted, was that "the immediate Motives which induced the commemoration of that day, do now no longer exist in their primitive force." Instead, the committee proposed that the fourth day of July, "a Day ever memorable in the Annals of this Country for the Declaration of our Independence, shall be constantly celebrated."[3]

Thus at a stroke the selectmen discarded an outworn tradition and validated a new one. The solemnization of the Massacre's anniversary had indeed "answered excellent purposes" in Revolutionary Boston by arousing and then fanning public hatred of British authority. Unlike the riotous outbursts of the lower orders during Guy Fawkes Day celebrations and the Stamp Act crisis, however, Massacre Day had marshaled public fervor in a controlled, respectable fashion of which all walks of Boston society could approve. With the achievement of independence, Massacre Day lost its utility. Fully aware, however, of the important function of properly regulated public ceremonies, the selectmen substituted the Fourth of July as an acceptable and constructive outlet for public expression.[4]

Uppermost in the minds of the Boston members were the "excellent purposes" that the Massacre Day orations (which were also printed for general sale) had served "in disseminating the Principles of Virtue and Patriotism" among Bostonians. American victory made Massacre Day pointless, but concerned Bostonians feared that the instructive effects of these exercises would soon be lost. Recognizing that "the Benefits resulting from the Institution [of a commemorative event] . . . may and ought to be forever preserved," the meeting proposed to do that, as they candidly expressed it, by "exchanging that Anniversary for Another."[5] Henceforth, Independence Day would carry a new but equally timely message for the people of Boston. Instead of fulfilling an immediate need (marshaling support for revolution), the "Institution" of the Fourth of July would accomplish a more lasting effect by extolling "the superior advantages of a Republican form of Government . . . and the necessity of Virtue and good Manners, and of an Education that tends to promote them."[6]

The Boston Meeting's concern for virtue and good manners was not mere rhetoric. In the closing years of the Revolution, concerned patriots expressed fears that the sense of danger and common cause that initially brought the colonies together were an insufficient bond or basis for a lasting republic. Writing to Benjamin Rush in the fall of 1779, Charles Lee insisted that "unless a proper education of the rising generation is adopted, a new way of thinking and new principles can be introduced among the People of America, there are little hopes of the present Governments or anything like republican governments being of any duration."[7]

Almost as soon as the war was over, the revolutionaries sought to pass on the virtuous principles of the Revolution to "the Rising Generation" through political institutions and an educational system.[8] As the Revolution retreated farther into memory, concerns for proper republican education increased. Benjamin Rush favored using the schools to infuse the nation's youth with the necessary qualities. Through their agency, he wrote, it would be possible "to convert men into republican machines." John Adams agreed. "Public virtue is the only Foundation of Republics," he wrote, and such virtues had to be taught.[9] The members of the Boston Meeting clearly felt that Independence Day could help meet this need for republican indoctrination by reminding succeeding generations of the self-sacrificing qualities that had given birth to their republic and that were the only hopes for its continuance. Instead of justifying the Revolution (no need for that now), Independence Day would memorialize it as the heroic struggle for self-realization; the national saga. The new holiday would be a constructive exercise in citizenship as well as patriotism.

But in recasting Independence Day, the Boston men wanted no return to the Pope's Days of pre-Revolutionary times. Samuel Adams and other Boston leaders had worked hard during the 1760s and 1770s to control the volatile lower orders of the town, and they were not anxious to let that influence slip. By the time the Revolution began, Pope's Day had been suppressed for a decade. During the long American siege of Boston, bored soldiers planned a Pope's Day revival, but General Washington would have none of it. Citing the offense that

Canadian Catholics and the French would undoubtedly take, Washington wrote a general order forbidding any such demonstration.[10] Boston's officials even feared the exuberant, orderly, but undirected July 4 celebration of 1777. Remembering the patriotic chaos of Boston's first Independence Day, an observer of the 1778 activities was "greatly pleased" with the "good Order of the Day."[11] But such restraint could not always be counted upon. The town oration and the ceremonies surrounding it would provide focus and context for positive, constructive expressions of enthusiasm. The records of the Boston Meeting demonstrate that they had indeed learned much from the Revolution; when it came to calculated and deliberate manipulation of the body politic, they had not lost their touch.

Boston's first official Independence Day in 1783 began as it had in 1777, with cannon fire and bells, but the rest of the day's program was more prescribed, "in a manner becoming the happy occasion." Instead of being delivered privately to the assembly as it was six years before, the oration was now open to all who could fit into the Brattle Street Church. Instead of keeping mostly to themselves, the lieutenant governor, council, state senators, and representatives marched in a public procession from their chambers to Brattle Street. There, Dr. John Warren took up the approved theme of republican virtue in "a most ingenious and elegant oration." Accompanied by an artillery train, the state officials then returned to the Senate chamber for "an agreeable entertainment." Musket and cannon fire continued throughout the afternoon, while the militia officers dined at the Bunch of Grapes and the Exchange Taverns.[12] The program was a complete success, setting the pattern for future observances. Instead of relying upon popular whim and enthusiasm, the Boston selectmen made Independence Day a familiar and predictable civic ritual of procession, oration, military exhibition, and orderly imbibition.

POSTWAR OBSERVANCES IN PHILADELPHIA

The comparatively lackluster observances of Independence Day in Philadelphia after the British occupation did not go unnoticed by some of that city's more demonstrative patriots. There, the postwar years were marked by an eventually successful campaign to revive the Fourth as a commemorative festival. In Philadelphia's newspapers citizens read accounts of the celebrations in other towns, particularly Boston and New York. They could hardly miss the incongruence of failing to celebrate the anniversary of the Declaration in the very city in which it was drafted, adopted, and signed. The Congress did not seem eager to bestir itself on that account; the members made no provision for observing the day in 1783 or 1784. In 1784 the Fourth fell on a Sunday, so the only public recognition given was thirteen changes rung on the bells of Christ Church. In Boston and other towns the celebration was merely postponed until Monday, July 5, but in Philadelphia the delay quite dampened what little spirit for celebration there may have been. Over the next two days only a few private dinners honored the occasion. A correspondent for the *Independent Gazetteer,* disgusted by Congress's apparent unwillingness to set an example, chided that body for its political torpor: "It is very extraordinary . . . that this illustrious event did not strike the notice of our *public* bodies— at least in the distinguished manner it has hitherto done in *uniform* periods within the memory of us all, —O! INDEPENDENCE whither hast thou fled! Into what happier region hast thou retreated! Or rather, more pointedly, have the guardians and directors of our country forsaken thee?"[13]

Some Philadelphians, at least, were as concerned about the effects of patriotic amnesia, especially upon the young, as were their Boston counterparts. "The spirit and character of a republic," declared the Pennsylvania Council of Censor in 1784, "is very different from that of a monarchy, and can only be imbibed by education."[14] Taking this principle to heart, the University of Pennsylvania held its 1785 commencements upon the Fourth of July, and encouraged the students to submit patriotic orations for recitation at the ceremonies. An observer thought it "not to be improper, to combine the taste for literary application and excellence, with the love of civil liberty." Indeed, he continued, considering the occasion, "a finer opportunity for that purpose there is not to be met with in the records of the world, than the anniversary of American Independency affords." Reflecting the formula for the Boston orations, the students' papers "shewed much propriety and elegance of sentiment, with respect to our political advantages, and the proper method of improving them."

The exercise was almost a disaster. The number and length of the essays read caused the ceremonies to go on far longer than antici-

pated, and in the July heat the audience grew restive and uncomfortable. The students, especially those whose papers came last, felt the
"uneasiness" of their position. Nevertheless, the crowd stuck it out to
the close of the ceremonies with "patient countenance and condescending attention."

The only other celebration the city papers thought newsworthy
was that of the Society of the Cincinnati, a veteran association of Revolutionary officers founded in 1783. The Cincinnati represented one
body at least that was committed to the annual recognition of Independence Day; the Society held its annual meetings and elections on
the Fourth of July in every state in which there was a chapter. The
Pennsylvania chapter met at City Tavern for their business dinner, and
Independent Gazetteer printed their patriotic after-dinner toasts.[15]

Gradually the "suspicious reserve" that one observer noted as a
legacy of Philadelphia's war experience wore away.[16] The examples
set by the Cincinnati and towns such as Boston, and a growing sense of
the appropriateness of a patriotic holiday, produced a celebration in
1786 that was markedly more to patriotic tastes, and would have been
more familiar to any visiting Bostonian. "No sincere well-wisher to his
country," wrote a correspondent, "can have been insensible to the
uncommonly great attention paid in the city this year, to the anniversary of our glorious day of political independency and freedom."[17]
The uncommonly great attention was due to the efforts of the Society
of the Cincinnati, in close cooperation with the city's volunteer militia.
Following the example of their Boston counterparts, the Philadelphia
militia gathered early that day in the fields just outside the city for
a formal muster. That done, several companies paraded into town,
pausing to fire a salute of musketry before the house of the state president. Their destination was the City Tavern, where, like the previous
year, the Cincinnati held their meeting. Together, accompanied by the
ringing of city bells and a marching band, veterans and young militiamen proceeded to the Reformed Calvinist Church in Race Street for an
Independence Day oration sponsored by the Society. After a "patriotic
and judicious prayer," the Reverend William Rogers, a member of the
Cincinnati, addressed himself to "the memory of the principle political
and military occurrences of the late revolution, and of those heroes
who fell in defending the liberty of their country and the rights of
mankind." Afterward the procession—drawing the "Hazzas and ad-

miration of the multitude"—returned to the City Tavern for dinner; those militia officers who did not accompany the parade dined instead at a country house outside the city.[18] Even Congress came around this year, taking the day off from their work to attend a levee. The whole was characterized by an "admirable order and decorum." An observer hoped that the transactions of the day "may form a model for future celebrations of the same august festival." More revealingly, he trusted that the renewed attention paid to Independence Day in Philadelphia would "prove to the world that the day becomes more and more dear to Pennsylvanians—Time enhances its value."[19]

CHARLESTON AND THE "RETALIATORY SPIRIT"

Any regular patriotic celebration in Charleston approaching the scale of those in Boston or Philadelphia faced a unique jumble of difficulties, especially in the immediate postwar years. The Revolution in the Carolinas had exhibited a particularly vicious quality, a combination of harsh suppressive measures and bitter partisan warfare. Here, too, the memory of the conflict was fresh: the last major campaigns before Yorktown had crisscrossed the Carolina interior, leaving a legacy of hatred between Whig and Tory unmatched in the more northern states. An English visitor discovered that the legacy had lost nothing in the telling even after two decades, and had probably gained a good deal. "The people of this state," he told a friend,

> have not yet got over the baleful effects of the revolutionary War. Their Independence cost the Carolinians, much blood and treasure. Pillage, fire, & sword, are said to have marked the footsteps of the British army in these States. Frightful tales of woe, the almost inseparable companions of civil warfare, are yet fresh in the minds of the Americans, and the name of Cornwallis, your Irish viceroy, is seldom mentioned without a hearty curse.[20]

Unlike Boston or Philadelphia, both of which had suffered occupation for less than a year, Charleston hosted its British conquerors from mid-1780 to nearly the end of the war. The effects of that occupation were more severe than in the other two cities, both of which had at least had some time before the war's end to restore their economies.[21] By the time the British left, much of the Carolinas' interior was devastated by regular armies and partisan bands. Houses and barns had been put to the torch, food and livestock seized, and farm equipment stolen or destroyed. Much of the planters' remaining capital had been tied up in slaves, and some 25,000 thousand of these had been "liberated" and carried away by the British.[22] Many Loyalist families, such as Lucy Wells's, had left Charleston or been banished, depriving the town of many of its "most estimable citizens."[23] Customary markets had of course been interrupted by the war and, perhaps worst of all, the British subsidization of indigo production was lost. It was no wonder if South Carolinians and their leaders felt "dazed" in the aftermath of occupation and war.[24]

Dazed—and angry. Helpless to punish the now-absent British, Charlestonians turned on each other. A violent, anti-British and "anti-aristocrat" sentiment boiled, especially in the lower and artisan ranks. Charleston merchant and political hopeful Alexander Grillon, together with Dr. James Fallon, managed to transform their Smoking Society, one of Charleston's many social groups, into the pugnaciously named Marine Anti-Britannic Society, with themselves as president and secretary, respectively. Into the formerly genteel club Grillon and Fallon attracted many of Charleston's Anglophobic elements, "mostly of the city's unpropertied class," according to one historian.[25]

Those planters and merchants who had maintained close ties with their British connections, and who used them to advantage in the brief import boom in 1783, became the special targets of the bitter and the disaffected. When some of the prominent moderate men of Charleston suggested that all but the "most obnoxious" Loyalists (perhaps fifteen out of a "black list" of 150) be allowed to return, the "lower and rougher class" vehemently opposed the measure, "with a veritable raging obstinacy; they breathed nothing but the bitterness of vengeance, and would hear of no forgiveness."[26] A month before July 4 of that year, a Charleston judge expressed his fear that the postwar agitation would cause Charlestonians to descend into factional infighting. Four men, he claimed, had been killed in the town since the British departed, and many more in the country, on account of the political tensions. A "retaliatory spirit" was abroad and could be easily fanned into further mayhem, warned the judge.[27]

Frustration, a sense of betrayal, and a desire for revenge threatened to make a mockery of Charleston's first tribute to the benefits of recognized independence. After having been suppressed for three years by the British conquerors, the Fourth of July, 1783, should have been a happy affair. But the dawn broke without the accustomed ringing of Saint Michael's splendid bells, for "amongst other property wantonly and wickedly taken away by the British, these made a part." Nine months before, when it became clear that Charleston was to be given up to the Americans, officers of the Royal Artillery claimed their rights according to the customs of war and made off with the bells (bronze was highly prized as "gun-metal"), as well as those belonging to the Presbyterian meeting house. Saint Michael's vestrymen protested in vain that the bells were private property, and so not legitimate spoils of war.[28] Charlestonians would have liked to celebrate their independence with pride; instead, in the acoustic vacuum caused by the loss of the bells, Charlestonians remembered their defeat and humiliation. Still, many inhabitants celebrated as best they could; there were the familiar dinners in the afternoon, and in the evening fireworks returned to the Exchange at the waterfront, and illuminations lit houses that for the past three years had been dark on this night. But all was not well, and some revelers were aware of that fact. At the statehouse, one after-dinner toast prayed: "May the harmony of the day not be interrupted by quarrels, tumult, or licentiousness."[29]

The supplicant got his wish; the storm broke several days later, in the afterglow of patriotic fervor and antiforeign sentiment. According to the official report, a "fray" between two small groups began when a British subject named Thomas Barron "impudently and grossly" insulted a citizen as they passed in a street. Whatever the actual circumstances of the initial incident, the anti-British elements were aroused to action, and for the next two evenings gangs roamed the town searching for Britons or their American supporters to terrorize. The Anglophobes seized four or five "persons who were thought obnoxious to the state," roughed them up and "pumped" them—drenching them under a water pump—before letting them go. Having transferred their humiliation to their victims and cowed the rest of the "aristocrats" in town, the gangs did little more damage, and the tumult petered out.[30]

But it returned the next year, again after a tense but apparently restrained Fourth of July. This time, according to an anti-British newspaper, the trouble began when a group of harmless, innocent apprentices were "attacked" by some presumably pro-aristocratic thugs. Someone summoned help by pealing Saint Michael's bells (returned by the British the previous November), and soon pitched street battles ensued between the forces of the magistracy and its supporters on the one side, and the Marine Anti-Britannic Society on the other (encouraged no doubt by the fact that their president, Grillon, had translated his popularity into a lieutenant governorship the year before). That evening, mounted pro-magistracy vigilantes patrolled the streets, occasioning frequent scuffles, in which at least one citizen was wounded, when he resisted what he regarded as an unlawful arrest.[31] With its virulently anti-British element, Whigs and Tories, and smoldering resentments threatening to break out into street battles, postwar Charleston must have seemed more like prewar Boston or Philadelphia.

THE RITES OF INDEPENDENCE DAY: AN ANATOMY

When the people of the seacoast towns came to adopt an annual festival of independence, whether they did so spontaneously, hesitantly, or by design, they adapted a variety of ritual practices from their cultural repertoire to fit the occasion. None of these practices, whether ceremonial or celebrational in style, was particularly new. In fact, most were positively old, harkening back to pre-Revolutionary forms associated with the king's birthday or accession day. The ritual *forms* displayed far more persistence than did the ritual *content*, however: while independence destroyed the royalist associations of the old rites, the ritual practices survived the demise of monarchy in America intact. On the one hand this phenomenon may suggest only that in eighteenth-century America, form was more immediately compelling than substance. On the other hand, the ease with which so many Americans adapted assertive, politically regicidal associations to traditionally conservative rituals of passive submission suggests that "monarchial culture" may not have run very deep in eighteenth-century America after all. For Revolutionary Americans, apparently, the medium was not the same as the message, and on Independence Day the old rituals could mean precisely what people wanted them to mean.

Certainly Americans were not shy about contributing as many of their most positive secular (and even religious) ritual forms as possible to the solemnization of their nationhood. Each element of formal celebration contributed toward the goal of building enthusiasm for order and national consciousness. Americans increasingly spoke and wrote

1. Charles Fraser, "South View of Fort Mechanic—Charleston, July 4th, 1796." The guns of the fort are firing a salute. Bathers are in the water at the center. (The Gibbes Museum of Art / Carolina Art Association.)

of July 4 in reverent, even religious, tones; for them the Fourth was a "Jubilee," the "brightest day in our calendar," and the "Sabbath of our Freedom."[32] As with a religious Sabbath, according to Catherine Albanese, Independence Day became an event "during which one left the profane time of ordinary activity and participated in a reality which had happened *in illo tempore*." By making the Fourth of July a holy day in a national calendar, the day itself possessed a liminal quality, standing "outside the ordinary sequence of days and hours because it was sacred time."[33] Just as religious holidays set aside special time for ceremony and reflection for the faithful, so Independence Day became the occasion for "a lesson in history and a reminder of duties."[34]

Cannon fire and the clamor of bells made the very dawning of the day significant. Normally the use of cannon and bells was closely regulated; traditionally they functioned to alert the town, usually in the event of emergency such as fire or invasion. But the din also had a celebratory function; it was used to announce good news such as military victory or royal birthdays. It is in this second context—a *birth* day—that bells pealed and cannon thundered. The noise politicized the very air, establishing liminal time and space wherever it was heard, and firing citizens with anticipation for the celebrations to follow (Fig. 1).

A military muster was often the first such event, providing most of the pomp and pageantry for the day. Because force of arms and the virtue of republican men had secured independence (or so ran the popular belief), it was only fitting that the militias of Boston, Philadelphia, and Charleston turn out to share vicariously in "the Spirit of Seventy-six." "This was the most proper emblem that could be given," wrote a Philadelphia observer in 1786, "of the means by which independencey [*sic*] was first affected, and since has been secured, so that many wished, that in future, this day might be set apart as a regular field day."[35] The obvious convenience of scheduling a regular militia day for the Fourth, when the duty would seem less onerous, made the wish an easy reality for many of the amateur soldiers.

Not all of the militia took part in the military ceremonies. For one thing it was logistically impractical, if not impossible, for virtually the entire grown male population to do so. For another, not all militia companies were equal to the dignity of escort duty or showy drill

The Boston Troops, *as reviewed on President Adams's birth day on the Common by his* Honᵉ Lieuᵗ Governor GILL *& Major* Genᶥ ELLIOT, *under the command of Brigadier* Genᶥ Winslow; *also a view of the New State House &ᶜ &ᶜ*

Published by Charles E. Goodspeed, Boston, 1903.
re-engraved by Sidney L. Smith

2. "The Boston Troops, as reviewed on President Adams's birthday on the Common. . . ." This 1799 view depicts many of the same activities that took place in this space of Independence Day (and to considerably larger crowds). Note the uniform appearance of the volunteer units and the socializing of high and low in the foreground. (Massachusetts Historical Society.)

before the public. Instead, special volunteer militia companies performed those coveted tasks. These were associations of young men of wealth and status, such as the Artillery Company and Independent Cadets in Boston, the City Cavalry in Philadelphia, and the Charleston Battalion of Artillery. The specialized nature of their units generally set them apart from the hoi polloi in several respects. Volunteer units were usually artillery, cavalry, or rifle companies—expensive to equip and maintain. Since the states generally provided little or no funding for militias, only the well-off could usually afford to belong to volunteer companies. The young men took pride in their appearance and expertise; members were expected to furnish their own colorful uniforms and equipment, and they trained more often than their plebeian counterparts. The results were predictable. After the first Independence Day in Boston, one journalist noted that, although the "Independent Company" performed *admirably* well," "nothing can be said in praise of the Militia, who perform'd *worse* than ever."[36]

Hours were required for the men to rendezvous, inspect arms, and dress in preparation for their ceremonial role in the public procession. As some units became proficient in their preparations, there was often time to practice maneuvers and fire volleys to entertain the crowds that collected to watch them. The musters and parades became increasingly elaborate. In Boston, the glass-rattling cannonading in State Street was discontinued after the mid-1780s—perhaps there had been complaints—and the center of military activities shifted to the Common to accommodate the growing number of militia companies mustering that day (Fig. 2). At least half a dozen companies paraded on the Common in 1787, watched by the governor and the usual dignitaries, with the addition of the French and Dutch consuls. The presence of the foreign emissaries inspired a particularly grand pageant, described by the *Independent Chronicle* as "brilliant, beyond anything of the kind, ever before exhibited in this town." After their review, the companies paraded through the town, returning to the Common and performing military maneuvers and musketry, to the delight and applause of thousands of townspeople occupying the rising ground. Afterward, "mutual congratulations passed between the several militia corps, and displays of conviviality, friendship, and good fellowship closed the day."[37] Later Fourth of July musters included cavalry troops and even visiting companies from outlying towns, swelling the ranks of militia celebrants still further.

The inclusion of the military on Independence Day did not simply add color and hearken to past glories. An organized military represents the coercive power of a government, the *ultima ratio* of a republic no less than of a monarchy. In a polity where the soldiers are the citizens, the militia symbolizes the consent of the people to their government. On Independence Day the people of Boston and Philadelphia hailed the citizen-soldier as the "founder of the feast," the means by which the United States allegedly secured its Independence, and the last and best hope for the continuation of the young republic.[38] But they were no rabble in arms; their attempts at precision and correctness as a body was political allegory, a fitting and very public representation of the need for personal discipline and collective order in a republic.[39]

As previously related, the Boston town meeting had determined that a public oration should climax the day's activities. But getting to the meetinghouse where the speaker would address his audience could be more than half the fun, and Bostonians turned this perambulation into a major event. Shortly before noon, the ceremonies began with a formal procession from Faneuil Hall. The governor, other state executives, and members of the legislature joined with the Boston selectmen and other town officials in a stately march to one of Boston's meetinghouses. To add color to this civic procession, the elite volunteer militia companies, in their most resplendent array, escorted the dignitaries.

Ritual processions of the sort seen on Independence Day have their roots in the distant past of many cultures; in Western culture, the procession of clergy, guild members, civil leaders, or of combinations of groups on certain saint's days is as old as Christianity. When, on the "sacred" Fourth of July, the civilian and military leaders marched in stately pomp before the respectful gaze of the citizenry, their procession was a symbolic representation, in small, of society at large. Through a sophisticated form of street theater, the community expressed, defined, and reinforced its social infrastructure for any and all to see.[40]

By its nature, a procession is an expression of order, and in turn

requires order to work properly. In a procession, the traditionally
communal space of a town's streets is temporarily taken over or given
up for a specialized use, and the citizenry is likewise given its place
to stand and watch.[41] This is in contrast to distinctly celebratory ritual, when the streets belong (at least temporarily) to the crowds. A
well-executed procession is a powerful, inclusive ritual: its message,
though unstated, is clear, and participation in the rite is virtually universal, if not as a part of the procession, then as spectator. Indeed, the
message of the procession is pointless without an audience. The civil,
military, and ecclesiastical elements of a procession are already aware
of their individual and collective authority; the voluntary attendance
of an audience gives the procession its meaning and signifies approval. In effect, the procession is a mobile liturgical ceremony that
declares "this is the way things are," to which the audience implicitly
replies "amen."[42]

The composition and arrangement of the procession indicates its
nature and message; place and symbolic association are very important. In Boston, the governor and his council typically headed the
parade, followed by members of the Massachusetts House and Senate.
It is not clear whether the Boston selectmen and other town officials
awaited the procession at the appointed destination, or regularly accompanied it. Since the attendance of the governor and legislature at
the town-sponsored oration was by formal (ritual) invitation, the former arrangement seems likely, but the town was apparently represented in the procession in either case. In 1787 the state dignitaries
were followed by the local sheriff and "respectable gentlemen" of the
town.[43] Certainly the selectmen accompanied their "guests" on the
return parade to the statehouse for the customary meal and ritual
toasts.

Smartly dressed companies of volunteer militia escorted the procession. Until 1787 the prestigious Artillery Company formed the
honor guard for Boston's Independence Day. Perhaps the train of cannon they customarily pulled with them proved unwieldy in Boston's
narrow streets, however; beginning in that year the elite and elitist
Independent Cadets, in their resplendent uniforms, took over escort
duty. The usual place for the militia seems to have been on the flanks
of the procession, with squads bringing up the rear and perhaps occa-

sionally clearing the way at the head of the formation. In later years, militia cavalry escorted the governor with drawn sabers, an honor traditionally given only to kings.

In Philadelphia, where Independence Day was not established by civil ordinance, processions were inaugurated by the Society of the Cincinnati, with help from the city's volunteer militia. Beginning in 1786, the Cincinnati preceded their annual Fourth of July meeting with a procession from City Tavern to the Reformed Calvinist Church in Race Street to hear their privately sponsored patriotic orations. The procession, marching in a column of two abreast, was headed by the vice president (George Washington, in temporary retirement, was honorary president of the Society), secretary, and treasurer of the state chapter. A marching band and three companies of militia infantry accompanied them, drawing a considerable crowd. At the head of the procession strode the revered and aging veterans, with the younger soldiers of the city following. The arrangement bespoke continuity, a "passing of the torch" from the Revolutionary generation to the next. The ideals that the Cincinnati members had fought for were now to be entrusted to, and maintained by, a new generation of (socially elite) soldiers.[44]

The processions in Boston, and to a lesser degree in Philadelphia, were familiar to the inheritors of European culture. Tangible representatives of civil authority, from governor to "respectable gentlemen," and in conveniently descending order, asserted their roles in society, preempting the customary use of the streets before returning them to the public. Similarly, the militia symbolically performed their function as protectors of the state. The crowds who observed the processions had no less vital a part to play, although that part was essentially (and significantly) passive. As an audience, they gave context and continuity to the civic pageant played out before them; most important, they gave their approbation to its message.

In all three towns studied here, the public oration was the intellectual and hermeneutical focus of Independence Day. In Boston particularly, all the morning's preparations aimed at this event, and the official procession literally led up to it. In its form, the oration ceremony was a secular version of a Sabbath-day service (and was almost always held in church buildings) that preached the "gospel" of the republic. After crowding lawmakers, officers, and as many citizens as possible onto the floors and galleries, the chaplain to the legislature opened with a prayer. Next, the audience joined a chorus in singing a patriotic ode composed especially for the day and circulated in hand-bills. Like Sabbath hymn singing, this part of the program was a par-ticipatory activity that established purpose for the meeting and put the audience in a receptive state of mind.[45]

Following the ode, the featured speaker delivered the oration/ sermon. The ordinance establishing Boston's annual Independence Day orations required the selected speaker to "consider the feelings, manners, and principles" appropriate to the occasion, but the speech itself was supposed to adhere to a precise formula. The discourse was expected to address five major points: first, the causes of the Revo-lution; second, the "distinguished Characters" who presumably di-rected and effected its successful conclusion; third, the "important and timely aid" received from the French alliance; fourth, the blessings and "superior advantages" of a republican government; and fifth, the supreme importance of maintaining personal and public virtue, "good manners," and the appropriate education without which all that had been gained would be lost.[46] Orations in Charleston could be equally didactic; a witness to William Laughton Smith's Independence Day speech in 1796 commented that "it was no doubt a studied piece" and in places "painfully long."[47]

If the orator's material was circumscribed and formulaic, his task was made easier by his listeners' "high regard for oratory as an intel-lectual activity."[48] By all accounts the Boston orations in particular were immensely popular events, consistently packing the places in which they were delivered.[49] During the 1790 celebration one Nathan Webb, a student residing in Boston, attended not only the town ora-tion, but also one prepared for the Society of the Cincinnati.[50] Nor was the audience limited to Boston residents; out-of-towners frequently braved the crowds for the chance to sit (or stand) in the audience.[51] Those who did not get to hear the town orations bought copies printed by the order of the selectmen that frequently went through several printings. Many of the town's most notable personages provided the orations, and some, like John Quincy Adams, delivered their first ma-jor public address on this day. Speakers like Thomas Dawes, Harrison Gray Otis, and Josiah Quincy attracted large crowds that, as with the Massacre Day orations, required a larger space than Faneuil Hall. The

selectmen employed several different church buildings for the first
decade or so after 1783, but they eventually settled upon the almost
exclusive use of the Old South Meeting House after 1800.

Historian Ralph Henry Gabriel recognized the striking similarity
of Independence Day oration ceremonies to Protestant religious services, with the prayer, ode, and oration assuming the order and place
of the benediction, psalm, and sermon.[52] The oration service performed functions similar to those of the Sabbath as well, fortifying
faith in the republic and uniting the "congregation" as members of a
political Elect. Like a Sunday sermon, the oration invited the listener to
"surrender idiosyncrasies and independence to some larger cause,"
for which he would be willing, presumably, "to fight, die, or pay
homage."[53] As in the religious service, participants at the oration ceremonies were supposed to leave their differences at the door, and collectively affirm their fundamental unity. A Charleston reporter recognized the purpose and power of these rites when he observed that
"the strength of language, the grace of utterance, the occasion, a numerous and brilliant assembly and the power of music, all united to
direct well selected sentiments to the breast."[54]

After the oration, the faithful departed to break bread together at
numerous private dinners. In Boston, the most regular of these was the
"collation" (a cold lunch) hosted by the governor after being escorted
back to the statehouse. There the executive and members of the legislature exchanged "mutual congratulations" and small talk amid the
food and Canary wine. Other groups, especially the militia, were
doing much the same at their favorite taverns and hotels. As one might
expect, eating and drinking establishments did brisk business on Independence Day. In Boston, private parties, civic societies, and hundreds
of thirsty militiamen retired to the Exchange Coffee House, the Green
Dragon, or the Bunch of Grapes to eat and share a convivial cup together. Thirteen patriotic toasts customarily followed dinner, that
number increasing as new states came into the union. Additional "voluntary" toasts often swelled the number of glasses raised to twenty or
more—no doubt contributing substantially to the general "hilarity" so
frequently observed in newspaper accounts.

In Philadelphia, the Congress gratefully set aside its business for
the day to enjoy a light meal together, occasionally interrupted by a
delegation of militia officers or members of the Pennsylvania chapter

of the Cincinnati extending felicitations. The prestigious City Tavern, the Wigwam, and the Old Hob in Walnut Street entertained Phila-delphia's celebrants throughout the warm afternoon. Some groups managed to escape the city's noise and smells by dining in the more bucolic settings of Gray's Ferry on the Schuylkill, and Lilliput on the Jersey shore of the Delaware River.

The regular and careful attention paid in the newspapers to the dinners testifies to the importance attributed to communal feasting on Independence Day. Sharing food is an age-old ritual of group har-mony, and in Christian societies, one with obvious resonances of the Lord's Supper.[55] In ritual eating, the satisfaction of hunger or the need for nutrition are secondary to the symbolic import of the social con-tact. Contemporary accounts glowingly describe the "good humor," "brotherly affection," and "universal love and friendship" that were at the heart of Independence Day dinners.[56] As with the Christian com-munion, and with feasting rituals in virtually all cultures, communal dining on Independence Day reinforced the identity and unity of the participating groups.[57] In both Congress and the state legislatures, bodies that institutionalized (that is, ritualized) conflict, members tem-porarily laid aside differences to celebrate as a unified whole.

Part of the bonding process of feasting required the imbibing of large quantities of spirits in patriotic toasts. These ritual pledges were of three general sorts, though not in a universally prescribed order: of faithfulness to the present body and its concerns, of attach-ment to the larger body of the state and nation, and of adherence to sets of abstract ideals and perceptions. In the first category were toasts to the group itself and to associated luminaries, as when the Society of the Cincinnati toasted George Washington, "The President-General of the Cincinnati—our late Commander-in-Chief."[58] Militia companies, civic groups, and, later, political parties likewise pledged their devo-tion to their fellows. In the second category were the more numerous toasts to civil authority: the state governor, the United States of Amer-ica, the Congress, and so forth. A French observer noted that, despite the original monarchic form of this custom, a republican shift in asso-ciation had taken place. "In America," he wrote, "they have always practiced the English custom of drinking to the health of the Sovereign after the meal. Before the Revolution, the first health was always for George III. 'The Nation' has taken his place."[59] In the final category came pledges to such timely and topical abstractions as "Agriculture, trade, commerce, navigation and fishery," the arts and sciences, public virtue, and "Union to the Confederated States."[60]

Toasts were complementary to the dinner, figuratively as well as literally. Ritual pledging is actually a form of oath-taking, in which an individual signifies his fidelity (toasting was performed by men) to a set of beliefs to which the group subscribes. As in the oath ritual, each individual must demonstrate his voluntary assent before the group. As with most ceremonies, proper performance of this ritual is essential to its success. When the toast was announced, each pledge stood, raised his glass, and drank, preferably draining the glass. Failure to perform any of these elements of the ritual would call into question the individual's adherence to the principles expressed in the toast, and thus his reliability to the group.[61]

The daytime rituals fall under the category of ceremonial performances, but the people of the port towns threw off a degree of restraint during the evening celebrations. The morning's preparations, and the afternoon's carefully crafted performances, readied the people for the evening's release of emotional patriotism. Customarily, true celebration occurs after fulfillment, when the necessary liturgy has been performed and the people are "whole." Indeed, Grimes suggests that all rituals *aspire* toward celebration as a *goal:* celebration substantiates the success of the preceding rites, and "proves" that the ritual message is "real" and accepted as such.[62] Understood this way, even celebration rituals "structure" society.

It is significant that Independence Day celebratory rites occurred chiefly late in the day and especially at night. Studies in other Western cultures reveal similar divisions of ritual styles. In his comparison of Brazilian Independence Day and Carnival, Roberto Da Matta notes that Independence Day "is a ritual carried out in the clear light of day and takes place in well-defined space." On the other hand, the manifestly celebratory activities of Carnival are confined to the night.[63] The American Independence Day combined rituals of ceremony *and* celebration, of day *and* night.

Independence Day celebrants filled the late afternoons and evenings with bell ringing and cannon firing (now serving a *celebratory* function), theatrical presentations, concerts, hot-air balloon demonstrations, horse racing, and especially fireworks. Celebratory by nature and almost universally admired, the official fireworks displays were carefully planned and executed for excitement and for maximum pedagogical effect. Huge transparent paintings depicting Washington and American military victories, dazzling ground displays and soaring rockets "not only gratified a momentary curiosity," noted one observer, "but excited a sensible interest in the feelings of the spectators."[64]

If municipally sponsored fireworks were not in the offing, the citizens of Boston, Charleston, and Philadelphia were quite capable of producing their own. While the 1788 Boston celebration was in progress, news of Virginia's ratification of the Constitution arrive by express rider. That evening the town's bells rang out the news, and a large group of townspeople paraded through the streets "with candles, firing rockets, loud huzzas, and other demonstrations of joy."[65] Potentially disastrous in towns built chiefly of wood, fireworks were supposed to be carefully regulated. The penalty for unauthorized shooting of fireworks in Boston was a stiff four-dollar fine, twice that of discharging a firearm in public, but the ban was generally ignored on Independence Day.[66] In 1806 the selectmen granted the petition of "a number of young men" praying liberty to throw "all kinds of fire works" on the Common on the evening of the Fourth, within certain bounds.[67] But most youngsters did not bother to ask permission, and the authorities were apparently resigned to their powerlessness in this regard, requiring only that squibs and firecrackers be kept away from the prepared fireworks and the public stands on the Common—a reasonable enough request.[68] Indeed, it is difficult to imagine how the town fathers could have wholly forbade the widespread use of fireworks when they were openly advertised for public sale; in 1811 the *Columbian Centinel* carried an advertisement for 26,000 "China Crackers," and numerous similar offers appeared in other newspapers.[69]

Emotional release on Independence Day was not an exercise in unbridled licentiousness, however. Although celebration generally encouraged spontaneity and loosened customary restraints, the expressions of pent-up emotions were still fairly formalized. Celebration is at the same time "spontaneous" and gamelike, directed by understood rules of play. For all the liquor that flowed on Independence Day, there was no drunken riot. Despite the nearly universal participation in the day's festivities, the merrymaking never got out of control.

In celebrations like those on the Fourth of July, public exuberance was "expected, cultivated, self-aware." Play was part of the structure.[70]

The function of Independence Day as an annual historical rite of passage becomes clear by recalling Victor Turner's three-phase composition of such rites. The dawn of July 4, marked by cannon and bells, was a "separation" from the normal calendar, setting apart a "moment in and out of time"—a "liminal" period, wherein participants shared ceremonial rituals of affirmation and group consciousness. The final celebrations completed the last step of "aggregation," confirming the parades, speeches, and dinners that made the participants "whole"— that is, united.[71]

The Fourth of July was a ritual extravaganza. The citizens of Boston, Philadelphia, and Charleston brought together the traditions of muster days, thanksgivings, Sabbath services, and seasonal festivals to form an extraordinary ritual compound. The observance of Independence Day actually contemplated a variety of discrete rituals drawn from different social experiences and creatively woven around a common theme. On the same day, Americans mixed solemn and decorous rites such as official parades, orations, convivial feasting, and pledges (toasts) with celebratory bells, cannon, fireworks, and limited excess.

"SPIRITUAL BLOOD": INDEPENDENCE DAY AS COMMEMORATION

In spite of John Adams's bubbling prophecy, and the public's initially enthusiastic response in the port cities, the continued observance of Independence Day after the Revolution was by no means certain. Indeed, it very nearly died in Philadelphia. Why did it revive? The willingness of Americans to perpetuate a revolutionary festival once the Revolution was over suggests that they felt it necessary and appropriate. What was their need, and what was the propriety of Independence Day?

Partly the need had to do with self-identification and self-definition. As previously stated, societies choose certain events to define them. Independence Day marked the "national birthday," the "political birthday," the point at which Americans "began to be free." The rhetoric surrounding Independence Day admits to virtually no past before July 4, 1776; it was as if Americans could wipe history's slate clean and start afresh. And the circumstances of their political moment of birth lent Americans value-laden terms with which to represent themselves: independent, free, virtuous. But these terms are not definitive; they possess relevance only in relation to their opposite conditions: subservience, bondage, corruption. Thus, Revolutionary Americans initially defined themselves in opposition to their supposed former condition; they defined themselves as opposed to all that they felt Britain stood for. During the early years of the war, when victory hung in the balance, Independence Day was the fitting occasion for ritual rejection of paternal authority and assertion of "adult" status.

But definitions based on opposites have limitations: if Americans were not one thing, what were they? The end of the war by no means ended the search for American identity. During the war it was enough to assert opposition to Britain on July 4. But with the coming of peace, Independence Day as originally observed lost its relevance. Its revival in the 1780s by the Boston leadership and by Philadelphians had to do with this uncertainty of national identity. The rites of Independence Day made men and women conscious of shared membership in a new republic (although they "shared" membership very differently). But the continuation of that consciousness "depended on the sustained relevance and vitality of its meaning." Americans would not continue to participate in nationalist rites unless they saw a reason for doing so. One reason, according to Barry Schwartz, was postwar America's need to "articulate and cultivate ideals that were enthusiastically accepted but not perfectly understood."[72]

Independence may have been won, but maintaining it was another matter. No republic was thought to be capable of longevity without a disciplined, virtuous, civic-minded citizenry. Such citizens did not occur naturally; they had to be educated, even indoctrinated, to their positions of civic responsibility. Benjamin Rush wrote unabashedly about producing "republican machines," and he was not alone in his opinions. Even the liberal arts—notably painting, architecture, and music—strove for distinctly American styles.[73] The newly independent Americans required an entirely new way of thinking if the republic was not to go the way of ancient Greece, or of Rome after the empire.

The key to the future lay in the past. Americans felt that their moment of definition occurred on the fourth day of July, 1776; that moment in time held the essence of their identity and provided the best guidance for their future. But that moment was gone, irretrievable in the literal sense. How could it be recaptured, at least figuratively, in all its original purity and power? Somehow, the moment had to be made to live again. Reflecting on the Independence Day celebrations of 1786, a Philadelphia correspondent thought the words of future French revolutionary Mirabeau pointed the way. Liberty, Mirabeau argued, "cannot long survive the moment when it ceases to be the highest and most sensible of enjoyments. In order that it may be preserved, your passion for it must never abate. Enjoyment must never weaken its charms. . . . [Y]ou must revive in your souls that spirit of intoxication, which you felt at the first shout of victory."[74]

Here, in Mirabeau's words, was the imperative for Independence Day in the new republic. It was to be a secular revival, a reanimation of an "intoxicating" spirit once felt and that must be felt again and again, if the republic was to survive. Freedom could not be experienced passively; one had to nurture a passion for it—and Mirabeau saw no inherent contradiction in rational passion. The fuel for passion had to come from empowering rituals. "A people who are new and rootless," writes Catherine Albanese, "must expend huge amounts of energy in maintaining their identity. Since energy dissipates as it is used, there is a need for an ever-charging supply."[75] As long as humanity went by the calendar, on July 4 there would be an annual "crack in time" through which one could glimpse again, and recapture, the vital spirit of the Revolution. The rememberers of that mystical moment "no longer merely recollected, but lived the event in its own moment with all the power which the moment unleashed."[76]

But what of those who were too young to remember or understand the events commemorated on the Fourth of July, or who indeed would be born in ages to come? Again, Mirabeau had the answer:

> Let the youth, the hope of his country, grow up amidst annual festivals, commemorative of the events of the war, and sacred to the memory of your heroes. Let him learn from his father to weep over the tombs of those heroes, and bless their virtues. Let his first study be your declaration of Independence, and the code of your constitutions, which were sketched out amid the clashing of arms.

Let the sword which his father once used in defense of his
family . . . be bound to his plough. Let the instrument of war, thus
united to the implement of peace, renew that language of signs,
which in ancient times was employed with such effect for less sacred purposes. Intoxicated with a love of liberty . . . let this young
hero, at frequent intervals, quit the toils of husbandry, to kindle
his public spirit amidst war like exercises; let him learn the use of
arms and accustom himself to discipline in the sight of the most
respectable citizens. Let him, in their presence, pledge himself to
defend his country and its laws.[77]

Mirabeau recognized clearly the educative potential of Independence Day so desired by Rush, Adams, and the Boston selectmen.
Ritual action maintains and transmits social bonds "from one generation to another. . . . Such cultural transmission is an enactment, a
drama in which the community is born and will be born again."[78] A
Philadelphia correspondent seconded Mirabeau: "Our youth will by
all means be trained into habits of thinking and speaking becoming
republicans; they will be reminded at least once each year of the glorious performances of their ancestors—of their heroes who are no more,
and of their duty to follow them with honour through such a career of
active life, as may entitle them to similarity of fame."[79] The revolutionary rites of Independence Day were not to be, *could* not be, the exclusive privileges of the Revolutionaries. For those who would follow,
"the remembrance of the new thing the founders had done would
unify and identify the citizen-heirs."[80] Americans endowed the Fourth
of July not only with perpetual life but with life-perpetuating qualities.

As with Christianity, the source of eternal life was rooted in a living
past. And, as with Christian revival movements of the eighteenth and
nineteenth centuries, the spirit of the ancients could be experienced
afresh with the correct combination of personal contemplation and
communal interaction. Thus, a Boston correspondent could relate accurately that the town oration in 1789 was *"well calculated* to *revive* the
principles and feelings which effected the Revolution." Similarly, in
far-off Charleston on that same day, celebrants enjoyed an *"exotic delight,* having *experienced a renovation* of those ideas naturally arising
from a review of the circumstances through which they had passed."[81]

The ability to reconnect with America's original liminal period was
all the more important because concerned Americans could already

see the Revolution slipping deeper into the past. Only three years after the end of the war, Philadelphia's *Independent Gazetteer* reported the activities surrounding the dinner of some "select citizens" and members of Pennsylvania's Society of the Cincinnati: "the occasion was celebrated with that joy and festivity that the ever memorable idea of independence *must have* created and inspired."[82] In a similarly nostalgic context, war veterans increasingly became the subjects of public veneration on the Fourth of July. A week before the 1784 anniversary, a Philadelphia newspaper recounted a "military anecdote" allegedly from 1777. Two soldiers of Washington's army, the moral counterparts of World War II cartoonist Bill Mauldin's "Willie and Joe," attend two different sermons on a Sunday. One preacher espouses a doctrine of universal salvation, the other a more traditional Protestant creed. "Tom," says one, "do you hear how different these fellows preach? Which of them do you intend to believe?" "I'll be d——n'd," replies Tom, "if I believe either of 'em yet a while, till I see it come out in General Orders." In the relative safety of the postwar years, the Revolutionary soldier's smoldering cynicism was an object of genial picaresque humor. A more direct and positive endorsement of the veteran appeared in 1787, when a correspondent covering that year's celebrations noted that "the fond recollection of past dangers, the veneration due to the memory of those heroes who have fallen in the defense of liberty and honor, and the respect that accompanies the characters of those patriots who have survived the glorious contest, naturally impresses the mind with sentiments of gratitude and exultation."[83] Even more telling are the wistful musings of a young orator at the turning of the new century, who may have had in mind Henry V's speech before Agincourt: "To us, my fellow citizens . . . there is a more interesting monument to commemorate this glorious day—in the wounds of those veterans who still survive—and some of whom form part of this festive circle—in these honored wounds, my friends, we should anticipate what may one day be our own fate. . . . Who is there among us who would not covet such glorious wounds?"[84]

Lester H. Cohen, in his analysis of Revolutionary histories in the early republic, argues that the "new historians" gave "voice and shape" to American historical consciousness. But the new history could be disseminated only so quickly in print. It was in public rituals like Independence Day that the great majority of urban populations first encountered their political and military history; the Fourth of July provided an important occasion for interpreting and remembering the Revolution, and enabling it to "pass into the vernacular."[85]

History is "spiritual blood," according to historian Lionel Groulx, "an incessant transfusion from the soul of the forefathers to the souls of the sons, which maintains a race unchanging in its core."[86] If so, then for Americans the celebration of Independence Day constituted the intravenous device. For those who actually experienced the Revolutionary era, the Fourth of July reanimated the old passion for liberty like a regularly administered stimulant. More important for the future of the republic, Independence Day was the occasion on which "the rising generation," and those to follow, would be inoculated with the same stuff.

LOCAL CONDITIONS IN THE SHAPING OF INDEPENDENCE DAY

The revival of Independence Day and its new ideological message addressed political and social needs, as well as cultural, in the seaport towns studied here. All three had a reputation—welcome or otherwise—for public political spectacles and crowd actions. The lower orders of Boston were particularly volatile elements, especially during the frequent economic tremors of the eighteenth century.[87] One of the singular qualities of Boston revolutionary leaders like Samuel Adams was their ability to divert the unfocused, often internecine energies of the lower orders of the town into political action. Instead of Pope's Day riots, Boston's crowds gathered for Stamp Act protests and nonimportation demonstrations. Even after the shooting of Christopher Seider and the subsequent Boston Massacre, when the wrath of the mob may have seemed inevitable, Adams and his cronies instead staged elaborate, emotionally charged, but peaceful political funerals for the victims. It was at this point that the town meeting instituted the annual Massacre Day orations, to keep the bitterness and the revolutionary message smoldering but under control. Moments of directed, focused violence such as the Tea Party were reminders not only of the mob's still-potent destructive power, but of the measure of control that Boston's leaders had come to exercise over that mob. Having seen how the emotions and energies of the people of Boston could be turned into constructive (and destructive) channels, the town meeting in 1783 explicitly and self-consciously exchanged a once-useful but now pointless ritual day for a more pertinent and, they hoped, more permanent one.[88]

Philadelphia's relatively more stable economy offered fewer occasions for large-scale expressions of discontent in the pre-Revolutionary era.[89] Perhaps for this reason the economic dislocation caused by the war, the experience of full-scale military occupation by the British, and the postwar depression demoralized the people of the city so severely. During the particularly bad year of 1779, economic hardship, political readjustment, and lower-order suspicion of the mercantile elite resulted in the ugly "Fort Wilson Riot," in which "silk-stocking" and more plebeian militias squared off in a brief but bloody fray.[90] That same year, in nearby Lancaster, an orderly Independence Day turned sour when a company of militiamen "behaved themselves as drunken madmen, cursed the Committee [of Safety], called them rebels and all the whigs that took their parts, paraded around the Court House. . . . Some of our people [from another company] got angry by the repeated abuse and kept as quiet as could be expected, though as some of them were struck at, they returned the compliment, so that a few blows passed."[91]

Visitors to Philadelphia in 1783 remarked that the city looked as though it had recently been through a tempest. Houses with peeling paint and broken windows lent a disheveled aspect to the once-tidy city. Pavement projects had been abandoned, and the streets turned to mud in the rain. Public buildings still stank, five years later, from their human and animal inhabitants billeted there during the occupation.[92] "Philadelphia boasted once of its especially good police," a German observer in 1784 commented, "and knew nothing of tumultuary and mutinous gatherings of the people, which were not seldom the case with their northern neighbors. This advantageous character . . . was lost during the war, when mobs took possession of the city."[93]

Outbreaks of violence and the depressed state of the city may have frightened the population into more conservative attitudes.[94] Incidents such as the Fort Wilson riot and the dangerous brawl between militia companies in Lancaster may be why Congress seemed so disinclined to promote Independence Day. Certainly it is not entirely coincidence that the revival of Independence Day in Philadelphia parallels the rise of the anti-Constitutionalist, or Republican, party (not to be confused with the Democratic-Republicans of the 1790s) in that city. The Constitutionalists, who secured for Pennsylvania the most radical state constitution in the union, had fallen from political grace by the mid-1780s. Their incipiently preeminent position was based chiefly upon war hysteria and anti-British sentiment, platforms that had small appeal once hostilities ceased. The more conservative anti-Constitutionalists found it easy to blame the economic woes of Pennsylvania, and especially of Philadelphia, on the now-redundant radicals; by 1786 the conservatives were in firm control of the city government. It was in that year, with the election for general assembly members only two months away, that Philadelphians celebrated their first notable Fourth of July in nine years.[95] It is too much to say that Independence Day that year was a purely political stunt by the anti-Constitutionalists, but clearly the conservative element was behind much of the proceeding that day, and made themselves more visible. For one thing, the Society of the Cincinnati, distrusted by democratically inclined Americans as an "aristocratic" institution, hosted and were featured in the focal activities of the day. Not only did they march in procession with the militia and sponsor the oration, they also, to the disgust of democrats, paid a formal call upon the Congress. "They [the Cincinnati] celebrate the Day with a splendor exceeding anything within the practice of Government," complained Rufus King. "The Chapter of these Knights appointed a delegation of four members to present the anniversary congratulations to the president and members of Congress. They attended the Levee, and [I] was witness to the degredation of Government in seeing them received."[96]

It is significant also that only part of the militia marched in the public parade with the Cincinnati and attended their oration and dinner, while the others declined the honor and went to their own reception outside the city. It appears that Philadelphia's conservatives recognized the potential of Independence Day to assert and reinforce republican values (of which they felt themselves to be the embodiment), at the same time responding to a public need for positive thinking. As we shall see, the lesson of that potential was not lost on them, nor on their political rivals.

As in Boston and Philadelphia, political, social, and environmental factors in Charleston shaped the specific form and content of that city's July 4 celebrations. One important factor was a concern for establishing discipline and maintaining it among the more obstreperous elements of society. After the post-Fourth disturbances in 1783 and 1784, in which the lower orders so ominously demonstrated their latent power, a return to order was as welcome to Charleston's elites and moderates as to their Boston counterparts. Charleston became a city in 1783, shortly after the July riots, with the resulting reapportioning of power favoring wealthy merchants and planters. They exercised their enhanced authority during the 1784 riots, when their hastily deputized police cleared the streets and arrested suspected troublemakers in spite of protest against this "unconstitutional and wanton behaviour."[97] The city fathers underscored their aversion to crowds when, days later, they announced that the same Saint Michael's bells that had summoned the mobs would henceforth have a special ring to warn the town and call out the guard in case of riot.[98]

The "friends of order" were quite frank about the reasons for their obvious concerns. Social disorder was bad for business. Charleston's decayed condition at the war's end could only be improved by restoring trade as quickly as possible, and that meant dealing with any and all foreign markets, even if those belonged to the former enemy. Beating up foreigners after Independence Day was the sort of misplaced patriotism that was "disgraceful to good government," and would convey "ill impressions . . . on the minds of the numerous foreigners amongst us, prejudicial to our rising commerce." In an open letter to the people of Charleston, "A Patriot" reminded citizens that their future economic well-being depended on their good behavior: "This country is evidently formed for commerce, and nothing can be more ruinous to its interest, than riot and disorders."[99] As it was apparently Independence Day that had inspired the unrest two years running, city officials and their cronies were alert to excesses of enthusiasm on July Fourth, encouraging "*decent* mirth and jollity" during the daytime and intervening occasionally to discourage evening entertainments.[100]

But other, more immediate factors affected Charleston's July Fourth celebrations. For one thing, it was (and is) hot in Charleston in July—unendurably and dangerously hot, according to visitors and native Charlestonians alike. Unlike Boston or Philadelphia, Charleston lies in a subtropical zone, where the summer's heat and humidity can persist for nearly half the year, causing one observer to remark that, during the period, Carolinians "may be said to bask rather than breathe." "As to walking out during the daytime," wrote Caleb Cotton, "at least before six in the evening, it is out of the question, it is even fatiguing to go out of one room into another." Applying more empirical methods, Cotton later reported that "we had the thermometer at 94 in the shade this summer, which is excessively debilitating, and it has stood at 90 at twelve at night. Warm work, you will say."[101]

Charlestonians said so, too, in their words, customs, architecture, and actions—or lack of actions. Carolinians had long recognized the dangers of the climate, and most low-country planters who had the means to do so fled to Charleston in April or May and stayed there for the entire summer, leaving their plantations in the hands of overseers. Charleston is miles from the open sea, but close enough for gentle southwest breezes to ameliorate the fierce heat somewhat. Permanent residents of the city as well as "summer people" favored narrow, well-ventilated houses, sporting covered porches and balconies, known locally as "piazzas," that generally faced into the prevailing breeze. It was in these circumstances that Charlestonians perfected now-famous summer drinks to replace body fluids lost by almost constant heavy perspiration, while avoiding any unnecessary exertions until evening, which was the time for attending parties and visiting acquaintances.[102] Even with these sensible responses to the prevailing climate, summer in Charleston was, according to one well-travelled Briton, only slightly less hellish than in the country. "No climate," he averred, "can be hotter than that of South Carolina and Georgia. In the piazza of a house at Charleston, when a breeze has prevailed, and there has been no other building near to reflect the heat of the sun, I have known the mercury in Farenheit's thermometer to stand at 101. In the night it did not sink below 89. I do not remember that the thermometer in the shade at Batavia exceeded 101."[103]

But it was not so much the tropical heat and humidity that so affected Charlestonians; Philadelphia and even Boston frequently experienced trying and dangerous heat spells in July. What was so "excessively debilitating" about the southern city's sultry climate was its long duration. Weeks and sometimes months of unrelieved heat and humidity left people in a seemingly continual state of torpor. Worse than the psychological debility was the very real physical danger of heatstroke (newspapers frequently warned their summer readers against overexertion), recurrent bouts with malaria, and almost regular attacks of yellow fever.[104] More than one visitor noted the sallow complexion of Charleston's citizens, women in particular, and even a Scotsman thought that the inhabitants in summer looked "pale and emaciated."[105] Johann Schoepf spoke for most observers of Charleston when he declared it "in the spring a paradise, in the summer a hell, and in the autumn a hospital."[106]

This healthy respect for the weather meant that Charleston's Independence Day parades, compared with those of more northern cities, tended to be of short duration, and as early in the morning as possible, often beginning at daybreak. Few fully dressed dignitaries and militiamen wished to endure more.[107] But processions in midsummer Charleston were not altogether enjoyable for audiences either. The streets were wide and straight, but with few trees to shade people or animals. Moreover, unlike Boston or Philadelphia, none of Charleston's streets were paved. There was little local stone for paving, and apparently even less interest on the part of city government for procuring any. Some homeowners placed narrow board footpaths alongside their houses, but such measures were wholly inadequate to protect large numbers of pedestrians. As a result, "in the middle of the street there is a single surface of sand, which is blown into the air . . . and causes great discomfort to the eyes." Almost every visitor to Charleston remarked on the severity of this inconvenience, which even the rain did not alleviate. "It is not unusual," wrote one, "to see the carriages rolling along up to the axle tree in mud and in less than one week after the wind whirling the Dust and Sand in such opake [sic] clouds as not to be able to perceive a person on the opposite footpath." On Independence Day, hundreds of marching feet must have thrown up clouds of dust that choked marchers and onlookers alike. And one did not even have to be outside to experience this unpleasantness: "Even the people in the front rooms of houses are exposed to this evil [the dust] because they must generally keep their windows open all the time because of the great heat."[108]

Conditions in Charleston's churches and meetinghouses during July 4 orations were probably more uncomfortable than on a regular summer Sunday meeting. Since the orations were nondenominational, these places of worship were likely more crowded than usual, making for a close, stultifying atmosphere that was too much for at least one orator, overcome by "the excessive heat of the weather and a crowded church."[109] Overall, Charleston's Independence Day was more restrained and less convivial in style than in Boston and Philadelphia. Charleston's severe summer climate was an important factor, as was the sensitivity of Charleston's political elite to the potential for public disorder. Another factor critical in shaping Charleston's public holidays was the "peculiar" nature of the city's population, which I shall address in Chapter 4.

A HOLIDAY FOR A NEW ORDER

Independence Day in the 1780s epitomized the changing nature of public celebration in the new republic. Although Americans built upon a steady foundation of familiar rituals, they departed significantly from late colonial practices. Independence Day was a synthesis of previously discrete ritual styles and occasions: it was neither the elite-dominated king's birthday/accession day, nor the plebeian-dominated Pope's Day, but a distinct compound. The celebration of Independence Day was neither elitist nor lower-class, neither conservative nor radical in itself. The different orders still tended to commune with their own kind, but precisely whom the festival was "for" or "by" was obscure and, occasionally, contested. The Fourth of July observances of Revolutionary Americans reveal the crafting of an explicitly "middling" popular culture, a departure from the more polarized political culture of the late colonial Anglo-American world.

The war's successful conclusion changed the message and function of Independence Day. During the Revolution, the Fourth of July served an immediate, pragmatic function, that of inspiring a people to prosecute the war. When hostilities ended, Independence Day became a commemorative event, one in which communication and performance were more important than any practical result.[110] With independence achieved, the Fourth of July lost its immediacy but gained perpetuity; it became "an annual witness of our enjoying undiminished the blessings which it gave."[111]

But with America's "liminal" phase apparently over, could the all-important *communitas* endure? Many contemporary Americans thought so. They would not have expressed it in Victor Turner's terms, but clearly they were aware that "rational passion" and "that spirit of intoxication" was necessary for the republic's maintenance. *Communitas*, they had learned, could be induced through the ritual observance of Independence Day.

The process of inducing spiritual regeneration, however, involved risks. If the Fourth of July festivals were not dominated by social and political elites, what was to prevent Independence Day from becoming a bacchanal, as in the case of Pope's Day? The officials, merchants, and planters of Philadelphia, Boston, and Charleston could never be in complete control of the day's transactions, and they knew it. In the throes of patriotic intoxication, who knew what the people were capable of? Did the general population possess the necessary virtue to practice festive restraint? The decision to institutionalize the Fourth of July called for a delicate balancing act between "intoxication" and civil reinforcement.

For assurance, concerned observers looked partly to the power of the messages contained in the rituals of remembrance. In contrast to the impulsive expressions demonstrated on the first Independence Day, the new celebrations emphasized an order and decorum congruent with the prevalent assumption that a republic was the logical and preferred government of rational people. Any "festival of reason" must itself be reasonable in its purpose, program, and execution. Rational (ritualized) behavior epitomized the abandonment of the fractious, disunited past. If the tree is known by its fruit, then an orderly and dignified Fourth of July was "proof" that the Revolution had been successful; that the American was indeed a "new man."

But to make doubly sure, the promoters of Independence Day took some of the potentially raucous edge off the festival by regularizing the component rituals. The splendid appearance of the elite volunteer companies eclipsed the contributions of the lower-order militias. Highly publicized, skillfully composed orations dominated the rhetoric of independence, while increasingly elaborate parades satisfied the public appetite for spectacle. Authorities attempted to discourage bonfires and home-made "squibs" in favor of responsibly sponsored firework displays. Lynn Hunt, analyzing the behavior of French revolutionaries a decade later, noted similar processes of official co-option:

> The popular classes gathered around the edges of the ceremonial space to watch as the tricolor cockade, the patriotic altar, and the

other signs of liberty were sanctified by their use in the new state ritual. The people's enthusiasm had invested those symbols with meaning in the first place; now official ceremonies regularized them. In this fashion, the popular contribution was at once recognized and partially defused.[112]

Newspaper reports of the "good order" that characterized Independence Day during its first decade sound like collective sighs of relief that public response tended to affirm the social and political order, rather than lampoon or challenge it. By making Independence Day commemorative and institutionalizing its forms, Americans sought to make the Revolution meaningful not only for themselves, but for all time. They adopted familiar forms of celebration and imbued them with new meaning, consciously balancing rituals of celebration with rituals of decorum. They rejected more boisterous forms in favor of an orderly, rational holiday suitable to their achievements. Thus, Independence Day was not only culturally structuring, but *super*structuring, in that the ritual observances built up and magnified the culture's good, virtuous, proper side to public view.[113] The inescapable message of Independence Day was that the American people were divinely guided, virtuous, successful, and united—just what Americans wanted and needed to believe in the 1780s. As Catherine Albanese relates, that belief, "already alive, received an infusion of power by being objectified in ritual action. When internalized it carried fresh authority as the story which was 'really real.'"[114]

Thus, although there was a mixture of ritual styles on Independence Day, there can be no doubt as to which style dominated. The Fourth of July was no Fifth of November; the "birthday of freedom" was not a day of social inversion and lower-class revelry. If anything, Independence Day celebrations flatly rejected the raucous, undisciplined parades of pre-Revolutionary times. The militia and civic authorities, the literal embodiments of order, took official command of the streets during the day. Processions and didactic ceremonies repudiated revel and frolic in favor of dignified restraint and social instruction. Even in the evening, a traditional setting for ritualized disorder, fireworks displays sent unambiguous signals that reinforced the message of patriotic propriety; the illumination of notable public and private buildings lent quiet dignity to the night, dispelling disorderly darkness. In Philadelphia a newspaper correspondent reported with obvious relief that "the entertainments of the day [were] conducted with a regularity and decorum *far beyond all reasonable expectations.*"[115] In Boston, "the day closed without the occurrence of any accident to allay the satisfaction conspicuous in every countenance." Statements like these reveal the recognized potential for "accidents" and disorder on a day that brought a large proportion of the population out to celebrate.[116] Thus, despite the mix of ritual forms and styles employed on Independence Day, a sense of order prevailed. Independence Day was a day of joy and festivity, but in a self-controlled temper befitting the pivotal moment in history that provided the occasion. Any "irregularity or turbulence" on the Fourth of July, declared the editor of the Philadelphia *Aurora*, would be a "disgrace." Rather, the day "ought" to be spent in *"well regulated and rational* festivity."[117] The writer was perhaps more correct than he knew. Revolutionary Americans generally agreed that the Revolution had been the product of a rational process in an age of reason, not the haphazard result of arbitrary events. That being the case, it *ought* to be celebrated in a rational, decorous manner. In celebrating Independence Day, Americans felt they commemorated, quite literally, a new order.

3

A Partisan Holiday

Abstract political symbols are not only used for their
integrative or community-building power, they also
function as powerful divisive forces.

DAVID PROCTOR, *ENACTING POLITICAL CULTURE*

Our anniversary [July Fourth] was spent . . . by no
means with that excess of pleasure I have observed
on former anniversary occasions.

WILLIAM READ TO JACOB READ, JULY 8, 1796

Beginning in the late 1780s, control of the rites and celebrations of Independence Day became the object of intense political
competition. Partisan groups strained mightily to direct the activities
of Independence Day to promote their agendas. Where they could not
do that, they organized alternative observances in direct competition
with those of their rivals. It was political war waged almost exclusively at the symbolic level, but the stakes were no lower for all that.

Independence Day commemorated supposedly definitive events
and values in the birth of the United States, events and values encoded
in patriotic symbols and their ritual use. During the Revolution, the
sense of urgency and shared danger prompted patriots to defer the precise definitions of "independence," "liberty," and "republicanism" to
another day. But Americans were far from agreed on the meanings and
consequences of these ideologically charged terms. Within five years of

the end of the War for Independence, Americans faced a crisis of confidence in the Confederation government and adopted a new federal Constitution. These rapid changes constituted nothing less than a political revolution. Sharp disagreement over economic and international policies gave birth to party politics, a situation most revolutionaries had hoped to avoid. Americans discovered that, far from sharing a monolithic political outlook, they held decidedly differing views of what the Revolution was supposed to have accomplished, or even whether the Revolution was truly over. Inevitably, committed partisans struggled to control the meaning of the Revolution and its fruits.

Doubts, fears, and partisan confrontation became focused on Independence Day. Because Americans had made the Fourth of July into a Sabbath of self-definition, the rites that defined American identity were prizes worth fighting for. Both sides in the contest realized the potential of Independence Day celebrations to shape public political consciousness. Like expensive coaches and political offices, control over crucial public rituals was (and is still) one of the signifiers of authority. It was also the means of communicating that authority. So the ability to manipulate the symbols and rites of Independence Day and their significance implied nothing less than the right to rule. Every July 4, as far as the contestants were concerned, the political culture and ideological future of the United States was at stake.

The "Federalists" who promoted the adoption of the Constitution set the precedents for politically charged Independence Day celebrations in 1788. On July 4, at a pivotal moment in the difficult ratification process, Philadelphia Federalists staged the largest, most elaborate piece of political propaganda yet seen on the American continent. The "Grand Federal Procession" was a tour de force of symbolic communication, unmatched in scale and sophistication for many years. A close examination of this dazzling pageant reveals how a dedicated, motivated minority both communicated and shaped political culture through public ritual.

"A FEAST OF THE MIND":
THE GRAND FEDERAL PROCESSION OF 1788

Francis Hopkinson could not believe his luck. The well-known Philadelphia judge, signer of the Declaration of Independence, poet, and wit had spent the last weeks of June 1788, busily planning a "Grand Federal Procession" for Philadelphia to coincide with the Fourth of July. Now, with dawn breaking on the appointed day, Hopkinson saw with relief that even the weather was going to cooperate. After sunrise the day turned cloudy, mitigating the summer heat. The clouds brought a refreshing southerly breeze, but without rain. Anchored in the Delaware, at the foot of Market Street, lay the ship *Rising Sun,* the flags of the United States and its allies fluttering gaily in the steady wind. That ship was a crowning touch; Hopkinson could not have guessed that there would be a vessel with that wonderfully appropriate and symbolic name in port for the Fourth. Its appearance was one more mark of heaven's favor on the Herculean exertions of Hopkinson, his friends, and about five thousand Philadelphians.

No effort had been spared to make this the largest, most lavish procession ever seen in the United States. Bostonians had set an example back in February, when Massachusetts had ratified the controversial new federal Constitution. Recalling a European tradition, Boston's artisans had organized an elaborate tradesmen's parade in support of the new government.[1] Carrying banners and the tools of their trades to distinguish them, the working men of Boston wound through the narrow, snowy streets before thousands of onlookers. Some of them towed a large model ship mounted on a sled, representing the new "ship of state."[2]

Hopkinson planned to beat Boston's procession, quite literally, by a city mile. The required nine state ratifications for the Constitution had been anticipated in June (a tenth, Virginia, ratified only days before the procession), and Hopkinson labored feverishly to get as many as possible of the military, professional, and trade organizations of Philadelphia and its environs involved in his triumphal procession. Scores of groups were contacted, acquainted with the plan, and allowed to let their imaginations soar for the big day. With the procession's route picked out, the city's street commissioners walked over the line of march to order pavements swept, obstacles removed, and intrusive tree branches lopped.[3]

As the sun broke the horizon, the bells of Christ Church in Second Street rang out in full peal. The *Rising Sun*'s cannon boomed out a salute. Further sleep was out of the question, and for many Philadelphians on that day, there was still much to do. The thousands who

would make up the procession began to assemble around the intersection of South and Third streets by eight o'clock. Horses needed to be
hitched, oxen yoked, and men and women dressed for their part in the
day. Dozens of units needed to be arranged in their respective places,
last-minute adjustments made, and a thousand details attended to.
Nine superintendents of the procession bellowed themselves hoarse
through their speaking trumpets to get everyone and everything in
place and ready for the signal to move. At half past nine the order
came, and the biggest show in America to that date lurched forward.

Whatever the people of Philadelphia had been expecting, this was
bigger: when fully extended the parade was five thousand strong and
a mile and a half in length. Hopkinson had organized the procession
into eighty-eight divisions, but the number of discrete units—civil,
military, and trade—was actually greater. Incredibly elaborate floats,
companies of brightly uniformed foot and horse soldiers, and dramatic tableaux dazzled the watching crowds. Hundreds upon hundreds of artisans and tradesmen displayed or actively demonstrated
their work as the procession moved.

Hopkinson's meticulous planning now paid off. Every unit in the
procession had been previously assigned a specific place in the line. As
the units arrived at the rendezvous that morning, the parade superintendents spirited them to prearranged places in the nearby side
streets. When the parade moved out, each group stepped into its designated place in line at the direction of a superintendent. In this manner the procession avoided descending into chaos as it grew ever
longer. Moving more or less steadily at the rate of a mile per hour, the
spectacular procession must have seemed endless to its awestruck
audience.

The structure of the procession was a masterpiece of political expression. The first thirteen divisions of the parade constituted a mobile
pageant-play of the Revolution, which culminated in the adoption of
the Constitution. Behind a vanguard of twelve axmen and a troop of
cavalry came "Independence": a mounted man bearing a staff from
which hung a white flag with the words "FOURTH OF JULY, 1776." Atop
the staff sat a "cap of liberty." Fifth in line came "French Alliance,"
another mounted man carrying a flag festooned with fleurs-de-lis and
thirteen stars over the words "SIXTH OF FEBRUARY, 1778." "Definitive
Treaty of Peace," another equestrian herald, came seventh. His staff

supported branches of olive and laurel over the date "THIRD OF SEPTEMBER, 1783."

Entirely ignoring the discredited Articles of Confederation, the next emblem, number 10, brought the audience up to date. Two horsemen heralded "A NEW ERA," which was the motto emblazoned on the banner they bore. Lest any misunderstand their role in the pageant, the horsemen blew trumpets and shouted their slogan to the crowd. Close behind (eleventh in line) came "CONVENTION OF THE STATES— SEVENTEENTH OF SEPTEMBER, 1787." In thirteenth place came "THE CONSTITUTION," which as far as the historical pageant, and Hopkinson, was concerned, was the closing act of the Revolution. This display was the first of many moving tableaux in the procession: three prominent judges, in full regalia, rode "a lofty ornamental car," thirteen feet high and shaped like an eagle, drawn by six white horses. Chief Justice Thomas McKean of Pennsylvania supported a tall staff bearing a framed version of the Constitution. Above the document hung another liberty cap and below it were the words "THE PEOPLE" in gold letters.

This first phase of the procession was "street theater" in its purest sense: a living, moving lesson in history and civics, a morality tale in the tradition of the ancient mystery plays. Interspersed with companies of militia, the mounted icons reviewed and interpreted the events of the past twelve years. According to Hopkinson's pageant, all that had come before had led naturally and inevitably to the adoption of the Constitution, the ultimate and logical consummation of the Revolution. "New Era" carried a pendant inscribed with verse that summarized the nature of the new age that was dawning:

> Peace o'er our land her olive wand extends,
> And white rob'd innocence from heav'n descends;
> The crimes and frauds of anarchy shall fail.
> Returning justice lifts again her scale.

So far the Grand Federal Procession would have made the newspapers in any town in America. But the history lesson was just the beginning. The second phase of the procession, consisting of the next nineteen sections, was a testimonial and benediction on the new frame of government. Following behind the "Constitution's" honor guard came ten gentlemen walking arm in arm, "emblematical of the union," each carrying a flag bearing the name of the ratifying state he represented. Next came groups representing American allies and state and local dignitaries, interspersed with militia companies.

Now the ever-growing crowd of Philadelphians saw true marvels of workmanship and showmanship. Twenty-fourth in line towered the "New Roof, or Grand Federal Edifice," intended no doubt by Hopkinson to be the centerpiece of the entire procession.[4] This was a classic-design structure of thirteen Corinthian columns supporting a dome ten feet in diameter and four feet high. The frieze was decorated with thirteen stars; significantly, three of the thirteen columns were left unfinished. Atop the dome was a cupola, and surmounting this was a figure of "plenty, bearing a cornucopia." The whole structure was thirty-three feet high; the carriage on which it rode, drawn by ten white horses, added another three feet. Around the pedestal was the motto, "IN UNION THE FABRIC STANDS FIRM." Incredibly, the work had been accomplished in just four days.

Watching from his house along the parade route, Charles Willson Peale had every right to feel proud as well as exhausted. For while Hopkinson planned, Peale had rolled up his sleeves and set to work. He had been a member of the committee that had surveyed the route for the procession. He had also procured (with no little difficulty) the flags that flew from the *Rising Sun*, had sketched the plan for the figure of Plenty, painted it the next day, and from morning until late in the evening of the third had been painting the Federal Edifice. Now, weary but anxious, he had the satisfaction of hearing his handiwork praised by the crowd, although he knew the paint could not even have been dry yet.[5]

Behind this lofty symbol of the new government walked the proud builders, including sawmakers, file-cutters, and members of the prestigious Carpenters Company, an impressive four hundred and fifty in all. Following them came members of the Pennsylvania Society of the Cincinnati (never ones to miss a parade), city militia officers, and the Agricultural Society. The Manufacturing Society put on a rolling demonstration of the fledgling American clothing industry that "was viewed with astonishment and delight by every spectator," and no wonder.[6] On a carriage measuring thirty by eighteen feet and drawn by ten bay horses, two men busily carded cotton on a new machine, while next to them a woman—a rare sight in the procession itself—

tended an eighty-spindle spinning machine. Two looms were also at work, while the Hewson family (father, mother, and four daughters) printed designs on chintz. This mobile factory also sported prominently displayed examples of fine cloths, and a flag bearing the motto "MAY THE UNION GOVERNMENT PROTECT THE MANUFACTURES OF AMERICA." Marching behind the carriage, about one hundred weavers seconded the sentiment.

The best was yet to come. Thirty-second in line creaked the "Federal Ship *Union*," a thirty-three-foot-long, twenty-gun model frigate built over the captured barge of the British *Serapis,* John Paul Jones's nemesis. Twenty-five crewmen and boys worked its sheets and cannon during the parade. Like the Manufacturers' exhibit, the *Union* was drawn on a carriage by ten horses. At Charles Willson Peale's suggestion, the men who completed her added a clever touch: in order to hide the carriage and wheels, they tacked a large canvas around the model's waterline, extended it outward from the hull over a light frame, and let it drape almost to the ground. Peale then painted the canvas to represent water, "so that nothing incongruous appeared to offend the eye."

Hopkinson had probably intended that the Federal Edifice be the centerpiece of the procession, but he reckoned without the imagination and industry of the shipwrights and riggers of Philadelphia who built the *Union*. It was, conceded Hopkinson, "a master-piece of elegant workmanship, decorated with emblematical carvings, and finished throughout, even to a stroke of the painter's brush." What was even more impressive was the fact that the ship, like the Federal Edifice, was built and ready in four days.

The *Union* stole the show. "Nothing in the procession," declared Charles Biddle, "gave so much delight to the spectators as this ship."[7] The admiring crowd, which up to this time had observed the procession in respectful and awestruck silence, gave way to cheers. "The workmanship and appearance of this beautiful object," explained Hopkinson, "commanded universal attention and applause." The ship's crew responded enthusiastically, ceremonially setting sail as their turn to move came, taking on a "pilot" along the line of march, and working sheets, halyards, and braces whenever the ship "tacked" or "wore" into a new street.

Behind the *Union* came the marine tradesmen and merchants in their appropriate subdivisions. Not content to concede the marine honors entirely to their shipbuilding brethren, the boat builders operated a mobile shop eighteen feet long, eight feet wide, and thirteen feet high. On top of this frame was the *Union*'s elegantly finished barge, and underneath seven workmen were building a thirteen-foot boat, which was actually set up and nearly finished by the time the procession ended.

The third phase of the procession belonged exclusively to the trades and professions. Those connected with the marine trades or with the building of the Federal Edifice were allowed a special place, marching along with and behind their handiwork, but the remainder of the trades groups were assigned their place in the procession by lot, in order to avoid squabbles over pride of place. The next forty-three divisions of the procession were dedicated to Philadelphia's many trades, and each manifested its pride in its skills and accomplishments according to its ability and affluence. Some simply carried flags or banners, emblazoned with the devices of their professions, while others aspired to the showmanship of the manufacturers and boat builders.[8] The cordwainers, chairmakers, painters, whipmakers, potters, wheelwrights, saddlers, gunmakers, and many more demonstrated their crafts on horse-drawn platforms. Others interacted directly with the crowd. The blacksmiths operated a fully functional "manufactory" with real brick chimney, literally beating old swords into plowshares and pruning hooks, making horseshoes "and other work, on demand." Nailers forged, finished, and sold examples of their work, still warm from the coals, directly to the crowd. The printers struck off hundreds of copies of an ode composed for the occasion by Hopkinson and handed them to bystanders. The bakers sported a large bake oven, from which they periodically drew freshly baked bread and distributed it to the spectators. The large and elaborate turnout of the professions signaled to the crowd their confidence (or hope) that happy days would come again with the Constitution.

The last phase of the procession, rather anticlimactic after the spectacle just witnessed, grouped state and local officials with representatives of Philadelphia's clergy and students from the university. In contrast to Boston's Independence Day processions that stressed social hierarchy, these worthies walked in the rear, where they were left to pick their way through the accumulated animal dung and trash left in the trail of the parade.

From its starting point, the procession marched northward up Third Street to Callowhill Street, at the edge of the Northern Liberties of the city. There it turned west on Callowhill for a block, turning left again to march south on Fourth Street, and turned west again at Market Street for the last leg of the march to Union Green at Bush Hill. This route took the procession through Philadelphia's best and most populous neighborhoods. As Peale confessed, the route's comparative simplicity was greatly owing to the ship *Union*, "on the supposition that it would be the most difficult to move around the corners."[9] The long, serpentine path proved convenient: when the procession had passed through Third Street, Peale and undoubtedly thousands of others simply moved up one block and got to watch the whole thing over again. Everywhere the procession passed, the footways, fences, windows, and roofs of the houses were "crowded with spectators, exhibiting a spectacle truly magnificent and irresistably animating."

As the procession neared its destination (the rear of the line had not yet cleared the city), the crew of the *Union* began "casting the lead," then furled sail and "dropped anchor," after which the captain pantomimed the delivery of dispatches to the state president. An estimated 17,000 celebrants crowded onto the green, where James Wilson (whose house had been besieged by disgruntled militiamen nine years before) delivered an oration from the Federal Edifice. An awkward few minutes ensued. "Owing to some mistake, the cannon began firing just as he began to speak, so that no one could understand anything he said."[10]

A circular range of tables, five hundred feet in diameter, surrounded the Edifice and the *Union*. At these tables the leg-sore marchers sat down to a cold collation, with plenty of American porter, beer, and cider—but no liquors or foreign wines. Trumpets announced each of ten formal toasts following dinner; each toast was then drunk to the accompaniment of ten rounds of artillery, echoed by salutes from the *Rising Sun*, in sight a mile away in the Delaware.

Philadelphians had never seen anything like it. "They had a most superb elegant Parade . . . in the City," wrote one witness, "far exceeding any then [*sic*] I have seen in England, the whole conducted without the least Riot of any kind."[11] Foreign observers in the crowd reportedly agreed: "they all yield, in the effect of pleasure, to our hasty exhibition."[12] Words failed otherwise astute correspondents. A week after the event, Philadelphian Anna Clifford wrote to her sister traveling in Canada:

> The city has been much engaged lately with celebrating the
> federal union of the ten states of America and whether that union
> is to produce happiness or misery the pageantry of the day will
> not soon be forgotten, it was altogether a most magnificent shew,
> superior several english gentlemen have said to anything of the
> kind they ever saw in Europe—the papers of the 9th give a minute
> account of the procession but the brilliant effect of the whole
> cannot be easily conceived or described. Our little Clifford was
> particularly delighted with it, he attempted a description but
> like me found himself unequal to the task and gave it up.[13]

A boy in the crowd put the experience more succinctly. It was, he claimed, "undescribable."[14]

The entire point of the event was, as one witness correctly observed, "to express publicly an approbation of the new constitution, by all classes of the community, from the day laborer to the highest functionary of the commonwealth."[15] Hopkinson knew what he was about when he designed his procession; he understood the potency of public ritual. The Grand Federal Procession was a symbolic smorgasbord, in which virtually everything "stood for something else," and often possessed multiple significations. Benjamin Rush observed that "the connexion of the great events of independence—the French alliance—the Peace—and the name of general Washington, with the adoption of the constitution, was happily *calculated* to unite the most remarkable transports of the mind which were felt during the war, with the great events of the day . . . to produce such a tide of joy as has seldom been felt in any age or country."[16]

Federalist symbols abounded. The eagle emblem appeared everywhere: on flags, on shields carried by horsemen, in sculpture, and in the shape of one of the floats. The rising sun (symbolic of the ascendant American empire) was another popular Federalist motif, turning up with nearly equal frequency, and especially in the form of the ship that lay anchored at the bottom of Market Street. The "Federal Edifice" was itself an imposing, three-dimensional representation of the new union: solid, dignified, and in a form that recalled the democracy of antiquity. Its mighty pillars, even unfinished, easily supported the "plenty" that would surely follow in the wake of federal government. Likewise, the show-stopping ship *Union* was an oration in wood and canvas: the great "ship of state" sailing serenely, avoiding disaster with discipline, prudence, and smart handling, trimming sail to every change of direction. The *Union*'s strength was suggested by its twenty cannon, offering defiance to any who would attempt its dignity or thwart its trade. The audience could easily compare the appearance of this ship and its implicit message to the seeming impotence of the Confederation government.[17]

Hopkinson orchestrated familiar elements within the procession to reflect positively on the expected benefits of the Constitution, and to inflate its popular support. The militia companies, interspersed throughout the procession, did not merely give "a beautiful variety to the whole"; they "evinced that both soldiers and citizens united in favor of the new government."[18] Toward the end of the procession, "the clergy of the different Christian denominations, with the rabbi of the Jews," seventeen in all, walked together, most of them arm in arm, "to exemplify the union." Hopkinson gushed at the sight "which, probably, never before occurred in such an extent." But even this apparently spontaneous act of harmony had been calculated for political effect. "Pains were taken," admitted Benjamin Rush, "to connect Ministers of the most dissimilar religious principles together, thereby to shew the influence of a free government in promoting Christian charity. . . . There could not have been a more happy emblem of that section of the new Constitution which opens all its power and offices . . . to worthy men of *every* religion."[19]

Other signs and gestures were even more explicit. Some banners, especially those carried by representatives of the trades and professions, carried mottos that expressed plainly the opinions of those who bore them. The coachmakers' standard prominently featured a rising-sun motif with the words "THE CLOUDS DISPELLED, WE SHINE FORTH." The Manufacturing Society sported a blue silk flag with a similar device and the motto "IN ITS RAYS WE SHALL FEEL NEW VIGOR." The victuallers brought their message most tangibly to the crowd. Two burly axmen led a pair of fully grown oxen, which Charles Wilson Peale, again denied his sleep, was "call'd up very early to decorate."

One ox was labeled "Anarchy" and the other "Confusion." Overhead hung a flag declaring that "THE DEATH OF ANARCHY AND CONFUSION, SHALL FEED THE POOR." Later the beasts were slaughtered, providing more than a ton of meat for the city's poor, with bread bought from the sale of the tallow and hides.[20]

As on previous Independence Days, numbers acquired allegorical significance. Tens and thirteens figured prominently: in the numbers of horses drawing the carriages, in the columns of the Federal Edifice (thirteen, ten finished), in the number of cannon salutes, toasts, arrangement of the marchers, and even the dimensions of the floats themselves (the carvers and guilders rode "an ornamental car, on the federal plan; viz. it was 13 feet by 10 on the floor").[21] Thirteen-star arrangements decorated flags, banners, and carvings throughout the procession, often with ten stars embellished and three left plain. One flag displayed a partially visible fourteenth star for Kentucky (soon to be admitted to the union). Even the organization of the procession was allegorical, in the number of units composing the historical pageant (thirteen), and in the total number of units (eighty-eight).

As Federalist propaganda the Grand Federal Procession was a smashing success. Popular symbols—liberty caps, working-class mottos and emblems, white hunting frocks—mixed unjarringly with classical and conservative Whig allegory to provide what one witness called "food for the *understanding.*" The symphony of color, visual effects, and music "at once charmed the eyes and ears of the spectators and thereby introduced the body to partake . . . in a feast of the mind."[22] The Grand Federal Procession appealed first to the senses; once these were "charmed," the political restructuring took place. The procession's rich array of tableaux, banners, and music condensed an array of philosophical abstracts into signs and actions that could be readily digested by the spectators. The Constitution itself had been picked apart and debated—"deconstructed," a later generation might say—for the previous ten months, to the point where its very existence must have seemed academic to many Americans. The Grand Federal Procession made the Constitution visible, audible, tangible—in short, made it *real* again.

It was undoubtedly the most successful instance of induced *communitas* since the Revolution. Virtually every account attests to the transcendent state of mind of all participants, active and passive. "Political joy," wrote Benjamin Rush, "is one of the strongest emotions of the human mind. Think then . . . how powerful must have been its action upon the mind on this occasion." Rush observed that the spectacle "forced open every heart"; the sight of the ship *Union* "conveyed emotions to every heart that cannot be described."

Such powerful emotions found expression in spontaneous acts of charity and civic harmony, as when people in the crowd provided cooling drinks to the thousands of thirsty paraders. Adrenaline also kept people going through a demanding day. Although the marchers were on their feet from dawn until the late afternoon, "scarcely a person complained of fatigue, although there were many old and weakly persons in the procession." But, observed Rush the physician, "this sudden excitement of the vigor of the body left a corresponding debility behind it, for I scarcely met a person in the afternoon that did not complain of fatigue and discover a desire to retire to rest early in the evening."[23] Revolutionary War veteran Ashbel Green seconded Rush. When Green arrived home after skipping Wilson's oration, "I found myself nearly exhausted by fatigue, as I had formerly been in any one of my military marches." Even the normally chatty schoolboy Nathaniel Snowden had only enough energy to write breathlessly at the day's end, "At grand procession undescribable very tired."[24]

Communitas is also evident in the sense of oneness, of equality, that the ritual performance inspired. "It was very remarkable," commented Rush, "that every countenance wore an air of *dignity* as well as pleasure." In words that would one day return to haunt the Federalist promoters of the procession, Rush noticed that "every tradesman's boy in the procession seemed to consider himself as a principal in the business." Actual equality was far from accomplished fact; differences in status did not entirely disappear in the liminal moment. Still, thought Rush, "rank for a while forgot all its claims."[25]

Observers saw omens everywhere, and universally interpreted them as positive. The weather proved "uncommonly favorable." The dawn provided a natural rising-sun motif, but afterward the hot summer sun was hidden by cloud until well after the heaviest exertions of the day were over. More significant, in the evening an aurora borealis provided a heavenly illumination perfectly fitted for the occasion. Other signs of heaven's favor included the unplanned appearance of the aptly named *Rising Sun*, and the fact that, notwithstanding all the hasty construction, "the manner in which [the floats] were drawn through the streets, and . . . the great number of women and children that were assembled on fences, scaffolds and roofs of the houses," no one was hurt. As a result, claimed Benjamin Rush, hundreds of people remarked that "Heaven was on the federal side of the question." Not even a momentary breakdown along the parade route was allowed to cast a shadow upon the proceedings. When the carriage supporting the moving blacksmith's shop had an "accident" that stopped the procession for several minutes, starry-eyed soothsayers declared that even this "was all in *order,* for it was an emblem of the obstructions and difficulties the Constitution had met with in its establishment from the arts of bad and the ignorance of weak men."[26]

Philadelphians never saw anything like the Grand Federal Procession again until the middle of the next century. The spectacle of 1788 was the result of the convergence of national events, July 4, and a partisan agenda. Compared to the dominant theme of glorifying the Constitution, the celebration of Independence Day was decidedly secondary, but Hopkinson and his fellows obviously viewed the coincidence of the Fourth of July and the anticipated date of ratification as a fortuitous circumstance. For Hopkinson and everyone involved in the project, July 4 held special power. In the liminal moment re-created by the celebration of Independence Day, they sought to bring the Revolutionary cycle to completion. Their Federal Procession did not merely promote the Constitution, as those of other states had done; it celebrated the Constitution as accomplished fact. The procession was not only a rite; it was an event—the final event that officially closed the Revolutionary era. Philadelphians could not hope to repeat the 1788 procession on future Fourths of July—such an extraordinary confluence of circumstances was unique—but the memory of that event lingered long in the public memory. The spectacle showed Philadelphians to what heights public rituals could aspire. In one area, however, the 1788 procession set an example that Philadelphians improved upon in the years to come: that of making Independence Day observances explicitly political.

Cumulatively, the effects of the Grand Federal Procession were all that Hopkinson, Peale, Rush, and every supporter of the Constitution could have wished. For immediate purposes, the great performance was "the happy means of uniting all our citizens in the government."

Rush thought he detected a more enduring legacy in the new "catch-words" he heard on the lips of children like Nathaniel Snowden: "it [the procession] has made such an impression on the minds of our young people that 'federal' and 'union' have now become part of the 'household words' of every family in the city." Rush was seeing his "republican machines" in the making.

DANGER IN THE LIMINAL MOMENT

And yet, for all its undoubted success, the Grand Federal Procession introduces the topic of public rituals as *contested* performances. A careful reading of these same contemporary accounts enables the reader to look past the apparent harmony to find ambiguity, anxiety, and even latent hostility over the interpretation of symbols and their use in the parade.

The first point to bear in mind is that the procession was designed primarily to persuade. Although the new Constitution had been officially accepted, popular opinion of its merits was far from universal. Hopkinson was careful to surround the "Constitution" in the parade with symbols implying popular support. But Philadelphians knew better than anyone else with what secrecy the actual document had been drafted, and with what difficulty it had been ratified. Hopkinson's spectacle was not only a triumphal march but an invitation. By allowing the parade to become to a very significant degree a trade procession, Hopkinson hoped to draw in participants who may have been less than enthusiastic about a purely partisan exposition. Apart from the implicit and explicit Federalist messages and occasional swipes at the Confederation government, no effort was made to single out or castigate "anti-federalists" specifically. Inclusion was the goal; the more the merrier. Opposition to the Constitution was portrayed as a thing of the past, of no consequence, and accordingly was downplayed in the procession. In the hopes of winning over as much of Philadelphia's population as possible, and of sending an emphatically positive message to as yet uncommitted states like New York, the many unanswered questions about the new government were symbolically swept under the rug.

And yet, not everyone watching the procession, nor even all of those directly involved in its performance, received its intended mes-

sage. For that matter, it is difficult to speak of the procession as having
any single message, as so many brought their own concerns and understandings to the event and left it with different impressions. Hopkinson had a specific purpose for the procession, but collective ritual
of this type "invariably alludes to more than it says, and has many
meanings at once."[27] Here at once is both the power and the perplexity
of public ritual: while an excellent medium for mass communication,
the message that comes through in public spectacle is problematic. In
short, the message intended may not be the message received. While
viewing the procession, Philadelphians were bombarded with messages supporting a particular political ideology. But Hopkinson and
his Federalist friends only controlled those symbols they had crafted
with their own hands, and even then they could never control how the
messages in those symbols would be received. Although Hopkinson
preferred strictly political allegory, the tradesmen who made up the
bulk of the procession voiced economic and social concerns as well,
and apparently the spectators responded to these messages just as
enthusiastically.

The apparent unity of spirit symbolized by the procession, and the
much-publicized harmony that supposedly prevailed among participants and spectators, in reality concealed a patchwork of motives and
messages. When read carefully, the mottos and slogans on the banners
carried by the tradesmen of the city indicate a range of economic and
social anxieties. "MAY THE FEDERAL GOVERNMENT REVIVE OUR TRADE"
was the prayer of the biscuitmakers, who hoped for economic encouragement under a government that promised trade protection. The
coachmakers declared "NO TAX ON AMERICAN CARRIAGES," appealing
alike to economic concerns and patriotism. The banners of the Manufacturing Society ("MAY GOVERNMENT PROTECT US") and of the bakers
("MAY OUR COUNTRY NEVER WANT BREAD") betrayed similar incerti-
tude about the future. Other banners promoted the ideals of social
equality and working-class dignity, which, although earnestly sought
by many during and after the Revolution, were far from fact. Would
the new Constitution advance these causes? Philadelphia's tradesmen
wanted no doubts as to where they stood. Out with all distinctions of
birth and wealth, proclaimed the painters, "VIRTUE ALONE IS TRUE
NOBILITY." The printers projected their self-image as guardians of intellectual freedom by asserting: "WE PROTECT AND ARE PROTECTED BY

LIBERTY." But it was the bricklayers who were the most insistently democratic in their sentiments. "BOTH BUILDINGS AND RULERS," they declared, "ARE THE WORKS OF OUR HANDS." It is ironic that such egalitarian sentiments found expression in a parade organized by Philadelphia's elite.

The range of emotions and motivations caught the attention of the perceptive Benjamin Rush. "Perhaps a greater number or a greater combination of passions never seized at the same time upon every faculty of the soul," he wrote.

> The patriot enjoyed a complete triumph, whether the objects of his patriotism were the security of liberty, the establishment of law, the protection of manufactures, or the extension of science in his country. The benevolent man saw a precedent established for forming free governments in every part of the world. The man of humanity contemplated the end of the distresses of his fellow citizens in the revival of commerce and agriculture. Even the selfish passions were not idle. The ambitious man beheld with pleasure the honors that were to be disposed of by the new government, and the man of wealth realized once more the safety of his bonds and rents against the inroads of paper money and tender laws. Every person felt one of these passions, many more than one, and some all of them during the procession.[28]

Evidently, "the language of signs" was not always heard the same way by everyone. The inclusion of some symbols, or the juxtaposition of others, was disagreeable to certain observers. Rush, for example, was disturbed about one important characteristic of the ship *Union*: "She was a ship of war. I wish the procession could have been conducted without the blending of emblems of peace and war together." Doubtless many of the Quaker persuasion agreed, and interpreted the highly visible soldiery less favorably than Hopkinson did.[29]

Nor were the professions participating in the procession perfectly united among themselves. At one point along the route the Agricultural Society, considerably underrepresented by the difficulty of bringing farmers in from the country, passed the group of lawyers awaiting their turn to get into line. One agrarian seized the moment to fire a dart at the farmers' traditional adversaries: "We sow, gentlemen, but you reap the fruits of our labors."[30]

Hopkinson's claims that universal sobriety and concord prevailed among those involved in the procession seem too good to be true—and they are. At Bush Hill, he boasted, "American beer, and cider" were the only beverages served. The choice was not simply patriotic; "Foreign liquors" were also considerably more intoxicating. Benjamin Rush even dreamed of a monument commemorating the complete temperance of the event. In part the inscription he composed for his fantasy read: "Learn, reader, to prize those invaluable FEDERAL liquors, and to consider them as the companions of those virtues that alone render our country free and respectable." Alas, his dreams evaporated when he learned to his disgust that "two or three persons" became intoxicated at Union Green and "several quarrels" ensued. It would be surprising indeed if these were the only instances of inebriation or disaccord in all of Philadelphia on that day.[31]

Hopkinson intended the 1788 Grand Federal Procession to speak for all Americans, whether all Americans wanted it to or not. Hopkinson and his friends created their own "language of signs," not so much to express an existing cultural consciousness as to shape a new one. Through carefully structured symbolic language, the procession sought to reshape, to *transform* the "cultural persona" of Philadelphians.[32] Through ritual participation, the spectators were asked to give their support to new structures of political union and federal government. At least in the short run, the procession succeeded to no small degree.

But Hopkinson had taken a chance. In producing the Grand Federal Procession, he sought to promulgate a specific political persuasion as though it were incontestable, when in fact those things he wished to communicate were very much in doubt. The liminal moment that public ceremony creates is potentially an occasion of danger: while it is "often the scene and time for the emergence of a society's deepest values . . . it may also be the venue and occasion for the most radical skepticism . . . about cherished values and rules. Ambiguity reigns."[33]

Ambiguity reigns in spite of ritual, not because of it. Public ritual strives for wholeness in society, for oneness, not for multiplicity; ultimately, however, it can do no more than to mask ambiguity with the assertion of agreement. Public celebrations have the power to "make it appear that there is no conflict, only harmony, no disorder, only order, that if danger threatens, safe solutions are at hand, that political unity is immediate and real *because* it is celebrated, and so on. Ritual can assert that what is culturally created and man-made is as undoubtable as physical reality."[34] During the Revolution, Fourth of July celebrations promoted common cause against a common enemy despite traditions of intercolonial indifference and even hostility. Postwar Fourths glorified new "American" ideals and virtues in the face of persistent self-centeredness on the part of the states. Commonality may be the ideal of a given culture, and for that reason it is ritualized, but ritual cannot make differences disappear.

And where there is ambiguity, where there are differences, sooner or later there will be conflict. Public ceremony and celebrations can allay somewhat the public sensibility of conflict within a given society, but ritual possesses an equally powerful, darker side. Since ritual often attempts to hide social contradiction, it is "manifestly competitive, sometimes conflict laden."[35] Because symbols both invite "believers" and at the same time exclude "nonbelievers," the symbols manipulated in public ritual have the potential both to build communities and break them apart. In other words, symbols both unite and divide.[36] Ritual continues to function as a structuring event only so long as its unifying properties outweigh its divisive potential.

Ambiguity is inseparable from ritual; it is the reason that ritual exists. In planning the Grand Federal Procession of 1788, Francis Hopkinson sought to minimize ambiguity with new, explicitly Federalist symbols, or by adopting already familiar symbols and making them explicitly federalist. That he was mostly successful is due in large part to the forward-looking theme of the procession as a whole, and to the receptivity of his audience. Instead of relying upon the past to justify a less than satisfactory present, the parade (after the introductory pageant-play) invoked a vision of a rosy future under new government. By successfully directing public attention to unifying themes (like hope), social tensions were ritually suppressed.

But clearly, not everyone was fully convinced. Conflicts in motives, apprehensions concerning the future, and sporadic incidents of disorder testify to the divisive potential of community ritual. Even in the midst of their political euphoria, Philadelphians pondered the reality of Hopkinson's hopeful message. Anna Clifford was not alone in wondering whether the federal union would produce "happiness or misery." The uncertainty dogged Americans in the decades to follow. Instead of veiling the ambiguities of American republicanism, the yearly observance of Independence Day increasingly underscored them.

A PARTISAN HOLIDAY: INDEPENDENCE DAY IN THE 1790S

The Constitution's "honeymoon" period was brief. Although temporarily in bad odor politically, the outmaneuvered "anti-federalist" opposition to federal aggrandizement of power only awaited suitable issues on which to base a renewed attack. They did not have to wait long. A new economic agenda, sponsored by Alexander Hamilton, aimed at strengthening the national economy by creating reliable federal revenues, stabilizing the banking system, and assuming state debts. His programs got off to a promising start, and at first seemed to fulfil the expectations of the nation's businessmen, artisans, and tradesmen for increased domestic and foreign trade. Political upheaval in France also increased demand for American produce and shipping, which likewise benefited the port cities.

But Hamilton's economic recovery program may have worked too well, and too quickly. Accelerated growth in the mercantile quarters inspired a speculation boom that abruptly went bust in mid-1791. Less than a year later a more severe panic added to the economic disruption. Disillusionment in national economic policies shook public confidence in the Federalists. In Germantown, a suburb of Philadelphia, the Society for Promoting Domestic Manufactures chose the Fourth of July, 1791, for a meeting to protest the excise on distilled spirits recently approved by Congress. The date was chosen deliberately: "As the fourth day of July is held sacred to the liberties of our country, we have selected this day to take into consideration the Excise law," which the society deemed not "consistent with the rights and liberties of a free people." The disgruntled members of the Society discovered that irony gave protest an edge; for them, Independence Day was a perfectly appropriate time to oppose an unpopular tax.[37]

The French Revolution further polarized Federalists and their opponents. No longer opposing the Constitution, the anti-federalists had successfully shaken off that pejorative appellation and were becoming generally known as Democratic-Republicans, or simply Republicans.

Federalists deplored the excesses of the *révolutionnaires* and feared that their radicalism, if embraced by Americans, could threaten the existing social order. On the other hand, Republicans regarded the goals of the French insurgents as corresponding with those of Revolutionary America. They viewed the events in France as a kindred republican movement, and adopted or adapted much of the revolutionary rhetoric coming from France to American issues. One's position on the French Revolution was not merely a matter of choosing sides in an abstract, far-away contest. Sympathy for, or revulsion to, the revolutionists in France awakened Americans' awareness of a troublesome vagueness in their own understanding of republicanism. Most probably agreed that republicanism implied abandoning monarchy and European-style aristocracy. Republicanism also presumed the concept of governmental authority by the will of the people. But beyond that agreement vanished.[38]

The problem of satisfactorily defining republicanism was not merely academic. As far as contemporaries were concerned, its resolution would determine the future course of republican government in America. One strain of republican philosophy (generally favored by the Federalists) emphasized government by the republic's educated elite, duly chosen by a restricted electorate. Republicans preferred a variety that stressed equality of social orders in government, and looser voting qualifications. Bitter political confrontations over domestic and foreign policies brought Federalists and Republicans to the point of complete distrust in each others' motives and integrity. By the mid-1790s, "American political life had reached the point where no genuine debate, no real dialogue was possible for there no longer existed the toleration of differences which debate requires." Each side esteemed the other in terms of one-dimensional stereotypes that precluded rational discussion. To Republicans, Federalists were little more than monarchists intent on subverting American republicanism. Federalists regarded Republicans as "social levelers and anarchists," bent on mob rule.[39] Each thought the other dangerous for different, yet similar, reasons: each seemed to its opponents likely to destroy the American republican experiment.

The bitterness of the conflict altered former patterns of political and social intercourse. The Republican champion Thomas Jefferson wrote to a friend of the change in 1797:

You and I have formerly seen warm debates and high political passions. But gentlemen of different politics would then speak to each other, and separate the business of the Senate from that of society. It is not so now. Men who had been intimate all their lives, cross the streets to avoid meeting, and turn their heads another way, lest they should be obliged to touch their hats. This may do for young men for whom passion is an enjoyment, but it is afflicting to peaceable minds.[40]

Tensions born of such "affliction" soon infiltrated the observance of Independence Day. The earliest manifestations of conflict were fairly restrained, confined mostly to taking sides on the French Revolution. In Boston in 1791, the militia from the eleventh ward included in their dinner a toast to "our Gallic Allies." The *Independent Chronicle,* a decidedly pro-Republican newspaper, began running installments of Thomas Paine's *The Rights of Man* at the beginning of the month, considering its radical message appropriate not only to Independence Day but the times in general.[41] In Philadelphia the next year, fireworks scheduled for the evening of the Fourth had to be postponed on account of the weather. The rain date selected was July 14, "the anniversary of the French Revolution; on which day it is expected there will be general rejoicing in every part of the United States."[42]

Rejoicing was not general with Federalists, who objected to identifying the French Revolution with the American. In the drama unfolding in Europe and the revival of revolutionary rhetoric, however, Republicans discovered a new level on which to attack their opponents. And in the rites of Independence Day they found effective tools for waging ideological warfare. Republicans organized throughout the country, and challenged Federalist domination in Boston, Charleston, and Philadelphia. As they did so, the rhetoric accompanying Independence Day became steadily nastier.

Republicans warned Americans that political dangers still threatened the young republic. Abandoning the "anti-federal" stance that some of them held during the Constitutional debates, Republicans now represented themselves as the true defenders of American liberty *and* federal government. Federalists, they claimed, were wolves in sheep's clothing: would-be aristocrats, Anglophiles and "new Tories" who used the Constitution to protect the interests of their "class." The same Boston militia company that toasted their "Gallic Allies" also proclaimed: "May the emanations of *Federalism* be as a *Pillar of Fire* to true Republicans, and as a Cloud of Darkness to Aristocrats."[43] Republicans lost no opportunity to identify Federalists with aristocracy, linking them to images of opulence, greed, and corruption. "However pleasing the ideas of Monarchy may be to *some* people," wrote a Philadelphia correspondent concerning the 1791 celebrations, "the citizens of Philadelphia are too strongly attached to their present happy Constitution, to pay the smallest regard to the arguments that are broached in favor of arbitrary government, and hereditary succession."[44]

Far from being respectable statesmen, argued Republicans, the Federalists were actually enemies to America's most sacred values, and Federalist attitudes toward the French revolutionists betrayed their real natures. In 1793, a Republican correspondent warned fellow Bostonians to beware how they associated with "enemies" who "promote the interests of Tyrants and their satellites." The Federalists were ungrateful, he claimed; France had helped secure the independence of the United States. Now France was struggling against all of Europe for liberty, and America was her only friend in the world. Nevertheless, the writer continued, on this Independence Day "you may observe a *Bold Indifference* and *disgraceful pusillanimity* among some, *on whose head* [France's] *Troops placed the laurel of victory and applause.*"[45] Criticism like this went right to the top of the nation's polity.

Ingratitude was bad enough, but Republicans throughout America saw far more sinister implications in Federalist hostility to revolutionary France. "The cause of France interests every friend of humanity, liberty and the Rights of Man," argued a Charleston advertisement for a celebration. If so, it followed that anyone *not* interested in the cause of France must be an enemy to humanity, liberty, and the Rights of Man.[46] Agreeable to this logic, Republicans labored to make American response to the French Revolution a touchstone of American patriotism, especially on July 4. Tapping a favorite Republican theme, an Independence Day correspondent in Boston outlined an eighteenth-century version of the domino theory, directly linking America's future with that of France. A monarchical conspiracy existed, he claimed, that plotted to undermine and eventually crush republicanism wherever it appeared. The kingdoms of Europe were already arrayed against France; if she fell, America would be next. Therefore, the ultimate success of the French Revolution was essential.[47] That same July 4, a

Charleston orator echoed the argument of his northern countryman: "The eyes of the world," he assured his listeners, "are fixed on this country and on France."[48]

At a time when British outposts still threatened American claims to the Ohio Frontier, conspiracy theories found plenty of believers. Sometimes these theories linked foreign monarchists with American elitists. Suspicious minds transformed whiskey excises into a plot to keep Americans on the frontier impoverished and weak. The joy that should have accompanied July 4 in 1792 was blasted, according to one observer, by the disgraceful conduct and disastrous events of the Indian war in the Ohio territory, which was waged for no other purpose than "to aggrandize a few individuals."[49]

Republicans gathered on July 4 *and* 14, to reaffirm their ties with the cause of France, excoriate Federalists and aristocrats, and to recruit. The Democratic Society of Philadelphia held its first Fourth of July meeting in 1794, to which they invited "other patriotic citizens." There they toasted "our allies and brethren, the Sans Culottes of France" and "The Patriots of Poland" (which was then in the throes of its own revolution).[50] That same year, French citizens in Boston invited "those of their Allies who are the real friends to the general principles of Liberty and Equality" to join with them in celebrating Bastille Day.[51] The French Patriotic Society in Philadelphia linked the American and French causes more tangibly. Their room at Lesher's Tavern was decorated on Independence Day with the American flag and the revolutionary tricolor, "joining under a cap of liberty, on which the national cockade was fixed."[52]

Federalists disdained at first to respond in kind on Independence Day. They generally regarded Republican pretensions to represent the real interests of Americans as beneath contempt. Rather than fight fire with fire, Federalists invoked the nearly deified image of Washington, or tried to convince readers of their newspapers that the country was already sanctified with "the greatest national and individual blessings, that were ever realized by nations or individuals. . . . We are now in the full enjoyment of every blessing which could possibly have been contemplated, and even more than probably had entered the heart of man to conceive."[53] To a growing proportion of Americans, however, such rhapsodizing seemed out of touch with reality.

In both Boston and Philadelphia, Republican challenges met with some success. Boston Federalists were compelled to bear the governorship of Massachusetts favorite son Samuel Adams for three years. In Philadelphia, Republicans steadily loosened the Federalist grip on the city's wards.[54] Federalists sensed trouble, but nevertheless maintained a policy of ridicule and self-righteous superiority toward their opponents. A Federalist correspondent to the *Gazette of the United States* simply dismissed the July 4, 1794, meeting of the Democratic Society, rhetorically asking his readers, "are they not rather a few, discontented with the small station which their small talents fit them for, and who are endeavoring thro' a covered way to sap the foundation of the government of the United States, under the pretext of finding out faults in its administrators, in order to obtain that rank and consequence which their own vanity and self-sufficiency render them ambitious of?"[55]

In contrast to their brethren in Boston and Philadelphia, Charleston's Federalists were fewer in number, smaller in proportion to the city population, and divided into several distinct cliques. But composed of pro-British merchants, prominent lawyers, bankers, and holders of the public debt, they were collectively a powerful group.[56] Also in contrast to Boston and Philadelphia, Charleston in the 1790s was no longer the capital of the state. Previously, planters in South Carolina's low country (of which Charleston was the economic hub), combined with city-dwelling lawyers and pro-British merchants, had formed a powerful bloc in the state legislature. Because of a representation scheme that heavily favored them, the low-country voters, with only a fifth of the white population of the state, elected nearly two-thirds of the state's legislators. More white planters moved into the backcountry during the 1790s, however, forming a powerful new network of their own, and by 1790 had succeeded in moving the state capital to Columbia. Charleston Federalists were now physically distanced from the center of political power in the state; nevertheless, until broader suffrage acts came to South Carolina, they dominated the political scene in the port city until the end of the 1790s.[57]

Certainly they could not count on much broad-based local support. Charleston's large artisan and mechanic population overwhelmingly favored the cause of revolutionary France, and they had long enough memories to see that the same "aristocratic" elements who had suppressed post–Independence Day protests were much the same men who so strongly opposed debtor relief in 1788 and who viewed the French Revolution with disgust. Supporting the laboring elements were merchants who "looked to France . . . rather than England, as a trade partner." Together they formed one of the most active Democratic-Republican societies in the nation, second only to that of Philadelphia. Despite their impressive numbers and activity, Republicans in Charleston could make little headway against the Federalist bloc. The French Revolution's violent turn, and especially the emancipation of France's slaves in the West Indies, cost the Republicans much-needed support from political moderates. With impunity, Federalists simply heaped scorn on what they regarded as a party of disgruntled have-nots.[58]

The strategies adopted by Republicans and Federalists for marking the Fourth of July reveal fundamental differences in their understanding of the American Revolution. Federalists considered the Revolution over, its goals realized and forever enshrined in the federal Constitution. The war that followed the Declaration of Independence, wrote Benjamin Rush, was "nothing but the first act of the great drama."[59] As the opening pageant-play in Philadelphia's Grand Federal Procession demonstrated, the adoption of the federal Constitution was for Federalists the closing act of the Revolution. " 'Till this period," declared New Hampshireman Aaron Hall in 1788, "the Revolution in America, has never appeared to me to be completed; but this [the ratification of the Constitution] is laying the cap-stone of the great American Empire."[60] Rush agreed. "T'is done," he concluded, "We have become a nation."[61] Federalist newspapers took up Rush's phrase "T'is done!" on Independence Day as a sort of mantra, reminding readers that the Fourth of July only marked the beginning of a process that the Constitution consummated.[62]

Republicans did not share the Federalists' complacency. For them, the American Revolution represented the opening shots in a worldwide republican movement. The independence of the United States, followed hard by upheavals in France and then Poland, convinced the more radical Republican elements that the old monarchies were on the way out. "May the same spirit prevail throughout the globe that actuated the heroes of 1776 in America," toasted Philadelphia's "Volunteer Greens." When Boston Republicans flew the French and Dutch colors alongside those of the United States on Independence Day, they wanted their fellow citizens to understand the Revolution as American in origin, but international in scope.

For that matter, Republicans were unconvinced that the American phase of the great Revolution was as neatly concluded as the Federalists wanted everyone to believe. Republicans had always been suspicious of Federalist motives in creating a strong central government. Federalist policies, especially Hamilton's financial reforms, convinced Republicans that their rivals distrusted and despised the American people, and were insidiously garnering autocratic power under the mere guise of republican government. As far as Republicans were concerned, the country's greatest enemies were in fact those running it. Until those enemies were defeated, and true republican balance restored, the American Revolution was not yet won. Both nationally and internationally, Republicans viewed the struggle for liberty as incomplete.

So on Independence Day, two competing interpretations of the American Revolution came into sharp focus. The Federalists regarded the Fourth of July as a commemoration of a historical rite of passage, fully consummated. The Revolution was accomplished fact, and in the past. Republicans considered the Revolution a fact also, but perceived Independence Day as a moment in a dynamic historical process that was still unfolding. In effect, the American nation was still in its "liminal" state. Two such opposing interpretations could not coexist; one had to dominate at the expense of the other. In the rarefied moment of Independence Day, Republicans and Federalists found an especially favorable opportunity to capture the "hearts and minds" of Americans and to shape American political culture. With the stakes so high, with the activities of July 4 so charged with manipulative potential, and with political controversy so continual throughout the 1790s, Independence Day activities and rhetoric became more confrontational, especially in Philadelphia and Boston, and the atmosphere of potential violence more palpable.

Negotiations with the British culminating in Jay's Treaty heaped fuel on the political fire. Britain's impressment of American seamen for her wars against France and her continued presence in the Northwest Territory of the United States plagued the foreign policy of the Washington administration. American mercantilists also wanted Britain to relax its restrictions on trade with the West Indies. Republicans viewed the discussions with hostility, convinced that the Federalist-dominated government would sacrifice America's best interests and conclude terms most favorable to its constituents. In June 1794, just days before Independence Day, crowd actions in both Boston and Philadelphia seemed to foreshadow a contentious Fourth of July. In a scene recalling the Stamp Act riots of 1765, Boston mobs broke into homes in the North End, smashing furniture and even pulling down whole houses. The outrages went on for several days, reaching their climax on June 27, when a crowd, reportedly numbering in the hundreds, readied to descend on the South End. With perhaps more nerve than sense, a lone justice of the peace met the mobs at the Mill Bridge dividing the two ends of the town, and somehow talked them into dispersing and going home. The next day the *Columbian Centinel* printed a proclamation by Samuel Adams, former Son of Liberty and now governor, deploring the behavior of the "Persons unknown" and calling upon all peace officers to do their "utmost" to apprehend the offenders. Details of the causes and course of the disturbances are unclear, but the spree appears to have been politically motivated, and directed at suspected "new Tories" by Boston's lower orders. If so, the incident bespeaks a serious erosion of Federalist support among the laboring people of Boston.[63]

While these disturbances rocked Boston, Philadelphia Republicans broadcast their displeasure with the British negotiations less ambiguously, though more peacefully. They focused their fears and frustrations by vilifying Chief Justice John Jay, who led the American delegation. Stuffing an effigy of Jay with gunpowder, they placed it on the platform of the public pillory in Market Street. After several hours, the figure was taken down, beheaded by a makeshift guillotine, and then set afire. The resulting explosion blew "Jay" to tatters and concluded the ritual execution.[64] Citizens in both towns must have wondered what confrontations Independence Day might bring. The disturbing marriage of symbols from the Terror in France and the Gunpowder Plot seemed to promise anarchy. In the end, nature may have aided the cause of peace; July 4 was "a rainey day, with frequent showers with thunder and Lightening." At any rate, the day passed without any further disturbance, although the toast rhetoric warmed considerably.[65]

The next anniversary was another matter. News that the Senate had ratified the treaty on June 24, 1795, drew howls of protest from

Republicans everywhere. Not only, the Republicans charged, did the treaty capitulate on American commercial interests; it also placed the United States in a position of virtual partnership with Britain in her war against revolutionary France. The French agreed, and intimated that economic or even military retaliation would be the consequence.

Republicans in Philadelphia determined to turn July 4 into a day of protest against "the illegitimate imp, the abortion of Liberty . . . a Treaty . . . so replete with hostility to a generous and magnanimous ally [France]."[66] The editors of the *Independent Gazetteer* and the *Aurora General Advertiser* proposed that outraged Americans should henceforth keep the Fourth of July as a day of mourning, "since George III had at last administered a dose of poison to 'Mrs. Liberty.' "[67] The proposition prompted a gibe in verse from the Federalist *Gazette of the United States:*

> To Celebrate the Day—
> The Governor says yea;
> The Aurora says nay:
> Whom shall we obey?[68]

When the day came, Republicans were divided over the proper response. Some feared that simply to celebrate the anniversary as though nothing had happened would be construed as approval of the treaty. On the other hand, to do as the Republican newspapers suggested could place them symbolically outside the ritual brotherhood of the day. Many resolved the dilemma by honoring the day but letting their toasts speak their protest. The officers of the Philadelphia County Brigade wished "A perpetual harvest for America; —but clip'd wings, lame legs, the pip, and an empty crop to all Jays." Purloining an image associated with President Washington, they hoped that Thomas Jefferson, "the illustrious framer of the declaration of American independence, like Cincinnatus be called from retirement, and . . . save us from the calamities which threaten us." Not far away, artillery officers sang a patriotic ode to the tune of "the Marseille hymn."[69]

Other Republicans heeded the words of the *Aurora* and *Independent Gazetteer,* and deliberately flouted the customary rites of Independence Day. Their aim was to generate resentment and opposition to Federalist policies by inverting the approved use of ritual time. Instead of rejoicing, Republicans affected "funeral solemnity." They encouraged Philadelphians to regard the day as "more like the interment of freedom than the anniversary of its birth."[70]

But they did more than mourn. In counterpoint to the Society of the Cincinnati's customary procession on the Fourth, the Republicans organized their own, rather more pointed exhibition. Ship carpenters who just seven years before had figured so prominently in the Grand Federal Procession now trooped a large "transparent painting" of John Jay through the city's streets. The painting depicted Jay in savage caricature, carrying in one hand a set of scales in which "British Gold" heavily outweighed "American Liberty and Independence." With his other hand he held up a copy of the treaty before a group of fawning senators, to whom he declared, "Come up to my price and I will sell you my country." The procession gathered followers as it marched from its starting point in Kensington southward on Front Street to the city limits, westward one block and then southward again, toward the city center on Second Street.

Whether they knew it or not, the carpenters were taking a big chance, both in symbolic and real terms. Their route took them through a part of town containing many of the artisan and laborer class that Republicans had begun to siphon away from the Federalists. Even so, considering the obvious twist the carpenters were giving the usual rites of this "sacred day," spectators might easily have interpreted the display as unpatriotic, as symbolic blasphemy. This time the effigy might have blown up in the Republicans' faces. As it was, admitted the *Independent Gazetteer,* the "great concourse of people" who turned out to see the parade viewed it with "scarcely a whisper"—a reaction that could as well indicate horror as respect.

There was a dangerous moment when the procession reached Market Street. Arrayed in their finery, fully armed and mounted, the City Cavalry blocked the carpenters' route south toward the financial and governmental districts of the city. A rumor, perhaps true, had reached the ears of Governor Mifflin that the carpenters intended to march to President Washington's house to burn their effigy. Mifflin called out the trusty "silk-stocking" cavalry in response.

Men on both sides may have recalled the "Fort Wilson" incident sixteen years earlier. Faced with the real possibility of bloodshed (and apparently unarmed themselves), the carpenters wisely chose discretion. Instead of trying to force their way through the Federalist horsemen, they turned eastward, toward the river, and retraced their steps north on Front Street, shadowed by the cavalry. Back in Kensington, at least, the procession's return was greeted with wild cheers.

But the confrontational mood had not been defused. On safer ground, the gathering crowd once again vented its anger and frustration on Jay's effigy. That evening, amid the "acclamations of hundreds of citizens," the transparency was ceremonially burned. The light and noise again drew the nervous attention of the elite militia, especially after someone threw a stone through a window in the house of the Washingtons' friend, Mrs. Bingham. Some light cavalry under an officer named Morrell appeared on the scene and attempted to disperse the crowd. The response was a hail of stones. Outnumbered, out of their neighborhood, and faced with determined resistance this time, the cavalry withdrew. Republicans hailed the carpenters and the supporting crowd as heroes; the next day someone placed a wooden marker commemorating the spot as the site of "Morrell's Defeat." A sword allegedly dropped by Morrell in his flight was first advertised for sale as a trophy and then contemptuously sold for four cents.[71]

Boston was also ripe for violence on the Fourth in 1795. Two weeks before, and apparently with the encouragement of the French consul in that town, a crowd attacked a British vessel in the outer harbor. Though the ship's master protested that the ship was simply a merchantman, the few small cannon and swivel guns produced in a search of the ship convinced the Boston men that they had caught a Bermudian privateer. They then brought the ship into the mouth of the Charles River opposite the North End. Stripping the hold of anything valuable, they chopped down the masts, set the hull ablaze, and let her burn to the waterline on the Charlestown shore.[72]

It was Boston's turn to be spared a potentially raucous Independence Day, this time because of the limitations of eighteenth-century communications. Despite the best efforts of Philadelphia Republicans to spread the word, news of the terms of Jay's Treaty did not reach Boston until July 6. Two days passed before the *Independent Chronicle* could get the text in print. The monster demonstration that followed came on the tenth, almost a week after Independence Day.[73]

Bloodshed was avoided for the moment, rather narrowly in Philadelphia, but the war of words went on. The election of John Adams in 1796 and subsequent Federalist legislation aimed at squelching opposition raised the level of political tension still higher over the next four years. In Philadelphia, Republicans continued to toast "the Day," but added "may apostate Whigs, old Tories, and British hirelings be disappointed in their endeavours to convert it into a day of mourning"—forgetting that it was their own party that had introduced the funeral motif.[74] Sensing a Federalist dynasty, the Federalist press grew increasingly virulent, styling all those who opposed established (Federalist) government as traitors. Referring to pre–Independence Day editorials in the *Aurora,* the *Gazette of the United States* screamed: "monstrous impudence! a few desperadoes vomit through the medium of the Aurora a perpetual cascade of abuse against the people, their government and its administrators." Although Federalists had long ago expunged any polite mention of France in their July 4 toasts, they did not forget Francophile Thomas Jefferson when raising their glasses: "John Adams: may he like Sampson slay thousands of Frenchmen with the jawbone of Jefferson." As for Jefferson's disciples, Federalist toasts seemed to promise Republicans' worst fears: "May the man who would stop the wheels of government, be crushed under its wheels."[75]

Partisan fervor disrupted the decorum of familiar Independence Day rites. In Boston, Governor Adams refused to attend the customary dinner with local and state dignitaries (mostly Federalist) after the town oration, pointedly preferring to dine with "strangers and private citizens at his house."[76] When a Boston militia company mustered on the Fourth the next year, one Captain Laughton refused to say part of a toast prepared for him by a committee of militiamen for the dinner later that day. After the customary toast to "the Fourth of July, 1776," Laughton was supposed to add: "May no insidious instrument ever consign the liberties of the country into the hands of those who oppose them." Apparently a Federalist sympathizer, he declined. The company was prepared for Laughton's refusal, however. Immediately they voted to publish all toasts as written. Laughton was not about to have his name associated with sentiments he did not share; humiliated by his soldiers, he walked away and later resigned his commission. The company took another vote and resolved to finish the day's schedule without him.[77]

The incident is instructive. The members of the militia company used one of the rituals of Independence Day first to identify, then to exclude, an "enemy" in their midst—in this case, their commanding officer. Their strategy was as effective as any "test oath" administered to Quakers a century and a half earlier. The episode also sheds light on procedures for presenting toasts. Their content was deemed important enough to require prior approval by members of the body to whom the toasts would be addressed. Collectively, the sentiments expressed in toasts represented the political creed of the group. Those who did not agree with the creed were purged from the group or discouraged from joining. Instead of uniting Americans, the rites of Independence Day were becoming tools of exclusion and the means of polarizing political allegiances.

WAR OF SYMBOLS

In this atmosphere of competition, distrust, fear, and downright hatred, words constituted "the foremost instrument" of symbolic expression, but the written or spoken word was not the only weapon in the rhetorical arsenal.[78] Visual symbols were potent communicators in the discourse, and crucial to identifying groups and their values.

Visual symbols form an efficient nonverbal language. They derive their efficiency and their effectiveness from their ability to combine a wealth of information and signification into a single sign. *Sign* is a generic term for a kind of rhetorical shorthand, coming closer to David Zarefsky's "anything that stands for something else"; dark clouds could be a *sign* of rain, for example. Under the general heading of sign are two subcategories: *symbol* and *signal*. A *symbol* distills information, values, and beliefs into a single sign that then represents the cumulative information, values, and beliefs. Symbols are informational. For example, a black mourning dress declares a person's state of grief and is a substitute for actual weeping; a road sign may indicate the direction to a destination, or the proximity of railroad tracks. A *signal* is a type of sign that expects or requires a response.[79] Returning to the language of road signs, a stoplight at an intersection of two or more roads is more than merely informational. It is a demand for precise and immediate behavior. To put the distinction between symbol and signal in eighteenth-century terms, a national flag accompanying an army is a *symbol* signifying the allegiance of those who march under it; in this case the flag is informational. In battle, lowering or surrendering a flag is a *signal* for fighting to cease.

Eighteenth-century Americans employed new symbols or reshaped old ones in order to understand and deal appropriately with their world. When conditions or understandings changed, the symbols changed also. Symbols were always part of the Revolutionary rhetoric, but they did not simply mirror change in the sociopolitical landscape. Symbols were also instruments of change. They were "a means of persuasion, a way of reconstituting the social and political world."[80] "Liberty caps," "liberty trees," cockades, eagles, and flags did not simply replace kings, crowns, lions, and other flags; they communicated different values and world views.[81]

The adoption of the national flag in 1777 provides an explicit example of how Americans symbolized their new political order, and how they communicated that new order to themselves and to others. A member of the Continental Congress later recalled how meticulously the flag had been designed to embody as many symbolic associations as possible:

> The stars of the new flag represent the constellation of States rising in the West. The idea was taken from the constellation Lyra, which in the hand of Orpheus signifies harmony. The blue in the field was taken from the edges of the Covenanters' banner in Scotland, significant of the league and covenant of the United Colonies against oppression, incidentally involving the virtues of vigilance, perseverance, and justice. The stars were in a circle, symbolizing the perpetuity of the Union—the ring, like the circling serpent of the Egyptians, signifying eternity. The thirteen stripes showed, with the stars, the number of the United Colonies, and denoted the subordination of the States of [to] the Union, as well as equality among themselves. The whole was the blending of the various flags previous to the Union flag, viz.: the red flags of the army and the white of the floating batteries. The red color, which in Roman days was the signal of defiance, denotes daring; and the white, purity.[82]

The power—and ambiguity—of the "stars and stripes" as a symbol lies in this plethora of meanings infused in one sign. With its combination of mythological and historical allusions, its reference to "American" values such as purity, justice, equality, defiance to oppression and daring, the new flag appealed to heroic sensibilities so valued in European-American culture. It was designed specifically as a Revolutionary banner, to identify patriots in all colonies and inspire them with the will to resist everything that was supposedly antithetical to the values expressed in the flag.

After the Revolution, however, the flag's symbolism shifted subtly. The flag identified the new nation, of course, but no longer called for defiance and daring—at least, not as far as the new leaders of the nation were concerned. With independence won, the paramount values they saw in the flag were purity, justice, and especially harmony. These were the qualities the national flag communicated on Independence Day when it was trooped in the streets, hung from windows, or flown on the masts of ships at anchor.

Republicans challenged that message. In their hands the flag became a symbol of defiance once again. Because they believed that the Revolution's goals were not fully realized, the flag for them was still a call to arms, although this time on the ideological level. Independence Day focused attention on symbols of nationhood, and it was on these occasions that Republicans employed the American flag in ways that its designers had not anticipated. At their celebration in 1793, a group of Philadelphia Republicans displayed the French and American flags, joined at the top under a French liberty cap, to which was affixed an American cockade. There was a multitude of meanings and associations in such a seemingly artless tableau. The neat balance and arrangement of the revolutionary symbols of both nations communicated instantly a message whose whole was greater than the sum of its individual parts. The legitimacy of the French Revolution, the kinship of causes, an ongoing struggle against tyranny—all could be "told" at a glance.[83] Boston's Republicans also knew how to use the American flag creatively. Celebrating at Faneuil Hall in 1796, they hung the flags of France, Holland, and the United States together to signify, and to salute, a growing international brotherhood of republics.[84]

Federalists and Republicans displayed the same flags on Independence Day, but they "said" different things when they did so. The ambiguity of the symbol permitted this, and permitted the Republicans in particular to graft new associations onto the flag. Federalists were powerless to attack a symbol they also used, and they could not prevent their rivals from attaching to it whatever significance they pleased. Federalists continually deplored Republicans as "factious," and vice versa, but it could not be "factional" to wave the national flag.[85] Federalists could denigrate the Republicans' principles but not the Stars and Stripes; they could only compete with their rivals for control of the popular associations made by it. Republicans in the 1790s learned what Federalists had known in 1788: that symbols could say a great deal without being explicit. Both parties now understood "the language of signs" as well as the spoken or written word; they had become rhetorically multilingual.

The flag is an example of a shared symbol masking competing political agendas. Little direct confrontation was possible unless one group actually desecrated the symbol, and neither side was prepared for that. But when different symbols competed, when signs were less ambiguous, conflict was less restrained. In 1798 a controversial piece of apparel threatened Boston with a Fourth of July donnybrook.

On official or festive occasions, people adorned their hats with patriotic cockades. The official American cockade (like the flag, standardized by Congress) was a black rosette. To show their sympathy and support for revolutionary France, Republicans sported a blue or tricolor cockade on Bastille Day. Some took to wearing the colorful ribbons generally, especially as relations between France and the Federalist government deteriorated through the end of the 1790s. War with France appeared increasingly imminent. Adding to this tension was the passage of the unpopular Alien and Sedition Acts, designed to rid the country of foreign revolutionary elements and silence the Republican opposition. Republicans in the eastern seaboard towns determined to show their disgust and defiance on Independence Day by wearing the French cockade in place of the American. Federalists readied for a showdown; here was a more controversial symbol they could attack directly. Sensing the advantage, the *Columbian Centinel* warned Bostonians that the "improper" emblems would not be tolerated on the Fourth. Even the *Independent Chronicle* advised its Republican readers, "the real friends of order, not to assume any badge liable to misconstruction," concluding that "this would answer no possible good and might be attended with mischief." One correspondent retorted that it was "because the war with France is to be a war of *Extinguishment* that the *black* cockade has been made our national emblem!" Many Republicans agreed to leave their blue cockades at home, but just as many wore them anyway.

During the celebration, Boston merchant Eben Parsons spied the hated emblem on the hat of a man in the street. Parsons accosted the man roughly, seized his hat, and tore the offending symbol from it. The victim turned out to be an elderly Frenchman in the consular office.[86] Perhaps because of the irony of the encounter, there was apparently no reprisal, but clearly Boston's 1798 celebrations had possessed the potential for large-scale disorder.[87]

Again, the incident reveals dynamics of symbolic association and response. The violent response to the blue cockade acknowledged it as a symbol worth taking very seriously. The Republicans purposely wore the improper emblems in competition with the more traditional symbols for Independence Day. On any other day, the blue cockade simply indicated sympathy for a cause. But on the Fourth of July, the decision to wear the controversial emblem in public was a calculated act of defiance, not only to Federalist philosophy, but to actual repressive policies. The special nature of the day itself raised the level and the stakes of debate. Republicans intended the symbolic inversion to compel reexamination of the official American cockade and the government that stood behind it. They argued that the national cockade had become a symbol of Federalist injustice and subversion of American liberties. Without saying a word, each wearer of the blue cockade made a claim on the control of public space, asserted the right of free expression and assembly, and essayed the will and the means of their opponents to do something about it.[88] To Federalists, the blue cockade carried an unmistakably un-American message and violated the sanctity of Independence Day. For them, the blue cockade was transformed from a *sign* designating rivals to a *signal* for suppressive counteraction.

Plainly, cockades could be much more than mere scraps of cloth. They represented competing ideologies and those who held them. Like flags, the cockades were closely related in the minds of Americans to two divergent political realities they represented. Whether hostile or friendly to the color, opponents treated the symbol as though it were the reality itself. Black or blue, the cockade made identification of friend or foe simple and demanded appropriate responses.[89] To other Republicans, the blue cockade denoted a comrade. To Federalists, it signified an enemy to be shunned or, alternatively, to take action against. When Eben Parsons laid violent hands on the old Frenchman's cockade, he felt he was attacking the alternative reality it stood for. Action against the cockade was a substitute for action against real persons.[90]

By the end of the 1790s both Federalists and Republicans had given up the possibility of convincing the other of their errors. Increasingly, their rhetoric turned more toward winning over the uncommitted thousands around them. Pamphlet and newspaper wars continued, as did the poisoned oratory, but both parties continually explored the potential of symbols and ritual action for capturing the allegiance of Americans. Symbols generated the most effective responses when employed strategically, at times of focused political consciousness. For that reason, Independence Day was an occasion for intensified ritual activity. On that day, Federalists and Republicans either competed for control of the same symbol, or countered each other's symbols with signs distinctly their own. The symbols they chose efficiently communicated to themselves and to the public they sought to enlist an interpretation of America's political reality. The rituals of Independence Day became more explicitly persuasive exercises.

When people responded to the symbols, they made political choices. All the flags, cockades, liberty caps, and effigies were "food for the understanding": means by which people became aware of and molded their political culture.[91] Federalists and Republicans understood this, and scrambled to test new symbols or to hone old ones for battle on July 4. For the most part these battles remained in the symbolic realm. Partisans developed alternative rites for Independence Day, as in the case of the Jay effigy processions, or when Bostonians took to the streets with differently colored cockades. But increasingly, public ways became openly contested spaces where violence threatened and occasionally erupted. At stake was nothing less than the power to interpret America's past "correctly"—and in consequence to mold its future course.[92]

4

OBSERVING THE FOURTH

I believe, sir, that no city or town in the union is more
distinguished for the orderly and decorous
deportment of its citizens, than Philadelphia; nor do I
believe that, since the ascendency of the
democracy . . . there has been a single instance of riot,
disorder or outrage committed on the fourth of July,
nor on any other festive day.
  AURORA, July 3, 1806

This is a day of riot and Drunkenness—Independence.
  ELIZABETH DRINKER, *DIARY,* July 4, 1804

T homas F. Pleasant was a Philadelphia lawyer and a
member of the Washington Guards, a Federalist volunteer company.
His day on July 4, 1814, began at half past six; little more than an
hour later he was at the statehouse yard, dressed in his uniform and
fully accoutered, to muster with the rest of his company. Frictions of
long standing within the unit surfaced almost immediately. Pleasant's
friend Anthony made a bid for the command of the company over its
current Captain Raquet via an impromptu company election, but was
rebuffed. Humiliated, Anthony told Raquet he did not expect to turn
out with the Guards again. The amateur soldiers kept busy for the next
hour, drilling within their cordoned-off area of the yard while a crowd
of spectators looked on. At nine o'clock they joined their brigade in
Sixth Street for a two-mile parade through the city.

After the parade, the Guards wanted to attend an oration for the Benevolent Society, a Federalist political league. Captain Raquet refused to march them there, "expressing his disapprobation of the junction of the Civic and the Military." When the rank and file protested, Raquet dismissed them, telling them that they could now do as they wished. Spurned by his comrades only a few hours before, the disgruntled Anthony now received the command from the exasperated soldiers. With Raquet not yet out of earshot, Anthony held an immediate election on the subject of attending the oration. The vote was unanimously in favor, and "the Capt. was thus openly censured by the corps."

After the oration the remaining officers of the Guards indulged in some private character assassination. One was sure his captain "was turning democrat," another that he "displayed littleness of spirit and *mean*ness." The whole company rendezvoused at a tavern for their dinner and toast ceremonies. Customarily, the volunteer companies sent delegations of officers to visit other celebrating units and exchange respects. It was considered an honor to be a delegate, and Pleasant, along with several fellow officers, received the honor that year. Pleasant recalled making a short speech to the prestigious Second Troop of the City Cavalry.

He returned to his own company's dinner to find his fellows already deeply into their cups. When Captain Raquet left after a brief reappearance, Pleasant took the chair as master of ceremonies. Thus it became his embarrassing task to make apologies to a reciprocating delegation from the City Cavalry for the behavior of his men, who were "very unruly and tumultuous." Testing the limits of his new popularity, Anthony tried to get Pleasant to surrender the chair to him, but Pleasant would not give it up, "especially as he [Anthony] was a little boozy." The rest of the entertainments were a disaster. "Tom Davis was so much by the head he could scarcely get through a song." To Pleasant's mortification, more delegations arrived, whom the Guards received "as politely as our situation would admit." When it came time to solicit volunteer toasts (those exceeding the prearranged toasts), Pleasant was bombarded with demands, indicative not only of the citizen-soldiers' "ambition . . . to see their names in print," but their determination to drink still more. Some men maneuvered shamelessly to be sent on specific delegations, or to avoid being sent with certain fellow militiamen.

Pleasant was clearly relieved when the party began to break up. He was not yet in the clear, however. Anthony accosted him in the crowd, but with ambitions forgotten in alcoholic good cheer, he showered Pleasant with "a wonderful deal of affection." Then Pleasant could not find his hat. "The members being nearly all tight, someone took it in a mistake," leaving in its stead a seedy replacement," considerably the worse for age. With mounting annoyance, Pleasant snatched this dilapidated substitute from its place and was almost to the door when two of his men waylaid him to arbitrate an argument in which they were hotly engaged. Pleasant "could not get at the merit of the dispute," as the logical faculties of the opposing parties were clearly not at their best, and frequent loud interruptions of each other's arguments did not help, but whatever the matter was, Pleasant was sure that it was trivial. Nevertheless, the contestants were in dead earnest. One threatened to throw the other out the window; the intended victim dared him to try it, for "if he had attempted it he would have put his bayonet in his guts." More words passed; one accused the other of not behaving "like a gentleman," to which the aggrieved replied "you are a liar" several times, evidently trying to provoke a duel. Pleasant had endured enough. Pretending to be engaged elsewhere, he slipped out, leaving the others still nose to nose.[1]

Descriptions of militia dinners on Independence Day usually make up the largest portion of July 4 activities reported in the newspapers. These accounts give the reader the impression of sober, responsible young men conducting their affairs in an atmosphere of comradeship and goodwill. This impression is hardly surprising, since the accounts that appeared in print were prepared by members of those groups. But as Thomas Pleasant's diary entry attests, what actually went on at these affairs could differ significantly from what the public was allowed to read of them.

Generally, in fact, newspaper accounts of Independence Day proceedings give the impression of universal involvement, profound emotion, and above all, "perfect order." But how accurate is this picture? Published memoirs, personal diaries such as Pleasant's, and official (but less public) records provide evidence that frequently contradicts the glowing reports in periodicals. For one thing, not everyone got involved with July 4 activities; many were indifferent, and some studiously avoided the festival. Certainly the Fourth of July was an emotional time for many, but how profound was people's comprehension of what they celebrated? Did that understanding also change over time? And as for perfect order on Independence Day, if newspaper editors truly believed what they wrote, they must have turned blind eyes to much of what went on about them on July 4. An examination of more candid sources, in addition to journalistic accounts, reveals a wide range of activities available to urban dwellers, and broad differences in their degrees of emotional investment in the rituals of July Fourth.

FROM HOLY DAY TO DAY OFF

The transformation of the Fourth of July into a generally recognized holiday from work did not occur suddenly, but the fact that Pleasant, his comrades, the hundreds of rank-and-file militiamen, and the thousands of spectators who turned out to see them were also away from their regular jobs indicates that by 1814 at least, Independence Day was already well established as a modern-style holiday from the obligations of labor. Although people in Boston, Charleston, and Philadelphia had always marked the day with special behavior, the impulse to convert a day of ordinary business into a day devoted exclusively to ceremony and festive behavior did not immediately leap to their minds. Long acquaintance with a relatively uninterrupted work calendar accustomed urban dwellers to life without holidays beside the Sabbath. The French traveler Moreau de St. Mery, in Philadelphia on Independence Day in 1793, confirmed the bells and cannon fire, the parades of the Cincinnati and militia, but he did so in far less expansive terms than the newspaper accounts, observing that "more than three fourths of the stores remain open. There are no signs of gaiety."[2] A native Philadelphian agreed, and scolded his readers for not treating the occasion more reverently: "This NATAL DAY has hitherto been too slightly kept," he wrote, "and to our shame be it spoken."

> The Almighty hand is conspicuously seen in our political salvation, and gratitude calls upon us for a return of thanks to the Almighty Disposer of all events, for the favors bestowed upon this

land. . . . The European nations pompously celebrate the birth days of their Kings and Princes, with festivity and rejoicing; but how much more reason have we to celebrate this great event. It is the birth of a nation—a day on which FREEDOM, *Heaven-born freedom*, triumphed over *despotism, oppression, and slavery*—Ought not Americans then to celebrate the nativity of their nation! Fellow citizens—you are called upon to rejoice. . . . Let not the day be forgotten, but handed down to distant ages; let it not be spent in riot and debauchery, but with that decorum and harmony which ought to characterize a free people. Let the hand of charity and brotherly love be stretched out, and sobriety and temperance prevail at our boards. . . . It is likewise to be wished, that stores and shops might be shut on that day, and that the bell might ring as on days of rejoicing, and the day closed by a general illumination. Thus it would be wholly devoted to joy and rejoicing.[3]

In other words, the author claimed, Independence Day should be kept like a "holy" day, and not spent in mundane pursuits. Bostonians also wrestled with the question of a secular holiday. Although their celebrations involved more of their citizenry at an earlier stage, many shops remained open for business. The selectmen occasionally recommended stores to close, but could not or would not command the transactions of a busy port and business center to cease entirely. Increasingly, however, admonitions like that of the Philadelphia correspondent triggered readers' responsiveness to sacred associations. The Fourth of July was increasingly referred to as an "auspicious day," "a day that ought to be sacred to the union," "a sabbath in the calendar of liberty," and the "Sabbath of American Freedom."[4] Religious metaphors suggested responses appropriate to such times: joy, thanksgiving, harmony, charity, temperance—and abstinence from work. The editors of the *Gazette of the United States* implored tradesmen and merchants alike to "let the hand of industry be suspended" in Philadelphia on Independence Day.[5]

Highly visible employers often set the pace toward the achievement of that goal. Newspaper editors regularly gave their staffs the day off so that employees could practice on the Fourth what their bosses preached. Independence Day also became increasingly a bank holiday, as when in 1797 the Bank of South Carolina in Charleston announced it would close its doors in honor of July 4.[6] The newspapers encouraged businessmen to follow suit, and the decision to do so must have been made easier as the banks were closed anyway. The decision not to work and to release one's employees for the day was a personal one, and undoubtedly much depended on financial considerations—How much could one *afford* to take the day off?—but each decision to suspend work added momentum to the movement toward a more general holiday. So rapid and pervasive was the trend that in 1796 a Charlestonian reported that "all labor" in the city was "suspended" on July 4. Even in busy Philadelphia, according to the *Aurora*, "all ordinary business" had been "suppressed" on Independence Day by 1802.[7] Good economic times might occasionally beckon the conscientious businessman, but the trend they help set could not easily be reversed. Merchants occasionally even policed themselves; after all, if some of them were not going to work and make profits that day, they did not want their competitors to do so either. In 1806, a Boston "Merchant of '75" hoped that none of his fellow businessmen would be so "mercenary and mean" as to deny the day off to their employees, "of whom it may be said—a day of independence does not often shine." It was important, the writer claimed, to demonstrate that people of his class show themselves "equally liberal and patriotic" to any ordinary citizen.[8]

Even politics encouraged the trend; both Federalists and Republicans saw the advantages of promoting a vacation from work on Independence Day. Naturally, both parties were eager for more participants for their rallies and competing celebrations, and for larger audiences. Having more people at liberty from their vocations on July 4 allowed partisans to vie for a larger share of potential celebrants. It was not long before partisans began to equate largesse with patriotism. Federalists and Republicans strove to appear more sincere and more patriotic than their opponents by campaigning for universal suspension of work. When, in 1806, the banks and customhouse in Boston announced that they would be closed for the day, the Republican *Independent Chronicle* demanded that the curtailment of work be extended generally: "It is ardently desired, that all business may be laid aside on this glorious Jubilee and the energies of one and all directed to increase the splendor and hilarity of the day."[9] A writer for the anti-Republican *Boston Gazette* called upon the Federalist selectmen to recommend officially the closing of all stores so that "the large and respectable class of Young Men and Apprentices . . . may the more sensibly feel and understand the occasion of this yearly festival." By doing so, the writer argued, Federalists would be able to preempt Republican claims of liberal benevolence. If, in conclusion, the selectmen would not declare a holiday by ordinance, then he was confident that the patriotism of Federalist merchants "in this instance, will so far outweigh self-interest" as to accomplish the same end.[10]

Public response to calls for a Fourth of July holiday were mixed. Most undoubtedly welcomed the respite, but not all for the same reasons. No doubt many sincerely wished to honor the day. Many others looked forward to a day of sport and amusement. A few deplored the day entirely. However, there is plenty of evidence to suggest that the "festival deprivation" noticed by Peter Shaw and Dirk Hoerder was real. Contemporaries acknowledged it, as when the "Merchant of '75" confessed that "a day of independence" did "not often shine" for Boston's working people. A Concord farmer with the pseudonym "Peter Pencil" echoed the feelings of many of his urban counterparts: "Let the labourer suspend his scythe, wipe the sweat from his gladdened brow, and spend one day in festive gratitude, to those who have mitigated his task, by relieving from his hands the shackles of slavery." Challenging the farmer's tradition of unremitting labor, Pencil concluded that "the independent freeholder will not think the fourth day of this busy month misspent in celebrating the nativity of his freedom."[11] A city dweller concurred, judging it not unreasonable for urban workers to be allowed "one whole day of recreation in a year."[12]

Philadelphians lacked even Boston's pre-Revolutionary Pope's Day tradition. Having "few days on which they meet at the call of gaiety and pleasure," working Philadelphians took enthusiastically to the idea of a day of festivity.[13] Three years after the Philadelphia correspondent's appeal for a better-attended Fourth of July, a Quaker diarist wrote: "I think I never saw our streets more populous, this being the anniversary [sic] of Independence."[14]

Not everyone was enthusiastic about devoting every Fourth of July to gaiety and pleasure, however. Because Independence Day was never celebrated on Sunday, the annual interruption of the work week must have been irksome to some merchants in the midst of a busy season. They had to be browbeaten in the newspapers or, in the case of Boston, by the selectmen, before succumbing to patriotic duty. In Philadelphia, the still-considerable Quaker population could be counted upon to shun all public celebrations, as they had since before the Revolution. The Fourth of July was no "holy day" to them, as Elizabeth Drinker confirmed in her diary: "General Orders in News-paper this forenoon, for a fuss and to do—I think, orders for peace and quietness, would be more commendable and consistent, in a well regulated Government or state."[15] Some without a mercantile or religious axe to grind simply thought Independence Day silly and superfluous. In 1802 a Boston schoolmaster refused to suspend a class that fell on July 4, averring that "the 4th of July is an old thing; it would do ten or twelve years ago, but ought now to be given up." The *Columbian Centinel* denounced the schoolmaster's overstrict attention to his calling as mean-spirited and unpatriotic.[16] For most citizens of Boston and Philadelphia, however, Independence Day furnished them with something new: a full day off from regular work without the obligatory duties of the religious sabbath.

This novel situation presented problems of its own. With more and more people freed from the constraints of the workplace for a day, where would they go and what would they do? Some did swell the ranks of the partisan observances, but others used their liberty to celebrate any way they pleased. "Anti-Saturnus" pleaded with Philadelphians not to use the Fourth of July as an excuse for a bacchanalia, and Boston newspapers echoed the sentiment.[17] The concern for orderly celebrations stemmed partly from the fact that there was no single, universally accepted "liturgy" for properly observing the day. Instead, the people of Boston, Charleston, and Philadelphia created a variety of activities on their own with which to express and celebrate their patriotism. Only some of these activities found their way into the newspapers, and then not always for the best of reasons.

"ALL CLASSES OF OUR CITIZENS"

Certain individuals and groups performed on Independence Day as a duty. In Boston, this category included state and local politicians. Philadelphia did not require such official gatherings, although before the national capital moved in 1800, members of Congress occasionally gathered to observe the Fourth. In all three of the cities studied here, however, private clubs and political societies regularly kept the day, as did the Society of the Cincinnati.

Independence Day would hardly have been Independence Day without the gatherings of the militia clans. As demonstrated earlier, the militia's special place on July 4 brought out the officers and privates of both the high and the low by the scores and hundreds. When the "uniformed companies" of Charleston turned out in 1794, nearly one-third of the city's white males over sixteen years marched in review, "though some of the companies did not assemble half their men," and these were only the volunteer companies.[18] Militia units gathered not only to march, of course, but to partake of their combination business/social dinners, which, as Thomas Pleasant discovered, could quickly descend to rowdiness, even among associations of highbrow volunteers. It is possible, of course, that the July 4 dinner of the Washington Guards was not typical; the fact that Pleasant felt compelled to apologize for the company's behavior may indicate that their lack of composure was an aberration. However, it seems unlikely that the Guards was the only unit harboring petty jealousies, political renegades, and personal dislikes, or that they alone succumbed to the dissipating effects of large quantities of liquor. It is more likely that militia companies throughout the nation produced scenes similar to those witnessed by Edward Hooker, a northern visitor to South Carolina. Attending a Fourth of July barbecue, Hooker considered everything to go well until the liquor was broken out for the toasts, "the management of which was ridiculous enough. No notice was given when they commenced, and they were drank by about a dozen at the head of the table, while the rest of the company were, some of them, eating, others talking and laughing and others sauntering about, without knowing of any toasts being drank, except by the sound of the cannon."[19]

In addition to militia gatherings, some urban trade associations also viewed Independence Day as an appropriate occasion for yearly meetings, although this tendency was slower to develop. Groups of these workers occasionally met along the banks of the Delaware below or above Philadelphia. The Franklin Society of printers met for the first time in Boston on July 4, 1802.[20] Sixteen years later, the Charitable Mechanics Association sponsored an ambitious Independence Day craft demonstration and contest on Boston Common, awarding prizes to aspiring coopers for the best-quality casks.[21] Gradually, however, the relations between masters and journeymen became less harmonious. As master craftsmen became industrialists and entrepreneurs, they identified less and less exclusively with the corporate traditions of their trades, and the economic and social gap between workers and their employers widened. In the 1820s, groups of laborers began to hold regular meetings of their own on July 4 as they attempted to bring their grievances into the political arena.[22]

By comparison, farmers gathered on the Fourth of July far less frequently. Despite the frequent appearance of banners promoting "Agriculture" in Independence Day parades, the numbers of farmers actually in parades "holding aloft the implements of their trade" were rarely more than a representative few. Mostly this had to do with the nature of their calling; certain agricultural tasks simply could not wait. George Nelson of Philadelphia commented that the weather one July 4 was "excellent for Harvest which is now generally begun."[23] Another who dwelt close by the city observed that July 4, 1814, was "clear and beautiful—therm. at 74 . . . will be a fine day for harvesting."[24] After Elizabeth Cranch married a man from Hingham, Massachusetts, her oration-going days were over. She spent Independence Day thereafter haying and doing other work about her husband's farm.[25] While on his way to New York from Philadelphia on July 4, Charles Willson Peale saw "some industrious men spreading their grass that had been cut the day before." Not all rural people were so industrious; in addition to the hay cutters, a disgusted Peale witnessed "several lazy lubbers loitering" about a village center, waiting for the day's fun to begin.[26] Bad weather released even the most diligent farmers from their routine toil, however. Elizabeth Drinker recorded rain on one Independence Day: "bad weather for the harvest—good for the Annaversary frolickers."[27] Naturally, in the area about Charleston, where the farmers were overwhelmingly black and enslaved, the issue simply did not arise; no one was about to allow crowds of blacks to march anywhere, for any reason.

Private dinner parties and daylong picnics occupied many in the upper and middle social orders, particularly in Philadelphia. The city gentry had long subscribed to the practice of retiring to summer homes along the nearby Schuylkill River or even further into the country. Those who could not afford semipermanent retreats followed their betters' examples by making a day's outing to Gray's Garden on the Schuylkill, Lilliput on the Jersey Shore of the Delaware, or other bucolic retreats on special occasions. The general middle-class exodus to the country on Independence Day began far earlier than some historians have suspected, almost as soon as the holiday won general acceptance.[28] In 1790 George Nelson recorded that "numbers of people went out of town to celebrate Independence particularly to Gray's Garden over Schylkill."[29] Yearly, the proprietors of that establishment enticed Philadelphians away from the heat and smells of the city with "liquors of the first quality, the wines, &c. kept in reservoirs of water and ice, iced creams of great variety, fine cakes . . . and every exertion made to render the entertainment elegant."[30] Federal Point, "a pleasing situation on the Delaware," attracted "a number of citizens" on the Fourth in 1793, shielding its late-afternoon diners under a bower constructed for the purpose.[31] An establishment at Harrowgate even arranged a coach shuttle that ran from Race Street.[32] The ability to escape the city appealed also to discrete political groups who preferred privacy. On several occasions Nathaniel Snowden observed small groups of Federalists and "Antifeds" celebrating in these rural settings, far from the taunts of their hated rivals.[33]

Charleston continued to be a summer resort for many low-country Carolinians, but this seasonal in-migration was mitigated by an out-migration of many of the well-to-do and their families. Some of the wealthy preferred to spend their summers on Sullivan's Island, while an increasing number of planters enriched by the cotton boom opted to leave the state entirely for more northerly climes, such as Philadelphia or New York.[34] Movement in or out of Charleston solely concerned with Independence Day appears to have been minimal.

In Boston there was much less tendency to disperse on Independence Day, and it even appears that Boston attracted people from the surrounding towns *into* the city. Some came to hear the orations, as did Elizabeth Cranch and Nathan Webb (see Chapter 2). Many more came for the dazzling militia displays and fireworks over the Charles River or Boston Common.[35] The inclination to congregate rather than disperse for Boston's celebrations is due in part to the difference in climate between Boston and the more southern cities. There was simply less incentive to flee Boston for reasons of comfort.

Despite Charles Janson's unhappy experience with the heat, Boston's summers were generally more temperate than Philadelphia's, not to mention those of Charleston. Boston also escaped the seasonal bouts with yellow fever and malaria that beset the warmer ports and made Philadelphians and Charlestonians especially keen to leave the urban environment when they could. Population growth and ethnic makeup was another decisive factor. Although a bustling seaport like Philadelphia, Boston did not approach the prodigious growth rate of Philadelphia's population, which went from 44,096 in 1790 to 91,877 in 1810 to 112,772 in 1820. Much of this increase came from Irish immigration and black migration from slave states.[36] In contrast, Boston's population for those same years was only 18,320, 33,787, and 43,298 respectively, and its ethnic communities were relatively small.[37] Although Boston was pinched for space on its little peninsula, the population increase was not nearly so large or so rapid as Philadelphia's. Bostonians felt less compelled to escape the squeeze of a rapidly growing and increasingly mixed population.

Despite wide participation on the Fourth of July, there were those who could leave it alone. Benjamin Rush was one of those wealthy Philadelphians who "fled from the noise of the city" with his family "to our customary and delightful retreat on the Skylkill [sic]," not to celebrate but simply to get away.[38] The sentiments of Elizabeth Drinker represent those of most of Philadelphia's Quakers, who were averse to Independence Day on religious grounds: "the most sensible part of the Community, have more reason to lament than rejoice—in my opinion. . . . There has been 2 or 3 troops of horse by our door, this evening with a band of Music—rediculous doings."[39] Sarah Wister also preferred a contemplative Fourth at her family's retreat in Germantown. "I know not how it is in Philad. on this day of public festivity," she wrote to her uncle in the city, "in the village it is tranquil and serene. Not even the sound of [music] brings to our remembrance the 4th of July. Well does peace and quiet suit the temperament of my mind."[40] And there were always those whose ability or propensity to celebrate was at the mercy of forces beyond their control, such as fluctuations in the world market. In Charleston, William Read noticed that "Gen¹ P. whom I sat near in the Cincinnati was not himself—He had heard some disagreeable news—the fall of Rice in England was one cause of his gloom & discontent."[41]

FROM COMMEMORATION TO FESTIVAL

Those who did wish to participate and who did not belong to a military, political, or professional group had a great many options regarding ways to spend their day. They could always join in a parade, as did the Englishman Charles Janson or the scores that attached themselves to partisan processions. Independence Day was also a fitting time for expressions of civic pride as well as of the national variety. Indeed, the quasi-magical quality of July 4 seemed to bless almost any project connected with that date. In 1795, amid great fanfare, Governor Samuel Adams and Masonic lodge member Paul Revere ceremonially leveled and plumbed the cornerstone for Massachusetts's new statehouse as part of Boston's July 4 program. A similar ritual in 1818 officially commenced the building of Boston's famous General Hospital.[42] The Philadelphia Military Association awarded a medal to the winner of a patriotic song contest for Independence Day, while more scientifically minded urbanites experimented with a hot-air balloon ascension in 1785.[43] Charlestonians dedicated a toast to their dream of "Inland Navigation" and "the abundant advantages to the community" expected as a result. Independence Day might even bring good luck for those investing in lotteries for public works. In Boston, a newspaper advertisement suggested that "probably the 4th July may prove propitious" to anyone buying a ticket for the Amoskeag Lottery. The Fourth of July certainly was propitious for one Charlestonian; the winning ticket for the East Bay Street Lottery, drawn that day, made him or her more than ten thousand dollars richer.[44]

Charitably inclined persons considered the Fourth of July as conducive to humanitarian endeavors as any religious holiday. "Hilarity, Philanthropy, and Fraternity" were the watchwords for Boston's Republicans in 1806, but Federalists also made highly visible philanthropic gestures on the Fourth, as when the year before they donated the surplus food from their banquet to imprisoned debtors.[45] Wishing that "the *fatherless children of want*" living in Boston's Alms House "might partake in the festivity of the day," Governor John Hancock instructed their keeper to conduct them to the old Province House, "where a large number of those little innocents were suitably refreshed."[46] In Philadelphia in 1801, a "society for the relief of poor and distressed masters of ships, their widows and children" met at Carpenter's Hall on the evening of July 4.[47] The induced *communitas* of Independence Day inspired spontaneous acts of charity for some who might not have received it on another day. In 1820 a sponsor appealed to fellow Charlestonians on July 4 for donations for a destitute but deserving family—perhaps ruined by the financial panic of the previous year.[48] In Boston, on the same day that Governor Hancock practiced noblesse oblige with the orphans, a cannon aboard a foreign vessel discharged prematurely while returning a salute from Fort Independence, blowing off a sailor's hand. Even though he was a foreigner, the fact that he had been firing a salute in honor of Independence Day qualified him for special consideration. A correspondent to the *Independent Chronicle* suggested (with an appalling choice of words) that a collection be taken up to benefit the unfortunate man, and "convince the world, that freedom and generosity, ever go hand in hand." All along the eastern seaboard, Americans dug a little deeper into their pockets on Independence Day, confident that, as one expressed it, "philanthropy will add a charming zest to the rational pleasures" of the day.[49]

The number and variety of Independence Day amusements grew quickly to satisfy (and profit from) the throngs of citizens released from work. Philadelphians crowded to see a "Summer Circus" in Market Street one year and a "Grand Concert" at Center House Gardens the next.[50] "Lovers of rational and genteel amusements" could visit Boston's Washington Gardens near the Common or Charleston's Vauxhall Gardens.[51] The growing number of museums in all three cities opened their doors wide on Independence Day and kept them open well into the night. There the holiday crowd viewed rare animals, wax figures of celebrities, and panoramic paintings, many exhibits constructed expressly for the Fourth. There were also sensational attractions, such as two-headed and five-legged creatures.[52] Elizabeth Drinker's Philadelphia friends were not so reticent as she to take in some of the fun on July 4. She noted in her diary that some of them had gone "this forenoon to look at the rarey shew."[53] Air conditioning was essential to these indoor attractions, especially in Philadelphia and Charleston. In announcing a special opening for Independence Day, managers of the Charleston Museum promised their prospective patrons a "spacious, cool, and airy retreat" where they could comfortably spend "a few leisure hours . . . alike sheltered from the scorching heat of a sultry day, and damps of the evening."[54]

Specific references to dancing on Independence Day are rare, but probably it was a common activity where men, women, and music mixed in such profusion. In 1799 Nathaniel Snowden attended a Federalist party near Philadelphia that included dancing for "a number of ladies and gentleman." Living up to their reputation for gentility, upper-crust Charlestonians turned Independence Day into the occasion for a formal ball. At the other end of the social spectrum, groups of "young people" danced together in Philadelphia's open commons at the edges of the city (Fig. 3).[55]

One of the myriad ways that Americans traditionalized the Fourth of July was through the consumption of ritual food. Special foods often associate with seasonal holidays: goose at Christmas, turkey at Thanksgiving, fish during Lent. For Independence Day it was ice cream and turtle soup. Then as now, ice cream was a popular treat during the summer. With thousands of people out in the heat of a Fourth of July, purveyors of this cold confection were sure to do a lively business. They set up their stalls at museums, theaters, near Boston Common—anywhere that crowds were likely to be thick. A Mr. Shindles advertised his "iced creams, of the best quality" in four flavors, just in time for July 4, 1798, and celebrating Charlestonians desiring ice or ice cream from Vauxhall Gardens in 1806 were advised to come early.[56] The people of Philadelphia and Charleston appear to have especially savored turtle soup for Independence Day. Bush Hill Tavern and Anseby's Tavern competed for the business of the *Aurora*'s readers in 1804 by advertising turtle soup exclusively for the Fourth, even to the hour it would be available. Turtle soup was still a Philadelphia passion in 1817, when James Stell advertised the delicacy for "This Day, July 4," at 11:00 only.[57] In Charleston, this holiday favorite could be sampled at the Merchant's Hotel, or "gentlemen" could send their servants to the Federal Coffee House to buy some for home consumption. Charlestonians could also make their own for their July 4 feast; in 1806 Abigail Jones, a pastry cook, advertised turtle meat for sale for that day only.[58]

Independence Day entertainments often consciously supplied some kind of patriotic reinforcement for patrons, however obtuse.

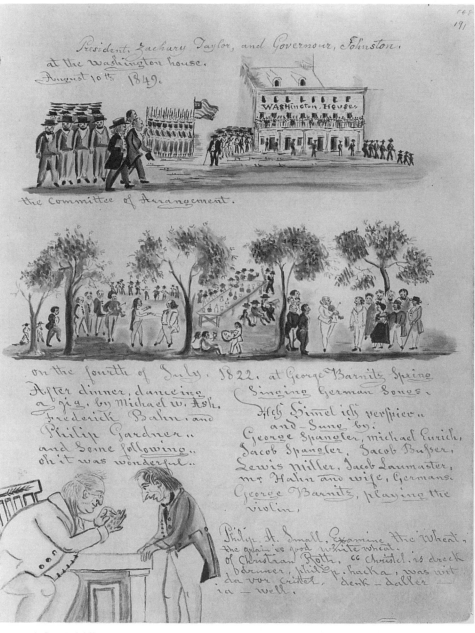

3. Lewis Miller, "On the Fourth of July, 1822." "After dinner, dancing a jig. . . . Singing German Songs . . . oh it was wonderful. . . ." (The Historical Society of York County, Pennsylvania.)

Concert bands played mostly popular tunes, but were sure to conclude their holiday programs with "Hail Columbia" or the "President's March." Amid their sometimes lurid tableaux, museums rarely neglected to display prominently wax figures of Revolutionary or contemporary heroes, especially George Washington. No popular attraction was more self-consciously dedicated to communicating the message of Independence Day, however, than theater. Independence Day inspired a genre of historical plays and stage performances written expressly for performance on the Fourth. These colorful and dramatic productions may have contributed more to the hagiography of the Revolution and its heroes, at the popular level, than the more intellectually structured public orations.[59] Through the immediacy of theater, audiences could suspended their disbelief for a time, indeed almost transcend time, and reconnect themselves with their historical and legendary past.

Some of the earliest July 4 theatrical expressions were produced by militia companies. On July 4, 1779, with the War for Independence still undecided, the Boston militia staged a mock battle on the Common. The "combatants" represented the American and British forces, and it is easy to surmise which side "won."[60] In 1794, at New Mills outside Philadelphia, several militia companies performed a "battle, in honor of the day." With tongue firmly in cheek, a correspondent to the *Pennsylvania Gazette* reported from the "front":

> The commanding officers displayed much ardour and military skill in conducting the battle, and the officers in general acted their parts exceedingly well; too much praise cannot be bestowed upon the privates . . . who advanced, engaged, and retreated, undaunted by the thickest fire. While victory [was] hovering with equipoised wings over the combatants, news was brought that dinner was ready.

On receipt of this intelligence, "the fire of the warriors suddenly ceased," and they marched to a nearby bower where "they suspended all animosity."[61]

On the one hand, large-scale pageant-plays of this sort were unwieldy, and the argument fairly simple. On the other hand, stage productions at once condensed time and action into manageable space, while enlarging the didactic content and elaborating the dramatic message. Significantly, the traditionalization of Independence Day coincided with a resurgence in American theater. Leaders in Revolutionary Boston and Philadelphia had prohibited plays, but petitions and popular pressure finally lifted these bans. Fine theater houses such as the Federal Street Theater in Boston and the elegant Chestnut Street Theater in Philadelphia catered to elite and middle-class audiences. For middle and lower-class citizens in both cities, more modest but still respectable theater houses rose to meet the general demand. Despite its smaller theatergoing population, Charleston still supported at least two playhouses of its own. The Charleston Theater, built in 1793, was favored by local Federalists and offered fairly refined entertainments; its rival, the City or "French" Theater (1794), featured more "democratic" fare: harlequinades, dances, and "stage acts." During summer, theater managers went to great lengths to keep their patrons as cool as possible in the crowded, enclosed spaces. They built fans or erected wind sails to direct any faint breezes into the stifling houses, and in one instance in Philadelphia even hired fire engines to spray water onto the roof.[62] The theatrical fare was generally of the "summer stock" variety, mostly lighthearted plays and farces, but the Fourth of July generated patriotic presentations as well. Boston's Haymarket Theater in 1799 presented "Washington" in three acts, a one-act play called *Independence*, and a musical comedy, *The Romp*. To keep the audiences in their seats between shows, the management provided entertainments such as a tightrope walk and a "savage dance."[63]

A French visitor to Charleston in 1817 left a vivid impression of his American theater experience. He may have had some trouble finding the establishment to begin with: on the outside the Charleston Theater appeared to his urbane view like "the unattractive home of a middle-class citizen." Once inside, he was no more impressed. The interior was "small and badly arranged," too narrow, and "composed of a pit with benches, with galleries round about, and two rows of boxes, which are more than sufficient for the resident or visiting connoisseurs." Nor did matters improve once he found his seat. "There is no good order or discipline in an American theater," he complained. "The back part of the boxes, instead of being closed in as is the custom everywhere else, has only a partial closure three and a half feet high, which offers a tempting support to the first person who comes in behind you. This annoys you all the more as the larger part of the honorable members, scarcely cured of their paralysis [from drinking] use rather crudely the facilities which are new to them." He was alternately bored and disgusted with the play itself. The only bright moment for him was when, "in the entr'acte, a girl danced," but her state of undress did not meet his standards. The Americans, he concluded, lacked "*savoir-vivre.*"[64]

Some patriotic presentations were not plays but allegorical mimes and music shows. The Old Theater in Philadelphia presented "A Historical story told in action, called *the ever memorable fourth of July, 1776*," featuring "a combat by an Indian and Brittania."[65] An 1802 advertisement for *The Federal Oath* in that same city was highly descriptive. *The Federal Oath* was "a Pantomimical Sketch, in one act, never performed here," and written particularly for the occasion. A rendition of "The Jefferson March," preceded "A DANCE. . . . During the Dance, the Approach of a Storm is Heard, the Women fly, the men run and fetch their arms, and go out different ways. When all are dispers'd PEACE appears in a flowing robe, a GARLAND on her head and an Olive Branch in her hand." A pedestal then appeared on which was largely inscribed "LIBERTY OR DEATH," followed by "an elegant transparent painting representing LIBERTY, COLUMBIA, AND JUSTICE. On each side are Soldiers, Sailors, &c." After playing the President's March, "the General advances and delivers an ODE TO THE UNITED STATES." "Washington's March" came next. At last came the Federal Oath. "Six principal officers march round the stage, draw their swords and place them on the Altar. Each takes his sword from the altar, kneels down, kisses the blade, repeats the words LIBERTY OR DEATH. When the oath has been taken by all, three Huzzas. To conclude with A NATIONAL INVOCATION AND CHORUS." The "pantomimical sketch" was a theatrical performance saturated with a number of ritualized (but clearly understood) expressions and signals, both verbal and nonverbal, inviting audiences by extension to share in an act of religio-patriotic renewal and rededication. The parallels with the Christian Eucharist ceremony can hardly be missed.[66]

Theaters also presented less allegorical productions. Between them, Charleston and Boston could boast two of the earliest full-scale armed conflicts of the Revolution; perhaps it was only a matter of time before someone thought of rendering these actions in dramatic form.

At the City Theater in Charleston, the "rising generation" as well as veterans of the war delighted in *The Attack on Fort Moultrie*. This appeal to local patriotism was apparently written to be performed for Palmetto Day, but its message made good fare for July 4—only a week away—as well. The climax of the play comes when "the Sergeant," a character obviously modeled on Sergeant Jasper, a hero of the battle, harangues a crowd momentarily awed by the sight of the British fleet:

> Come on my countrymen! 'Tis liberty demands you—'Tis freedom leads you on—Your bleeding country calls for your service. Think, if you live, what honors will attend you! —and if you fall, fall in the glorious fight! . . . My heart, though glowing warm with patriotic zeal, can feel as well as yours for female softness—can shed a tear to see a weeping parent, or a mourning wife; But next to your Great Maker, the High Lord of Heaven, love your country: She is your nurse—your guardian—your protector: therefore, fight for her. . . . Let the proud tyrants of the earth, now tremble to view the mighty resolution in your arms —Let future glorious legends bear records of your bright achievements. . . . Come on then—Let us be free! or perish in the cause.[67]

In Boston the most celebrated local event of the Revolution was the equally dramatic defense of Bunker Hill in 1775. The highbrow Federal Street Theater presented *Bunker Hill* in 1797, and with its rousing rhetoric, tragic characters, and exciting onstage reenactment of the battle in the final act, it was a persistent Independence Day favorite in New York and Philadelphia as well as in Boston.[68] The main characters are Abercromby, a British soldier (a surprisingly sympathetic role), his American lover Elvira, and patriot General Joseph Warren. The star-crossed lovers epitomize the tragedy of war: sweethearts compelled to oppose each other out of obligation to country. To Warren, on the other hand, the war is a glorious portal to a brave new age:

> The day is come for which through every age
> Sages have sighed; which like a magic spell,
> Shall dash down tyrants and their thrones together,
> And make their blood-stained idols fall before it. . . .
> And shall I then, inglorious, stay behind,
> While my brave countrymen are braving death
> To purchase glory; I too am fond of glory,
> And such a cause will make ambition, virtue.
> (19)

Revolutions will be so in use,
That kings when they behold the morning break,
Will bless their stars for living one day more.

(22)

Joining the Americans in their stand atop Bunker Hill, however, Warren articulates motives more noble and selfless than his personal ambitions:

To teach my countrymen contempt of death,
To kindle great ideas in their minds. . . .
This hill shall be America's *Thermopyle;*
Here shall her little band of patriot sons,
Oppose those modern Persians.

(43)

In the end, all are victims of honor. Abercromby falls amid the carnage of the battle, a good soldier in a bad cause. Elvira goes insane at the news. And Warren gets his wish, achieving glory even in defeat and death. In a pathetic final aria Warren reaches out to his audience's time:

O might I look into the womb of time
And see my country's future destiny:
Cou'd I but see her proud democracy,
Founded on equal laws, and stript entire
Of those unnatural titles and those noble names
Of King, of Count, of Stadtholder, of Duke,
Which, with degrading awe, possess the world,
My cheared soul . . . would singing soar to heaven

(53)

Tell the world, 'tis all I ask of thee . . .
That Warren did his duty: leave me now.
America—my country! bless thee heaven.
O god protect this land—I faint—I die.
Live the Republic. Live, O Live forever

(53–54)

The final scene is a dumb-show, with Warren's body brought back to the American camp and surrounded "with republican emblems, and popular devices," including "The Rights of Man," "Liberty and Equality," and "A Federal Constitution." As the curtain falls, "two Virgins" sing an edifying ode and the orchestra plays a dirge.

Bunker-Hill was powerful theater in its time; it played manifestly false with history, but on Independence Day it translated local events into national saga, and made that saga reality for its audiences. Orations appealed to the intellect, at least ostensibly,[69] but *Bunker-Hill* went straight for the emotions. The poetry, the unabashed sentiment, the pathos, and the spectacle brought the past dramatically to life in an American patriotic passion play.

The success of *Bunker-Hill* and other July 4 productions inspired calls and contests for more "national plays."[70] Whether indoor or on Boston Common, whether in lyrics, movement, or prose, patriotic theater on Independence Day made the past immediate. Theater provided the altar (the stage) and the liturgy of words and gestures that conjured forth the spirit (and spirits) of the past. In this darkened, mystical space, audiences connected tangibly with the past, using the liminal moment of July 4 to join hands across time with the patriots of 1776. Through the medium of theater, the thoughts, values, and virtues of those heroic figures could live again and inspire the present. Like the Siegfried legends, the Song of Roland, and Mummers' plays of Europe, Independence Day plays built and transmitted "histories" of national origin. As with Coventry's Corpus Christi plays, they contributed to "the welth & worship of the hole body."[71]

IMPERFECT ORDER

Charles Willson Peale was returning to Philadelphia from New York by stagecoach on July 3, 1801. When Peale was about halfway home, a coach from a different line approached from some distance behind. The occupants of this other coach seemed "fond of dashing on," Peale observed. As they came into sight, they began firing pistols into the air to signal their urgency and high spirits. Peale observed that these were travelers "of that class" that felt less inhibited in their behavior when released from social restraints. While they were far off, the firing was no more than an annoyance, but as they closed the gap between the two coaches and the firing intensified, the passengers in Peale's coach became nervous. The indiscriminate shooting "frightened our horses, and we were in danger of their running off—we desired our driver to hold and let them get . . . far ahead as our company would prefer safety to overmuch haste."[72]

Peale's rowdies were "dashing on" to be at their destinations in time for Independence Day, and were even celebrating a day early. The encounter along the road illustrates a growing divergence of celebration styles (along what Peale thought were class lines) and an element of danger and disorderliness that increasingly accompanied the Fourth of July in America. Newspaper assurances of "perfect order" on the Fourth are misleading. On a day with thousands of citizens on the loose, insufficient police, and a high level of consciously encouraged excitement, perfect order was perfectly impossible.

To begin with, some of the most popular and exciting forms of celebration on Independence Day contained an inherent element of danger. The most serious threat was from fire. Freak accidents or careless discharges of muskets, cannon, or fireworks could be disastrous. In 1785 Philadelphians read a cautionary account of a narrow escape for New York. During the nighttime celebrations, a "squib" (a homemade firework that either exploded or whizzed like a rocket) shot into the cellar of a residence in Queen Street. The burning missile ignited a pile of straw, which was only extinguished "after a good deal of confusion." Luckily, little damage was done.[73] Bostonians learned the hazards of Independence Day more graphically. A week before the 1803 celebration, artificers at Fort Independence in Boston's inner harbor were preparing fireworks for the upcoming display. A rocket accidentally went off, exploding eighteen pounds of gunpowder. The roof of the workshop was blown off, and an unfortunate pyrotechnist mortally burned. The resulting fire threatened the entire fort; in the adjoining room were seven full casks of powder, one with its head off. At the risk of suffering the technician's fate, soldiers from the garrison pulled the casks from the burning building. It was touch and go for a time; the women and children were evacuated to Governor's Island, and the soldiers needed the help of Dorchester's fire engine to put out the blaze.[74]

The selectmen of Boston and the city councils of Philadelphia and Charleston took measures to reduce the risks of fire and explosion on the Fourth of July. Charlestonians lived in particular dread of fire, especially in the summer, when private and municipal wells (the only sources of water in the city) were dangerously low. In 1783, the firemasters strategically deployed all of the city's fire engines "to prevent any danger of fire" from fireworks or illuminations; the next year the city council recommended curtailing illuminations in the city altogether.[75] The Boston selectmen categorically outlawed bonfires in 1797, and the city councils of Philadelphia and Charleston did the same six and nine years later, respectively.[76] Boston's officials encouraged formal fireworks displays on the large Common to satisfy the public, and Philadelphians gathered in broad Market Street for a similar exhibition. In the latter city these displays soon moved to Center Square, away from the crowded commercial district.[77] The same ordinances that banned bonfires also regulated the use of fireworks, but apparently with much less success. Not only were common firecrackers and rockets easily concealed, they were commercially available and could even be homemade in a pinch with a little gunpowder. And while laws might regulate the *use* of fireworks, no law prohibited their sale; merchants advertised "Sky Rockets of Superior Quality" and "India Crackers" openly.[78] Conceding the inevitable, Boston's selectmen instead sought to promote a relatively safe area for people to set off their purchased or handmade explosives. In 1806 the selectmen granted the petition of "a number of young men" to throw "all kinds of fire works" on the Common on the evening of the Fourth, within prescribed bounds.[79]

The people of the port cities may have been safer from fire for these measures, but a day generating so much cannon fire and musketry was bound to produce accidents of another sort. Two men were loading a cannon on one of Boston's wharfs in 1810 when the gun went off unexpectedly. The blast blew off one man's arm, while his companion lost both arms and half of his face.[80] The same sorts of accidents happened with small arms. A group of Philadelphia militia met in the orchard of a tavern on the afternoon of July 4, 1804, "for a frolic more than for a military exercise." They were "shooting in a careless manner" that cost young John Ball his life. "One of them fired his gun before the ramming-rod was taken out, this rod struck the lad who was very near on one side, penetrated his body and broke within in many pieces beside breaking his arm. The frolics on the 4th of July . . . have seldom passed without some such accidents."[81] Elizabeth Drinker learned of a similar instance in 1801, when "one Man [was] wounded by a gun." People were occasionally hurt even when militiamen used blank charges in their salutes. Drinker reported that on one July 4 "a boy had his eye hurt, or put out, by the wading [wadding] of a gun."[82]

The fact that at least one of these accidents occurred at a tavern exemplifies a potentially serious problem: the dangerous combination of guns and liquor. Philadelphia shopkeeper Henry Orth probably saw nothing incongruous in his 1805 advertisement for thirty casks of gunpowder and five hundred gallons of Tennessee peach brandy three days before the Fourth of July, and neither, apparently, did his neighbors.[83] Excessive drinking on Independence Day compounded the difficulty of preventing accidents. Whether indulged ceremonially, as in the case of Thomas Pleasant and the Washington Guards, or extempore in orchards and taverns, urban Americans consumed large quantities of alcohol on Independence Day. Christopher Marshall was in Philadelphia for the Fourth in 1780 and witnessed "bell ringing, guns firing till the evening and until numbers were so drunk as to reel home."[84] In 1798 the editor of that city's *Porcupine's Gazette* mused that the relative calm of the Fourth of July that year may have been due to "less toasts drunk than usual, that there was more public spirit and less Jamaica spirit afloat, than has been usual on like occasions for some years past."[85]

Porcupine was indulging in wishful thinking, however; as a former Bostonian admitted of Independence Day years later, "there was more noisy mirth after dinner than comports with good taste, but it was the fashion of the day to drink hard and then kick up a row."[86] Certainly, if the burial records for Philadelphia's Gloria Dei Church are any indication, the problem of excessive holiday drinking showed no sign of rapid improvement. In 1805, a twenty-eight-year-old man with a reputation for intemperance became violently ill after an evening of dedicated carousing on the Fourth. He died two days later. A year later, Margaret Barion of Catherine Street became so intoxicated on the Fourth that she "fell or leaned from a trunk on which she sat & never spoke afterward." She may have suffered a stroke, for there was "no bruise or other hurt." In 1812 an inebriated journeyman blacksmith suffered convulsions while wading or swimming in the Delaware River and drowned.[87]

Liquor may or may not have contributed to the shooting accidents mentioned above, but drunkenness was certainly a factor in several violent crimes committed on Independence Day. Two drunken men beat a Penn Street woman when she refused to sell liquor to them on the evening of July 4, 1798. When an elderly neighbor came to her aid and escorted her away, the drunks followed the women, "abus[ing] them with vile language." Finally they knocked the older woman to the ground, kicking and trampling her to death. Neighbors apprehended the felons. In 1807 Titus Roberts, deliriously drunk from the night before, killed his mother "in a most cruel manner" on July 5.[88] Drink may also have been involved in a rape that occurred on Independence Day, 1785, in Frankfort, north of Philadelphia.[89]

Charlestonians also had a reputation for being a hard-drinking lot. Just as travelers rarely failed to expound on the excessive heat of the city, so they almost invariably commented on the propensity of the natives to drink. As discussed earlier, the two characteristics were related; alcoholic drinks were generally thought to ameliorate the effects of the fierce climate. Nevertheless, the practice may have been taken to extremes. A Scotch visitor thought that "with respect to drinking the Carolinians may be compared with the Persians of old, for the more wine he can swallow the more accomplished he conceives himself. . . . Hence few of the men are robust and healthy." "Most of them," reported another of his Charleston hosts, "hasten their death by the incautious use of spirituous drinks, in which they seek refreshment and fortification against the relaxing effect of the hot climate. . . . [I]t is the doctrine here that during the summer months one should think and work little, and drink much." Still another correspondent thought that the excessive drinking of Carolinians accounted for their quarrelsome nature, which in turn led to many duels.[90]

Charlestonians did not let their famous reputation suffer on the Fourth of July, and indeed many started early. "We began the celebration of Independence Day," reported Edward Hooker, "in the Carolina way, this morning, by participating in a *flowing bowl* of Egg-Knogg." If not celebrating at home, the people of Charleston had recourse to nearly a hundred taverns, alehouses, and liquor parlors in the city— nearly one for every twenty-eight men over sixteen.[91] The annual inebriations were notorious enough for one native of the city to remark that the prevailing attitude seemed to be that "every free white man had a *right* to get drunk on the Fourth of July."[92] John Calvert Davis apparently thought so. The Charleston ship-carpenter fell asleep in a storehouse attic after an evening of July 4 tippling, leaving the doorway over the street open for air on that steamy night. Awakening in the wee hours still "in a state of intoxication," he "insensibly walked

out of the door . . . and fell about 35 feet perpendicular." The incident would be comic if it had not ended so tragically; Davis was killed
by the fall. Three other persons died that same day, two of them
young men, but whether by drink, violence, or some other cause is
uncertain.[93]

The Fourth of July was a field day for some of the criminal elements. With attention diverted and often in semidarkness, crowds of
well-dressed revelers made tempting targets for pickpockets. In 1799
the Boston *Independent Chronicle* advertised a reward for the return of
a pocketbook containing thirty dollars stolen on the Fourth of July.
During the celebrations of 1807 in Boston no less than three pocket-
books were "lost," one containing the very large sum of four hundred
dollars. Another was reported stolen near the Common three years
later.[94] In Philadelphia in 1798, Elizabeth Drinker heard of a little
boy caught stealing a handkerchief from a man's pocket on July 4. In
searching the lad, his captors discovered seven or eight more. Reportedly, the mayor ordered the boy sent to jail.[95] Thieves occasionally
employed bolder methods. On the evening of the Fourth in 1798, a
man strolling near a wharf at the bottom of Cross Street in Boston was
"knocked down, stunned, and robbed."[96] Independence Day in 1815
was apparently a bad one for robberies in Philadelphia. A "mulatto
servant boy" apparently broke into a shop to steal an English gold
watch and chain, a "young man calling himself Joseph Moore" "hired"
a horse and gig, never to be seen again, and an art lover stole a painting of the *Constitution/Guerrière* battle from a tent at Center Square.[97]
In 1812, for a group of Charleston criminals including several bank
robbers, swindlers, and one murderer, the evening of July 4 supplied
the perfect cover for their successful jailbreak.[98]

Some disorderly acts were more the result of high spirits than
criminal intent. On the night before the Fourth in 1806, a sideshow
charlatan in Boston exhibited a shaven bear as a "nondescript biped
from the East Indies." When the imposture was discovered, the "mobility" released the poor creature, "who attempted to make his escape
on all fours," and chased it through the streets.[99] In 1805, after several
canceled performances, an exhibitor calling himself "the Flying Man"
received warning in the *Boston Gazette* that "if he [did] not *fly* in the
town" on July 4 as promised, "the wrath of the populace will oblige
him to *fly* out of it." The Flying Man had to cancel his "Aerial Excur-

sion" when some overcurious revelers wrecked the levitating appara-
tus.[100] On the July 4 following the British occupation of Philadelphia, a
"dirty woman" with "a very high Head dress" attracted "a mob after
her, with Drums &c. by way of rediculing that very foolish fashion."[101]
On a more serious level, some bonded laborers adjudged the anniversary of independence an appropriate time to achieve their own liberty.
A seventeen-year-old apprentice cordwainer ran away from his Philadelphia master on that date in 1787, as did fourteen-year-old James
Bolton in 1805, and "a negro man named Bill" two years later.[102]

The traditional peacekeeping functionaries in the port cities were
woefully inadequate. Boston retained an outmoded system of law enforcement that was manifestly deficient for controlling crime or containing social disorder. There were only ten sworn constables in the
whole town, and on Independence Day in 1798, when tensions between Federalist and Republican partisans were dangerously high,
four of these covered the town ceremonies. Again, two years later,
only four could be spared "to preserve good order in the Common that
Day." In 1803 their number was increased to six, but that was still far
too few for the throngs and the area they covered. An 1805 notice in
the *Independent Chronicle* assured readers that "the proper Officers will
be stationed to prevent any irregularities," but in fact there was little
that they could have done by themselves had the worst fears of Boston's authorities ever materialized, as the editor of the *Boston Gazette*
admitted. "We are highly gratified," he wrote, "with the great decorum and propriety observed on this occasion, at a time when rudeness and vulgarity were justly to be expected, and might have been
practiced almost with impunity."[103]

Philadelphia's police was little better. With a population three
times that of Boston in 1811, Philadelphia had only fourteen constables, one for each ward. The chief duties of the poorly paid night
watch were to light lamps, take up vagrants, and report crimes after
they had already occurred. The Northern Liberties of the city did not
even receive a night watch until 1810, and Southwark not for two
years more.[104] Charleston's constabulary, according to John Hall, was
particularly mediocre, unenthusiastic, or corrupt.[105]

Nor could civil officers and social superiors be counted upon to set
good examples consistently for Independence Day behavior. In 1778,
on the morning of only the second Independence Day, Generals John

Cadwalader and Thomas Conway met in a public park in Philadelphia to settle their differences once and for all. Cadwalader wanted to get rid of the namesake of the infamous "Conway Cabal," which had sought to replace General Washington, by challenging him to a duel over "some disrespectful words" allegedly uttered by Conway against Cadwalader. We can only guess at the reasons why they thought July 4 a particularly appropriate day for their combat. Cadwalader won the first fire, and he shot to kill; his ball passed through Conway's face and lodged in his neck. Amazingly, the wound was not fatal.[106] On the evening of another July 4, members of Charleston's City Guard, ostensibly a peacekeeping body, severely beat "a poor fellow who had enjoyed himself to too great an excess," until a number of private citizens interfered. A reporter claimed that this was not the Guard's "first act of wanton barbarity."[107]

Small wonder that some people dreaded Independence Day. Elizabeth Drinker was not merely being cranky when she reported "riotous doings at Grey's Ferry" on the Fourth, or noted that "these days seldom pass without some melancholy accident occurring from riotous doings." Even during daylight hours, and when the weather was pleasant, some refused to go out. Visiting friends from the city hurried back before nightfall to protect themselves and their property, "as it is a night of Hubbub, or may be so."[108] The elderly Benjamin Rush very much preferred to spend the day with his family along the quiet banks of the Schuylkill, or talking with a widow a generation older than himself about bygone days.[109] For a growing number of people who disliked the popularization of July 4, self-exile was a safer way to pass "the birth-day of American freedom."

"THE AMERICAN FAIR"

In all three of the cities examined here, women composed half of the population, and at first glance their role on Independence Day appears to have been simply that of spectators and occasional symbolic figures. Female status was defined in part by pervasive male distrust in the extent of women's intellectual and moral capacity on the one hand, and of their economic dependency (which disqualified them for independent citizenship) on the other. Despite the prevailing attitude, however, women fashioned a competing image of "republican motherhood" in the decades following the Revolution. These women rejected the image of females as morally deficient, instead asserting that since personal virtue was crucial to the new republic, women played a vital role in teaching their children the necessary values. Far from being less virtuous than men, according to this doctrine women were even more so.[110]

Nevertheless, women were generally excluded from direct participation in processions and other public ceremonies. "In contemporary opinion," observes Susan Davis, "women made themselves 'public women' or 'women of the streets' when they assumed performative roles outside the home."[111] There were exceptions to this general rule. In the case of the Grand Federal Procession of 1788, women figured prominently in the carding and spinning demonstration. At the 1800 Independence Day celebration at North Farms, a Philadelphia suburb, "one hundred young ladies dressed in white" made up one-quarter of those in the procession.[112] Women also appeared in processions as allegorical figures, as when "the Goddess Independency, an emblematical transparent piece of painting, very large" embellished Gray's Garden in 1792.[113] Most male celebrants "included" women in the ritual process only symbolically, however, as was the case with toasts. Few of the hundreds of surviving lists of Independence Day toasts offered at state, military, and private celebrations fail to include a tribute to "the American Fair." One such toast proclaimed "the rights of women and the rights of men reciprocal," but less sexually egalitarian sentiments were more typical: "The Fair Daughters of America—may virtue, knowledge and industry render them useful ornaments to their country."[114] Whether real or symbolic, female appearances were overwhelmingly ceremonial presences rather than being assertive of any public roles.[115] While men acknowledged a place for women in public celebrations, that place was essentially passive.

Nevertheless, women looked forward to joining in the activities of Independence Day in any way they could. A correspondent for the *Boston Gazette* in 1787 noticed that the throngs watching the military exercises on the Common consisted largely of "the blooming fair." Years later, another "large concourse of spectators, particularly ladies" beheld the drills.[116] The Fourth was an important summer social event, particularly in Boston and Philadelphia, a day to see and be seen, as much for the women as for the men. Charles Janson's "boarding house misses" had hoped to promenade on Boston's Mall and attend the oration with their exotic guest; no doubt they were disappointed by his rather ungallant excuses. When Janson later went to the Mall without them, he saw "a great number of citizens of both sexes, and of all description." Regardless of the heat, Janson's subjects were dressed for the occasion: "The ladies appeared in the fashions of England about two years antecedent, but more gaudy . . . their clothes of the best materials. During the hot weather it is a custom here to wear light dressing or morning gowns, but very few were to be seen on this day of jubilee."[117] Near Philadelphia, Charles Willson Peale saw "ladies . . . ready drest in their best attire."[118] The temptation to go out, to see all the excitement, and to be a part of it, was occasionally too great even for those with Quaker backgrounds. "The light horse and Vollentears are to pearade, and to have dinner," fumed Elizabeth Drinker. "My daughter Ann, like many other Simpletons are gone to look."[119] The numerous little parties in the country around Philadelphia included women as well. Some found the opportunity to mix romance with patriotism; in 1814 William Wood Thackera attended a "Party of 25 Ladies and Gentlemen under the Liberty Tree —Had the pleasure of waiting upon ———."[120] There was even a Fourth of July ball—balls were rare events in summer—for the socially elite ladies of Charleston who did not choose to flee the stifling heat.[121]

Women eagerly took active parts in Fourth of July ceremonies and entertainments when given the chance. At one point during the 1790 celebration at Gray's Garden, "thirteen young Ladies and the same number of Gentlemen, dressed as Shepherds and Shepherdesses," came out of the nearby grove and sang "an ode to liberty by alternate Responses and a Chorus" under "the Federal Temple" (the same that Charles Willson Peale painted two years before?). A year later, the oration for the Cincinnati concluded with music "performed by a choir of singers of both sexes."[122] Women also found parts in the many theatrical productions performed on Independence Day.

Occasionally, women claimed more assertive roles in the ceremonies. Militia companies, especially the volunteers, usually had distinctive flags that were the symbols of each unit's pride. These flags were usually made by women, which they then presented to the assembled company in solemn rituals. In 1801 Philadelphia's Republican Blues received one such standard from the ladies of Lancaster. The flag sported an eagle, grasping a thunderbolt, from which streams of lightning dashed symbols of slavery, and the motto "Strike them with your thunderbolts." The women also prepared an address that a spokeswoman read on their behalf. After preliminary congratulations, the women charged the Blues to remember that:

> This not an unmeaning ceremony: the matrons and daughters of America ought to feel the strongest attachment to the militia of their country. They discern in that body, their husbands, their sons, and their brothers associated under the laws in the support of our constitutions. They perceive in those institutions a spirit of justice, quickened by the tenderest humanity, exempting the sex from those countless wrongs which perverted religion and the varied forms of civil policy in other countries have heaped upon them. . . . In presenting you with this standard, we solemnly charge you with the defense of those inestimable constitutions. The emblems which adorn our offering to the Republican Blues will excite them to the contemplation of other objects. . . . Should tyranny rear its head in our land, the Republican. Blues will read, in the device on their banner, the consistent expectations of their female friends.[123]

In Charleston in 1795, the Cadet Artillery paraded before the door of prominent Charlestonian Daniel Hall only a few days before Independence Day, to receive from his daughter the banner they would carry during the celebration. After a few selections by the company band, Hall's daughter, "with much elegance and propriety," delivered a brief address and presented her handiwork to the Cadets' Captain Drayton.[124] Flags were occasionally rededicated as well. In 1825 Philadelphia's elite Washington Greys rode out to a nearby town for an elegant Fourth of July ball. As the Greys prepared to return to the city, the wife of "a distinguished member of the bar" took their flag and refused to release it until, "supported by all the ladies assembled upon the occasion, [she] spontaneously advanced in front of the line and after an eloquent and inspiring address, presented it to the color bearer."[125]

These were indeed no "unmeaning ceremonies." The Lancaster women could hardly have shouldered arms with their men, but they nevertheless insisted on being included symbolically in the ranks of the Republican Blues. Their speech is remarkable not simply for its having survived at all, but for what it reveals about the ideals and concerns of those who wrote it. The women affirmed "the strongest attachment" to the same ideals encoded in "justice," "civil policy," and "constitutions" that their men professed—concerns popularly presumed beyond the female sphere. Whenever they looked upon their flag, the men of the Republican Blues were supposed to remember the "consistent expectations" of the women who made it. Thanking Miss Hall for her gift of a flag, Captain Drayton assured her that "should misfortune be our lot, we will then recal [sic] to memory, that it was presented to us by one of the Patriotic Fair of America, which will make us more strenuous for its support." When soldiers fought for their national flag, they were presumed to be fighting actually for the national entity the flag represented. In protecting their regimental or company flag, they presumably fought for the honor of their unit. In both cases they fought for an abstraction. But when those flags were presented in solemn ceremony by "the patriotic fair," then the men of the Republican Blues, the Washington Greys, the Cadet Artillery, and scores of other militia companies fought to protect something more personal: the respect and admiration of "their female friends."[126]

The fact that women did not regularly march in parades or direct July 4 rituals does not mean that their role on Independence Day was in any way insignificant, or that their presence at orations, parades, militia musters, or social entertainments was superfluous. As argued earlier, not only do spectators play a crucial part in any public ritual, usually the ceremony is more for the spectators than for the performers. An intended audience can ruin a ceremony or celebration, and simultaneously register their level of commitment, distrust, or skepticism, simply by denying their presence. Conversely, attendance implies approval. Women discovered that their attendance—and approval—at July 4 ceremonies were very much in demand by the men who choreographed the rites. "The fair were not excluded from our pleasure," a Charleston group boasted in 1793, "but their firmness, their resolution, their patriotism were again made an embellishment to their charms."[127] In 1805 the Young Republicans of Boston specifically solicited ladies to attend their Fourth of July oration and ceremonies at the Universalist Church, as did the American Republican Society of Philadelphia in 1810.[128] Also in 1805, the Boston committee for the town celebrations erected a stage in the middle of the Com-

mon for the accommodation of a band, fireworks, and the more genteel members of the audience. The *Independent Chronicle* exhorted its
younger readers "that the Ladies who may honour the exhibition with
their presence, may not be intimidated or endangered, the Committee
requests those young Gentlemen, who usually throw squibs on this
occasion to desist from firing any in the direction of the stage."[129] To
encourage female attendance at the overcrowded town orations, orga-
nizers reserved the galleries in the Old South for them, and opened the
doors to women an hour before the general public was allowed to
enter.[130] At Charleston's Orphan House, ladies attending the evening
fireworks there were given the lower suite of apartments "for their
convenience."[131] The militia wanted admiring women to perform for
as well. One observer noted that the presence of females in the crowds
watching the militia "inspired the troops with the ambition becoming
soldiers."[132] The Republican Legion of Philadelphia barred their camp
to most of the general public on Independence Day, but "ladies [were]
the only persons (out of uniform) tolerated to pass the lines."[133]

This deliberate inclusion of women in an otherwise male-
dominated celebration is significant of more than simply the apparent
expectation that the attendance of women would help curb excessively festive behavior. Female participation in Fourth of July activities
both confirmed and validated the self-image that men sought to maintain unchallenged. If the toasts to "the American Fair" represent long-
held "misogynist" impulses on the one hand, on the other they reveal
male responses to the conceit of "republican womanhood."[134] Toasts
gave voice to men's attempts to affect the contest between traditional
apprehensions of women as shallow, supercilious daughters of Eve,
and the assertive, morally superior image that women wanted to project. Toasts that cast women as "Life's first endearment—The best
friends of our heroes and patriots"; pledges that hoped for "the Fair of
America, in the arms of those who best deserve them," placed virtue
(as symbolized by women) within men's grasp.[135] When men proposed, "May the chains, that their charms impose, be the only ones to
which Americans will submit," they claimed those symbolic links to
virtue.[136] It was only one metaphorical step more to appropriate "republican motherhood's" claim to superior virtue by asserting a protec-
tive function over women: "The fair sex—Our delight in peace, in war
our reward, we'll defend them with our swords, they'll repay us with

their love."[137] Female patriotism was a commendable "embellishment to their charms," but it was not the efficacious variety of patriotism that men possessed and that actively defended the nation. By reaffirming their traditional roles as protectors of women, men placed women in the roles of debtors, and reclaimed the preeminent responsibility for affecting the future of the republic.

In the rituals of the Fourth of July, men and women pitted competing concepts of male / female roles against each other. It was an unfair contest, of course; men dominated the ceremonies and celebrations of Independence Day from the start. They ritually acted out their understanding of the Revolution, and that understanding clearly did not include any significant change in gender roles. Men could not allow women an active part in the rituals; nonetheless, to a great extent the rituals were *for* women. Men wanted women, as spectators, to judge the male understanding of republican womanhood and to approve of it symbolically with their continued attendance. "Woman—made to temper man, we had been brutes without them," ran one toast.[138] The statement implied that men were *not* brutes. On the contrary, only virtuous men could defend the republic, and in turn that protection made it possible for women to carry out their roles as republican mothers. "Tho' you are excluded from a participation in our political institutions," one orator told the females in his audience, "yet nature has also assigned to you valuable and salutary rights. . . . To delight, to civilize, and to ameliorate mankind—to exercise unlimited sway over our obedient hearts, *these are the precious rights of woman!*[139] Whether or not women understood it that way, their attendance at the rites of Independence Day gave their male contemporaries all the confirmation they required.

"SHAMEFULLY ABUSED"

The activities of the Fourth of July also reflected the ambiguous situation of the fast-growing black populations in Philadelphia and Boston. Despite the profession of the Declaration of Independence that all men are created equal, the prevailing white sentiment after the Revolution, north and south, was that innate inferiority and the irreparable degradation caused by slavery rendered blacks incapable of becoming responsible, republican citizens. Nevertheless, blacks flocked to northern cities after the Revolution, especially Philadelphia. In that city, the proportion of blacks to the white population shot from 3.6 percent in 1780 to about 10 percent by 1790, at which level it remained until shortly after 1820.[140] Instead of realizing the revolutionary vision of a racially harmonious existence, however, blacks and whites in Boston and Philadelphia discovered that emancipation demanded a reassessment of interracial relations for which whites were generally unprepared. Whites in northern cities increasingly placed blacks upon the margins of their society, physically and figuratively. The irony was particularly poignant on the Fourth of July, where mounting indifference, fear, and hostility between the races engendered a symbolic parting of ways that reflected the unhappy reality.

Initially, Boston's blacks joined whites to celebrate the July 4 festivities, as they had done for decades during other public events such as Election Week. On "Negro Election Day" (part of Election Week) in particular, blacks gathered on Boston Common to carouse, socialize, and gently mock white political elections.[141] They carried much the same sort of spirit into Independence Day, as in 1790 when Nathan Webb observed a "high parade in the common with the negroes &c."[142] Blacks occasionally featured more prominently in Boston's Fourth of July activities; in 1809 the Independent Cadets turned out to escort the oration procession to the Old South with "a new and full band of black music, in superb Moorish dress." Not to be outdone, the Young Republicans in 1810 preceded their Independence Day procession with an "African band" of their own. Black entertainers did not limit themselves to musical offerings; one Fourth of July horsemanship show featured trick-rider "Peter, the African."[143] Blacks in Philadelphia also turned out on the Fourth, apparently gathering in the southeast "square" (today's Washington Square) designed so long before by the city's planners as a public space. They were visible enough on Independence Day for a local poet to observe that "poor and rich, black men and free / All hold it as a jubilee."[144]

White attitudes hardened steadily toward blacks and their participation on the Fourth of July, however. In Philadelphia, a rapidly increasing black population, combined with economic hard times, resulted in burgeoning black poverty, indigence, and crime. Despite the presence in the city of a dedicated, hard-working black community, whites took negative indicators as confirmation of the pervasive opinion that blacks were shiftless, lazy, and morally deficient.[145]

Mounting tensions between the races surfaced in dangerous confrontations on two successive Fourths. In 1804, several hundred black youths met in Southwark on the evening of the Fourth of July. Brandishing clubs and swords, the crowd paraded the streets, roughing up white people they encountered and attacking one house to batter its white occupants. The next night the crowd was out again, this time threatening a Caribbean-style uprising by "damning the whites and saying they would show them St. Domingo." A year later whites retaliated, driving blacks verbally and physically from the square before Independence Hall (the old statehouse).[146]

White forbearance soon ran out in Boston, also. Celebration of diversity was not an issue in the early American republic, and the problem of how (or whether) to include legally free blacks in solemn observances of nationality must have nettled some white consciences. Moral unsettledness may have made whites more sensitive to what they saw as thinly disguised mockery from blacks on public days as well. The parodying of white institutions that made Election Week so much fun for black Bostonians was not lost on their white counterparts, and they did not like it. Certain ceremonies demanded prescribed decorum, and blacks seemed to whites to violate that decorum with their antics, and increasingly, even with their presence. Blacks might congregate safely enough on Negro Election Day, but on a "grave and martial occasion" such as Artillery Election Day, "woe, then, to the black face that dared be seen."[147] In his later years, former Bostonian Sol Smith remembered that in 1814 he, along with a gang of white youths, regularly "chased all the niggers off the Common, as was usually done on occasions of gatherings except on what was termed 'nigger 'lection,'" the only time blacks were left alone on Boston's premier public space.[148] Through this combination of hostility and physical intimidation, whites frustrated any attempts by blacks to participate equally in the rites of Independence Day. Prince Hall, founder of the first black Masonic Hall, reminded an audience at the African Lodge in Menotomy of "the daily insults you meet with in the streets of Boston; much more on public days of recreation, how [you are] shamefully abused."[149] "Is it not wonderful," mused a black citizen of Philadelphia, "that the day set apart for the festival of liberty, should be abused by the advocates of freedom, in endeavoring to sully what they profess to adore?"[150]

The symbolic separation of blacks and whites on the Fourth of July was mirrored by increasing physical separation in the cities in which they lived. Philadelphia's commercial center became almost a completely white domain, while blacks gravitated toward the cheap housing available in the "Cedar Street Corridor." By 1810, two-thirds of the city's black families lived in this southwest area of the city. Ten years later, the proportion increased to three-quarters. In Boston, blacks concentrated in the west and extreme south ends of the peninsula. Black response to increasing segregation and white hostility was mixed, but some were clearly for quitting. Scores of signatures filled a petition before the Massachusetts legislature for funds to "return to Africa, . . . [which is] . . . much more natural and agreeable to us . . . and where we shall live among equals and be more comfortable and happy, than we can be in our present situation."[151]

Driven into more discrete corners of the urban environment and increasingly barred from white Independence Day activities, blacks decided to hold their own exclusive commemorations. On New Year's Day in 1808, traffic in the slave trade became illegal. Black Philadelphians marked the day with divine worship and an oration, and declared January 1 to be a perpetual day of public thanksgiving for the black community.[152] In Boston the following July 14, members of the black community formed a procession from Elliot Street to the African Meeting House in the West End to commemorate the act of Congress. There, about two hundred persons attended an oration and dinner. In form, the day's proceedings closely resembled those of the Independence Day celebrations held ten days before by the white majority—uncomfortably so for whites. The *Independent Chronicle* admired the spirit and good order of the meeting, but suggested that such celebrations were in poor taste, and that annual repetitions were unnecessary. The editors of that Republican newspaper undoubtedly smarted from the irony inherent in the date of the meeting. The African Society insisted that July 14 was selected "for convenience merely," but observant Bostonians wondered at the coincidence of the observance with Bastille Day.[153] The separate black celebrations served notice to whites that, since they denied the equality asserted in the Declaration, black Americans would find more relevant holidays of their own.

The promises of Independence Day did not reach to northern blacks, however hard they worked to achieve the respect of northern whites. Their exclusion from the rituals of July 4 mirrored their increasing exclusion from republican political culture, and reinforced blacks' marginalization in early nineteenth-century America. That exclusion was fundamentally hypocritical, and both whites and blacks knew it. A whites-only Fourth of July denied the social aspirations enshrined in the nation's most famous document, and pronounced the failure of that revolutionary objective. In the case of northern black Americans, the propensity of ritual to gloss over society's contradictions appeared at its worst.

"WHAT AN INCONGRUITY!"

Edward Hooker was not a native South Carolinian, but he spent several years working and traveling in the state, and recording his experiences. The July 4, 1806, found him at an Independence Day dinner with about two hundred men and women. As the food and drink went around, Hooker was struck by what he, and probably only he, saw as a disturbing circumstance: "The tables," he wrote afterward, "were served by negro slaves under the superintendance of the managers. What an incongruity! An Independence dinner for freedmen and slaves to wait on them. I couldn't keep the thought out my mind, the whole time I was there feasting."[154]

Hooker was a Northerner, unused to a society in which slavery was the norm and the presence of blacks taken for granted. In Charleston the relations between blacks and whites were institutionalized, and more formally regulated than in northern cities. There was also much less ambiguity about the place of blacks in the American political culture. Simply put, they had no place, and so their active participation in the celebration of Independence Day was never even an issue. Hooker would have been even more puzzled had he heard the toast of a romantic reveler at a Charleston July 4 dinner: "The silken fetters of love—the only signs of American slavery."[155] Neither the drinker nor Hooker's diners were being hypocritical, strictly speaking. The "incongruity" that was so jarring to Edward Hooker was nothing of the sort to white Charlestonians; for them there was nothing contradictory in utilizing one's own slaves to celebrate American independence. Independence simply did not apply to slaves.

This does not mean, however, that blacks were ever far from the minds of Charlestonians on Independence Day. Indeed, in a city in which such a large proportion of the population was black, they were never physically far at all, establishing three crucial differences between the black populations of Charleston and those of Boston and Philadelphia. First, unlike the modest minority populations of the northern cities, Charleston's black population made up more than half of the city's total throughout the period studied here. Even with its minority white population, Charleston was a comparative island of whiteness surrounded by a low-country plantation population that was 84 percent black in 1800.[156] Second, Charleston's black population was overwhelmingly enslaved; free negroes never made up more than a small percentage of the total, and even these lost most of what few privileges they had by 1820.[157] Third, black Charlestonians did not dwell in segregated neighborhoods, as in Philadelphia and Boston. Owing to their status as slaves, they were distributed more evenly about the city, as the census records of 1790 demonstrate. In that year, 1,247 out of 1,933 heads of families—more than two-thirds—owned one or more slaves, and the percentage of slave owners may have been as high as 82 percent among Charleston's artisans and tradesmen.[158] These conditions, so different from those in Boston or Philadelphia, dictated much of what happened—and what did not happen—in Charleston on Independence Day. The entry of Charleston's blacks into the rites of Independence Day was never allowed—indeed, could not be allowed—but more than the oppressive heat, more than the uncomfortable conditions in the city for Fourth of July celebrations, the omnipresence of a large, enslaved population in their midst profoundly affected how white Charlestonians spent the day. This is not immediately obvious in examining the newspaper accounts of celebrations, where blacks are virtually invisible. However, a careful reading of these and other sources reveals that white Charlestonians celebrated, as it were, while glancing over their shoulders. More than in Boston or Philadelphia, white Charlestonians could never quite dispel their fears of what their enslaved servants might do while their masters celebrated liberty.

White Charlestonians were aware of the numerical disparity of blacks and whites in the city and surrounding low country, and were extremely sensitive to anything that might loosen the bonds of dependency and subservience that kept their slaves in control. In 1781 General Nathaniel Greene, desperate for more men to oppose the British in the Carolinas, suggested arming slaves to help the American cause. The strategy had proved successful in his native Rhode Island, where emancipation was offered as an inducement to military service. South Carolinian John Laurens endorsed the plan, but with the Rutledges spearheading opposition, nothing came of it, even in this year of emergency in the South. The opponents had what they took to be sound reasons for their position; the Stono Rebellion four decades earlier had left an indelible impression on the minds of Carolinians as to the likely result of putting weapons into the hands of slaves. Arm the slaves, they contended, and it would not be the British who would have most to fear.[159] After the bloody Saint Domingo insurrection in 1791, French refugees flooded into Charleston, bringing with them the horror stories that were sure to make their way to the ears of the city's own servile population. What made these stories worse, and what made the French Revolution so particularly fearsome to some Charlestonians, was the fact that France emancipated its slaves throughout the Caribbean several years later. If Carolina's blacks ever got the notion that liberty, equality, and fraternity could ever apply to them as well as to their Caribbean counterparts, there was no city in the United States more vulnerable than Charleston to a similarly determined uprising.[160]

For "proof" of their worst fears, white Charlestonians could look to their sad experience with fires—unmatched for frequency in the much-larger northern cities. In 1796 a devastating fire in the city center consumed some five hundred houses, according to one report.[161] From that year forward, as a native later recollected, "there was scarcely an interval of three to five years in which a large fire did not occur." What was more, Charlestonians were sure that these were not accidents: "It was a rare occurence," asserted one, "that a fire took place below the line of Broad street, on the south, and Market street, on the north, and Archdale street, on the west; and, what was no less remarkable, they embraced the business portions of the city . . . leading to the supposition that they were the work of incendiaries.[162]

White city-dwellers were pretty sure who the "incendiaries" were. Slaves, they felt, certainly had the motive (revenge), and though they might not dare raise their hands against their masters directly, the destruction of their masters' material wealth was a proven method of hurting them effectively. All that was needed was for one determined person to steal through the dark maze of alleys, quickly kindle a flame in the back of a building (perhaps conveniently abandoned for the summer by a vacationing family), and disappear into the darkness before the alarm sounded. Any slave could do it, and the slaves were everywhere. A fire could be simply a malicious destruction of property, or the perfect distraction for a planned revolt; whites could not defend their property and themselves at the same time.

Fires could "happen" any time of the year, but there were several attempts at arson during Independence Day observances particularly, and blacks were either directly implicated in these instances, or strongly suspected. Early in the morning following the 1798 celebration, neighbors managed to extinguish a fire in a house on Queen Street before it did any serious damage. The apparent cause was arson, as the house was unoccupied at the time, and investigators found combustibles under the stairs. Two black women were arrested, "on suspicion of having conveyed the combustibles thither," apparently under cover of the previous evening's festivities. Under "examination" they "confessed" their guilt. At their trial the next morning, one was condemned to be executed that very day in the Lower Market. Charlestonians noted that the house the "girl" had apparently attempted to burn belonged to her master, and that the other alleged incendiary was a "French," or Caribbean, Negro. On another occasion, arsonists fired a stable on the night of July 4, apparently with the intent of destroying the neighborhood. This fire was also extinguished before it got out of control, this time due to advance warning from a letter "evidently written and dictated by a Negro," who may have risked his or her life in betraying comrades. At least two other instances of arson, one of which caused "immense" destruction in an artisan neighborhood, were perpetrated on the night of July 4.[163] The poetic appropriateness of such destructive strokes upon the premier national holiday must have been obvious to both blacks and whites. So, along with the elation that was supposed to accompany Independence Day, the people of Charleston also had to accept the special danger that the day held for them. Every July 4 brought Charlestonians the possibility that arson, performed by their own slaves, might present to their view "a dreary devastation, and [shed] a transient gloom over this anniversary."[164]

White Charlestonians responded to their fears by supporting draconian ordinances designed to restrict the activities of Charleston's blacks severely. In 1789 the city council prohibited gatherings of any more than seven "Negroes or other slaves, for the purpose of merriment or otherwise" in any public or private place after dark. Anyone secretly allowing such gatherings or selling liquor to blacks courted a hefty fine. When the council noticed in 1801 that it had become "a practice with slaves to be whooping and hallooing indecently about the streets or on the wharfs, and to sing loud and obscene songs," they moved to curtail these daytime recreations as well. After 1807 no assembly of Negroes or "coloreds . . . for dancing or merriment" would be tolerated even in the daylight hours without the *written* permission of the local warden. The fine for tolerating any such unlawful gathering was raised a startling tenfold, from $10 to $100.[165]

Whites might be fined, but offending blacks, slave or free, would be handled more severely. The errant dancers or merrymakers taken up by enforcement officers were brought to the city's house of correction, known locally as the Sugar House because of its former use as a sugar refinery. The Sugar House was a place of terror for Charleston's blacks. "Here such scenes of flaggellation are witnessed," wrote one observer, "that one cannot threaten a Negroe with a more efficacious punishment than that of a visit to the Sugar House." If their owners (or family and friends if the prisoner was a free black) did not pay a fine to release them, the revelers would be flogged. For some offences there was not even the possibility of paying a fine; any black, slave or free, caught using fireworks received ten to twenty lashes. Even the whoopers and hallooers were ordered to receive ten lashes, and this number was doubled in 1806, the amount also given to any black smoking a pipe or cigar (which could start fires), or carrying a "cane, club, or other stick" in public.[166]

Giving teeth to the city council's ordinances was the City Guard, a quasi-military police force established after the 1783 riots to reinforce the meager and inefficient constabulary. Every night, the Guard was required to keep at least one sergeant, one corporal, one drummer, and eight privates on duty at the city guardhouse and on patrol, discouraging burglars and arsonists, and taking up prowlers or suspicious persons for fines or corporal punishment. Despite the fact that public disturbances of the sort that inspired their inception were rare after 1784, the City Guard grew by 1810 to a company strength of forty or fifty men, all uniformed and sporting the national cockade.[167] There is no evidence to indicate that Charleston's crime problems were any greater than those of Boston or Philadelphia, which made do with much smaller law enforcement agencies.[168] Nor was it the City Guard's duty to defend the city from invaders; the militia did that. The continued growth and refinement of Charleston's City Guard is best explained by the pervasive fear that whites held for their servile, but potentially dangerous, population. A foreign observer captured the essence of one of the seeming realities that shaped the world of white Charlestonians. "To a certain extent," he wrote, "necessity has re- quired that the Negroes must be kept very severely not only in regard to their subsistence but also in regard to the punishments executed against them. The number of whites is nowhere near as great as that of the blacks, therefore, a fear of the whites must be maintained con- stantly among them."[169]

Without the ability to congregate freely, dance, sing, halloo, be out at night and throw fireworks, there was not much left for Charleston's blacks to do on July 4, at least not lawfully. Nor did whites lift the onerous restrictions for the day in a display of largesse, as they did on the surrounding low-country plantations on Christmas and other oc- casions. Independence Day was for Americans only, and as far as white Charlestonians were concerned, blacks simply did not qualify. When the city amusement park known as Vauxhall Gardens adver- tised a special Independence Day program in 1799, there was to be "no admittance for people of colour."[170] For their own security, whites regarded it as vital to remind blacks at every opportunity that Inde- pendence Day could mean nothing to them. Even the limited and short-lived participation of Boston and Philadelphia blacks in the holi- day was unthinkable in Charleston.

Did the "incongruities" that so troubled Edward Hooker in 1806 ever occur to white Charlestonians? The attitudes and beliefs of a people are impossible to quantify, and in this case even anecdotal evidence is rare; to my knowledge, no Charlestonian left a record of his or her reflections on the subject. Inference is all that is left; tentative conclusions based on the interpretation of what Charlestonians did and what they did not do, together with a few clues. Public slave auctions in Charleston took place on Tuesdays and Thursdays, but I have found no record of any being held when July 4 fell on one of those days.[171] Of course this may indicate nothing more than that the auctioneers decided to take the day off along with other citizens, but the coincidence is intriguing: Would a slave sale on a holiday dedicated to liberty and independence simply have been too incongruous, even for a society that embraced a political economy built and based upon the institution? Would such an event have been just too provocative for the city's black majority?

A year after Edward Hooker first noticed the "incongruity" attending South Carolina's Independence Day, he was back with his former July 4 comrades, this time as one of the committee members charged with drafting the formal toasts to follow the dinner. He proposed several stock pledges that were accepted, then stumbled again into the invisible cultural wall that separated Hooker the Northerner from his hosts. He proposed (innocently he insisted) a toast that ran: "the principles of rational liberty—May the blissful period ere long arrive when they shall prevail throughout the inhabitable globe!" Congressman John Taylor, also on the committee, "took it up and looking it over a little at first seemed to find no fault, but all at once spoke out; 'O this will never do! Why 'twill include our cursed black ones,' or words to that effect." Somewhat taken aback, Hooker protested that he had not intended to be that specific, but that he "suppos[ed] there is none of us but would wish it to extend even to them at some period or other." There was an uncomfortable pause, and then another committeeman, the state surveyor general, said, almost as in a prayer, "I hope it may not be till we are gone." Hooker tried feebly to recover the initiative by offering to strike the words "ere long" from the text, but it was too late: "Taylor said the toast would not be an acceptable one at the Table, so we concluded to drop it."[172]

What Hooker considered innocent the other committee members regarded as insidious. Their sensitivity to Hooker's toast suggests that the southern members of the committee were also aware of the "incongruity" that Hooker had noticed the year before. But by and large they appear to have chosen to ignore the incongruity, or rather, to deny it. Such cultivated pretense might fool outsiders, but as Hooker's experience suggests, it did not fool the Carolinians themselves. Charleston's blacks affected the celebration of Independence Day more than the city's whites cared to admit publicly. If the large servile population could not be trusted in the absence of white overseers, how could any significant numbers of white masters leave the city for a shoreside frolic, as could Philadelphians? How could they leave their houses for the evening by the hundreds and thousands, as in Boston, and feel secure that their houses would still be there when they returned? The pervasive fear of their enslaved population necessarily limited the degree to which white Charlestonians could celebrate as a community. The labor system that had enriched white Charlestonians also held them somewhat captive on the Fourth of July; if that situation did not cast a "transient gloom" over Charleston's celebration, it at least prevented the kinds of activities that were possible in the northern cities.

Whether Americans celebrated Independence Day hesitantly or with abandon, they did so within the framework of celebratory styles shaped by conditions particular to their communities. It was all very well for some to boast that millions of Americans celebrated as one, but clearly that was not the case. Some no doubt truly kept the Fourth of July holy, a secular Sabbath. Others just as certainly were there, as Susan Davis has remarked, only "for the beer." Most regarded Independence Day as a legitimate festival of nationalism, but the variety of ways they celebrated, and the different companies they kept, suggests that "nationalism" may also have been differently understood between regions, and among the peoples within a region. With their familiar and formulaic reports of Independence Day celebrations in other localities, newspapers provided Americans with the mistaken impression that all of their countrymen and countrywomen celebrated and imagined as they did. For them, nationalism may have seemed little more than localism writ large.

Within the localities, some Americans were concerned that popularizing Independence Day and the democratization of celebratory forms would turn the Fourth of July into a lower-class bacchanalia little better than Boston's Pope's Days of pre-Revolutionary times. The popularization of July 4 seemed to test whether or not ordinary Americans possessed the self-restraint to be proper republican citizens. Some thought not, and withdrew from the popular rituals. The majority felt otherwise. They did not reject the ideology encoded in the decorous ceremonies established by their social betters; they added a wider variety of ritual forms to express their political understanding in ways meaningful to them.

Popularizing the Fourth did not mean democratizing it in the broadest sense, however. Manifestly, Independence Day was a white man's celebration. On the one hand, Americans generally rejected the racial applications of the Declaration's "all men are created equal." On the other hand, those who controlled the public rites of Independence Day agreed that *only* men could be equal; We have seen that men excluded women from actively shaping the rites. Nor did populariza- tion mean that Independence Day became a distinctly "working-class festival."[173] Citizens representing the whole range of the social spec- trum observed the Fourth, but they did not observe it in the same way, or all together. Many of the wealthy celebrated quietly with family in the country, or passed the day in the company of a few close friends.[174] In Philadelphia, middle-class social groups, political clubs, and militia emulated the wealthy and left town for the day in increasing numbers. Where Elizabeth Drinker in 1796 "never saw our streets more popu- lous" on the Fourth, another observer in 1811 remarked that "the city appeared about noon to have been entirely emptied of its popula- tion."[175] Bostonians experienced the opposite, although the different orders still tended to celebrate separately. With no large white popula- tion outside the city to attract, and with a potentially dangerous slave population in its midst, Charleston's July Fourth was the most insular of the three, but at the same time the least communal.

Despite the worst fears of some, the Fourth of July was never a lower-class charivari. The town and city leaders acquiesced to expres- sions of high-spiritedness (partly because they had to), but there were no rituals of social inversion, no attempts to attack the social order itself, certainly nothing even approaching Boston's Pope's Days. Inde- pendence Day relieved the "festival deprivation" of all social orders, not only that of the lower sort. As with rituals of social inversion, the significant function of the rites of Independence Day was not so much how they released social tensions, but how they controlled those ten- sions.[176] Town and city officials regulated the ritual matrix and many of the ritual forms of July 4 encouraging some and forbidding others. Many of the entertainments created by the public at large contained socializing messages encoded in the fireworks, stage productions, songs, and food. Many upper and middle-class Philadelphians gave up the city to the lower sort during the day, but only temporarily and only because the lower sort did not go on rampages while they were gone. Nearly everyone who left the city on the Fourth returned by

nightfall. When darkness came, attractions such as theatrical productions, museums, illuminated public buildings, and fireworks ensured that the lower orders did not rule the night. To all appearances,
Charleston promptly closed down after the fireworks were over, and
the City Guard made sure that no one, black or white, would be reveling long after dark.

From the semisacred to the profane, the diversity of activities on
the Fourth of July allowed almost everyone to express his sense of
patriotism individually or with the group of his or her choice. But
communitas was slipping away. The feeling of civic unity that the people of Boston, Charleston, and Philadelphia experienced during the
Revolution, and even the "induced" variety that came after, was being
lost in increasingly large and diverse urban populations. Popularization brought polarization of the social, political, and ethnic orders.
Communitas and its promise of unity and equality was an illusion, a
nagging ambiguity cloaked by ceremonial sleight-of-hand.

5

"Even to Blood"

> Party Spirit—it is the guardian of our rights—but
> may it never mar the bosom of friendship, nor
> interrupt the course of private affection.
>> Toast of the Democratic Young Men, July 4,
>> 1809

> The day was celebrated here with all the spirit of
> *party* if not of *patriotism.* To what a height has party
> spirit arrived in this country; that the event which
> equally concerns all should be celebrated distinctly
> by the different parties, and each avoid the other as
> pestilential.
>> Leverett Saltonstall

The year 1800 marked a turning point in American politics. Thomas Jefferson's election to the presidency (not confirmed until March of the next year) was only the best known in a series of Republican triumphs at state and local levels throughout the nation. More victories came in the following years, until the defeat of the Federalists became almost a rout. That dramatic transferal of power seemed to signal victory for the Republican interpretation of American politics.

The great shift did not come all at once, as the examples of the three cities examined here demonstrates. In South Carolina, where Federalists lost ground quickly after 1798, Charleston became virtually a last refuge of Federalism, surrounded by a state that enthusiastically supported Jefferson and his party. But the waning of "party spirit" there was aided in large measure by the cotton boom in the decades after 1790. Cotton, and the wealth it produced, worked to accommodate the interests of low country and backcountry as mere ideology never could. Instead of bringing about the social revolution that many Federalists feared, the cotton industry created a backcountry aristocracy that seemed far less threatening to their coastal counterparts. Also, since Charleston was no longer the political center of its state (the capital moved to Columbia in 1790), political competition at the highest levels was far less focused in the city. The result of these factors was a relaxation of political tensions in Charleston after 1800.[1]

Federalism, and party spirit, was more persistent in the northern cities. The collapse of the Philadelphia Federalist party in 1800 seemed complete, but a sizable Federalist minority remained, eager to regain preeminence if possible. Republicans held political sway for the moment but seemed unsure of their strength. Their fears of a Federalist resurgence prompted them to treat Federalists as a serious threat long after they had ceased to be so. In Boston the Federalists were the most solidly entrenched, and held on the longest. In the years following Jefferson's reelection in 1804, the Federalists' dominance of the Massachusetts government steadily weakened, but they clung tenaciously to the mastery of the Boston town meeting until well into the 1820s. Federalism in Boston did not so much collapse as erode.

The political climates in these cities affected their Fourth of July celebrations differently. In Charleston, where political lines became increasingly blurred or irrelevant, there was little apparent change in July 4 activities occasioned by alterations in political winds. Boston and Philadelphia were different matters entirely. After their defeats in 1800, much of the spark seemed to go out of Philadelphia's Federalists. Now in the minority, they lacked the broad support, and increasingly the inclination, to challenge and provoke their opponents on Independence Day as Republicans had done. Nevertheless, Republicans kept up the battle to redefine Independence Day, and to make it an annual testament to the Republican vision. Republicans wanted not merely to defeat, but to crush Federalism utterly, so they continued to fan political partisanship on July 4.

Boston was still the only city to have officially ordained observances and there the impulse to celebrate communally was strongest. As a result, there was no diminution in the pattern of bitter competition over the annual festivals begun in the 1790s. With their party brethren victorious elsewhere, Boston's Republicans hoped to assume the town's official Independence Day rites as well. When they were balked in their attempts, they resolved instead to give Bostonians a choice between the traditional, Federalist-dominated town ceremonies, and alternative observances of their own. The contest became fiercer still, and violence on the Fourth of July remained a real possibility.

"A VAST PILE OF COMBUSTIBLES"

The central feature of Boston's official celebrations remained the patriotic oration decreed by the 1783 town meeting. Over the years many of the town's most illustrious personages had performed the duty. As with the Massacre Day orations, the popularity of these events required a space larger than that provided by Faneuil Hall (its appearance today is the result of Charles Bulfinch's extensive enlargement of the original structure). The selectmen tried several different church buildings for the first decade or so, but after 1800 they settled upon the almost exclusive use of the Old South Meeting House. That venerable building held a number of Revolutionary associations, the most famous being the meeting place for the crowd that perpetrated the Boston Tea Party.

The speakers selected for the town orations were supposed to give strictly patriotic speeches evoking the "feelings, manners, and principles, which led to this great event."[2] However, there was no way to prevent orators from mixing the feelings and principles of their political sympathies with the patriotic message; indeed, because of the precedent set by the Massacre orations, polemical outpourings may have been just what the audiences expected and desired. Since the Selectmen who annually chose the next year's orator happened to be overwhelmingly Federalist, the sentiments expressed in the town orations frequently rankled Republicans in the audience. Even when a speaker did not grind a political axe openly, the consistent choice of "federal" orators irked Republicans; only once after 1792 did the Republican press unqualifiedly approve of the selection of the speaker and his message.[3] Attempts to balance the Federalist rhetoric by substituting Republican speakers met with no success, and Republicans could only chafe in frustration. Josiah Quincy's 1798 oration "was received with general applause," grumbled the *Independent Chronicle*, "agreeable to the old adage, 'one story is good, 'til another is told.' "[4] Four years later, the editors of the same paper saw fit only to print the ode sung at the Old South, since at least that was "not disgraced by any marks of that party rancour, which influenced the orator."[5]

Denied equal access to the Independence Day pulpit, and disgusted with the "aristocratic" monopoly of the ceremonies in Boston, Republicans unveiled an alternative July 4 program in 1802 that was more to their liking. This began with a separate procession, about three hundred strong, that commenced at the Old State House and ended at Faneuil Hall with a dinner. The ceremonies at the Hall opened with the reading of the Declaration of Independence, a custom that became a hallmark of Republican celebrations everywhere. The feast began at two in the afternoon and went on into the early evening. In contrast to the many small, private dinners held throughout the town, the repast at Faneuil Hall was a public event, to which the Republicans hoped to attract new recruits. It was a noisy affair, with artillery blasts outside the Hall punctuating each after-dinner toast. At the name of George Washington, recently sanctified by death, six guns thundered in salute. Federalist hackles must have risen when a toast to Thomas Jefferson, very much alive and then president, merited three more. After the dinner, the celebrants donated the surplus food to the prisoners of Boston's jails, especially the poor debtors. The gesture recalled similar favors shown on royal birthdays in former times, and was calculated to signify the Republicans' benevolence and identification with the oppressed. After five hours of fortifying themselves with food, drink, and good fellowship, the celebrants reportedly "retired like rational freemen."[6]

The mustang Republican celebration was an open challenge to Federalist domination of Independence Day activities, and for the next decade the Republicans kept up the competition. Unable to wrest the official observances from their opponents, the Republicans set about supplanting them, beginning with the location for their July 4 activities. For nearly two decades the focal point for Boston's civic celebration had been the Old South Meeting House, where the town-sponsored oration was usually performed. Town tradition was squarely on the side of the Federalists; if the Republicans were to compete successfully with the Federalist-dominated ceremonies, they needed to establish a symbolic legitimacy equal to that of their rivals. The Federalists had successfully co-opted the Old South's revolutionary past, and neutralized its radical message of forceful resistance, by sponsoring the annual orations there. However, there were other historic sites the Republicans could use. In Revolutionary times Faneuil Hall had been a meeting place for Boston's radical Whigs. This crucial association with the past gave Faneuil Hall a special place in Boston's array of Revolutionary landmarks. Although often passed by for use on civic occasions because of its size, Faneuil Hall was transformed by the Republicans into a Revolutionary shrine rivaling the Old South. In their inaugural dinner there, the Republicans lauded the Hall as "the Cradle of Independence—rocked by the Republicans of Boston."[7]

Competitors they might be, but the Republicans did not attempt to mock or overturn Boston's customary Independence Day ceremonies, nor were their celebrations intended to lampoon the Federalist rites. Republicans stuck to most of the same traditional forms as did their adversaries: the procession, the public address, the convivial feast. They even sent a delegation to pay their respects to the aging veterans of the Cincinnati, a group once shunned by anti-aristocratic Republicans. The Faneuil Hall celebrants had no quarrel with the town's traditional observances as such, nor apparently did they wish to change them in any material way. Indeed, until they could dominate Boston town politics, there was little chance of their refashioning Boston's official activities. But they could challenge the Federalist message of July 4.

Boston's Federalists watched with concern as the Republican activities at Faneuil Hall attracted more people each year. Republican militia companies deserted the Common to add color, music, and muscle to the alternative observances, finding a place to parade more congenial to their politics. Following the form established by the Federalist ceremonies, the Independent Republican Fusiliers escorted the Republicans to Faneuil Hall in 1803, as did the Washington Infantry in 1804.[8] Quite apart from the fact that military escort implied legitimate authority, the presence of Republican militia at Faneuil Hall was symbolic of divided loyalties and pregnant with the imagery of opposing armed camps.

After several years of "traditionalizing" their own Independence Day activities, Republicans felt confident enough to begin chipping away at town traditions. The Republican press dismissed the Federalist celebrations as inconsequential, and refused to detail these events any longer. "To comment upon these annual instances of delusion," sniffed the *Independent Chronicle*, "would be superfluous."[9] Republican auxiliaries added to the denigration of Federalist rites. In 1805 a group of young Boston men formed the Young Republicans Society, holding its inaugural meeting on Independence Day. They noted with "lamentation . . . that the Anniversary Oration in this Town should be exclusively pronounced by what is insidiously termed a Federal Orator who merely used the sacred name of Liberty to deride her qualities and to excite jealousies and animosities between the different sections of our country." They made choice of their own "Republican Orator" for their first meeting that year, one whom they felt would more accurately reflect the feelings, manners, and principles of the occasion. Then they made sure that the minutes detailing their decisions were published in the Republican press.[10]

Republicans also changed their tactics with regard to symbolic associations. The decision to mingle French and American revolutionary symbols had yielded questionable results for the Republican cause. Certainly tricolor flags, blue cockades, and guillotines elicited responses from those who saw them, but those responses were not always favorable. Despite the rhetoric of the more radical Republicans, Americans were not inclined to view the French Terror as representative of a kindred political spirit. The quasi-war with France in 1799 and Napoleon's subsequent rise to power made further attachment to America's old ally a political liability. Although Republicans still preferred France to Britain, and considered America's best interests to lie with her Revolutionary ally, they downplayed the Franco-American connection after 1800. Federalist newspapers noted with smug satisfaction that the Republicans at Faneuil Hall did not fly the French flag alongside the American as they had done in the past. "If party distinctions were not forgotten," declared the *Boston Gazette*, at least "*no insignia of foreign attachment* was displayed to disturb the serenity of the day. Those who have heretofore carried it as a badge of patriotism, seem to be seeking some new colours and glosses to give it, before they put it on for future use."[11] Next year's display was much the same, and the Republicans admitted that they had studiously avoided any display that might "irritate the public mind."[12]

But the Republicans did indeed find new colors and glosses. As they had discovered when flourishing the American flag to get the public eye, symbols rooted firmly in the American past could hardly "irritate the public mind." Republicans now seized upon symbols that had lain dormant or been taken for granted since the heady days of the Revolution and breathed new life into them. Federalist opponents discovered to their chagrin that not only were the Republicans taking over more state and local offices, but the symbols of American political culture as well.

Most especially, the Republicans claimed the Declaration of Independence, the very basis for July 4 celebrations, for themselves. They hailed it as the font of American freedom, an "American Magna Carta." The *Independent Chronicle* annually devoted most of its front page to reprinting the Declaration's text, exhorting its readers to remember the principles that guided "the heroes of 1776." A solemn reading of the Declaration and the names of its signers preceded every Republican Independence Day meeting. Republicans claimed not only the Declaration's principles, but also its authorship, as the exclusive domain of their party, and credited Thomas Jefferson solely with its composition.[13]

More than that, however, they infused the Declaration with timely and, for Federalists, frightening political implications. Before this time, Americans on Independence Day had celebrated the *act* of signing the Declaration. However, the document that declared independence from foreign tyranny could not make Americans immune to domestic despotism. Instead of regarding the Declaration as a historic relic, Republicans fastened upon its assertions of "life, liberty, and the pursuit of happiness" as promises not yet fulfilled. For Republicans, the document was a summons to arms, a manifesto against tyranny *wherever* it was found. More than a historic but dead letter, for Republicans the Declaration still held immediate power and meaning; the words of the Declaration of Independence were not mere liturgy, they were the lyrics of "a kind of war-song," a call to action.[14]

Federalists were instantly hostile to the Republicans' demagogic interpretation of the Declaration. They feared the consequences of "the seductive doctrines of 'Liberty and Equality,' " convinced that the true meaning of liberty had been perverted by radicals and Francophiles.[15] But they never found an effective way to counter their opponents' ideological appropriation of Independence Day's raison d'être. Instead, the Federalist press chose to deal with the challenge by dismissing it. To the Republicans' annual printing of the Declaration in their newspapers, the Federalists replied that they were delighted, "as the greater part of them must have been entirely ignorant of the facts and principles upon which it was founded." The Federalists acknowledged that the Republicans were "striving to outdo the Federalists in the celebration of American Independence," but resolved to make no extraordinary effort to compete. Because they had been in the habit of celebrating the Fourth for the past twenty-six years, they explained, they needed "no extraordinary incentive to the performance of a pleasant duty." Indeed, huffed the *Boston Gazette,* when Republicans abused Independence Day for mere partisan purposes, "Federalists should not only neglect, but detest the festival."[16] As for the Republicans' "new modes and ceremonies," the *Columbian Centinel* concluded, "hypocrisy always overacts the part."[17]

The Federalists were stirred from their complacency, however, when their rivals next laid claim to the soul of George Washington. In their first meeting at Faneuil Hall, the Republicans raised their glasses to "Washington—the *Republican* general."[18] A year later, with the week-old news of Louisiana's cession to the United States further animating the celebrants, they again remembered "their" general: "While his *old* enemies claim the patronage of his name, his . . . *real* friends enjoy the triumph of his principles."[19] In 1804, the Republicans were joined at Faneuil Hall by a pro-Republican militia company styling themselves the "Washington Infantry."[20] Federalists naturally bristled at this Republican presumption to identify with their "immortal Washington," especially since the general was no longer alive to disavow any association with Republicans, as he surely would have. There was little the Federalists could do to stifle Republican efforts to arrogate Washington's symbolic mantle; they could only claim to speak for their deceased champion through toasts of their own: "May the memory of Washington be spared the *insult* of *praise* from those who defamed him while living, and who now pretend to wear his uniform."[21]

The Boston Federalists had good reason to worry about the Republicans' new tactics. The ability to appropriate and manipulate symbols has a direct correlation with power and legitimacy. Whichever side controlled the most effective symbols would eventually "win." Federalists recognized this principle too late. Having lost the Declaration of Independence to the Republicans, they now found that even those symbolic associations they thought most secure were slipping away from them. After 1800 they attempted to recapture a direct connection with the revolutionary past on Independence Day by annually publishing John Adams's "pomp and parade" letter of 1776 in their newspapers on July 4.[22] In imitation of the Republicans' glorification of the Declaration of Independence, Federalists insisted that Adams's letter deserved "to be read at least *once every year.*"[23] As Republican successes in both the symbolic and material realms continued, Federalist rhetoric betrayed a growing sense of desperation. One writer to the *Boston Gazette* advocated as a last resort using the still-potent Federalist legal machinery to muzzle Republicans, suggesting that more "vigorous execution of wholesome laws" would check "party spirit" on the Fourth.[24]

Political events in 1806 altered the pattern of partisan Fourth of July celebrations in Boston. The Federalist domination of Massachusetts politics had begun to slip two years earlier; the 1806 elections for state legislators provided Federalists with a chance to recoup their losses. For their part, Republicans naturally viewed the elections as an opportunity to consolidate their gains and to continue sapping their opponents' entrenched positions. The elections were set for June, just weeks before Independence Day, and the campaigning was particularly acrimonious. Sensing the worst, Boston Federalists employed every means at their disposal to influence votes. "Many go so far as to dismiss their truckmen, mechanics, and seamen who differ with them in politics," wrote one diarist. Boston, he claimed, was "a vast pile of combustibles, and a spark may produce a flame that will end in blood and destruction through the streets."[25] Despite their efforts, the Federalists took another pounding at the polls, losing more seats to their detested rivals. Although the Federalists still controlled the governor's seat and the Boston town government, the writing on the wall looked clearer than ever to them. Frustrated and embittered, the Boston selectmen were determined not to allow Republicans to turn the following Independence Day into a victory celebration.

Two weeks after the election, the Republicans applied to the selectmen as usual for the use of Faneuil Hall on the Fourth of July. They had been holding their meetings there for the past four years, and no doubt looked forward to using the newly enlarged edifice for a monster rally. Instead, to their amazement, they were told that the Hall was "preengaged by the federalists." With only days remaining before the Fourth, the Republicans scrambled to make virtue out of necessity. Meeting instead on the old burial grounds of Copp's Hill in the North End of town, they conducted their usual festivities as best they could. Very likely, the Republican ranks that day included bitter workmen recently deprived of employment. Fortunately the weather, though hot, was not otherwise unpleasant. A huge tent sheltered the celebrants from the July sun, and the tables were spread amid the ancient graves and over the remains of British earthworks built some thirty years before.[26]

Not surprisingly, Faneuil Hall was "preengaged" the following year as well, and every year after that. Republicans cried foul, claiming that the Federalists did not even use the Hall on two occasions when they had supposedly reserved it, simply to deny its use to anyone else. To Republicans, the selectmen's actions were further proofs of "aristocratic" abuse of power, and mean-spirited responses to Republican victories elsewhere in the state. But they found few ears in the town government sympathetic to their complaints.[27]

Finding all town facilities denied them, the Republicans met next year at the Boston Coffee House, but found that establishment too confining for the kinds of public rallies they were used to. Exasperated, in 1808 they decided to shake the dust of Boston from their feet and join the July 4 celebrations hosted by their party brethren in Charlestown. But they were determined not to leave Boston with their tails between their legs. Forming a procession at the statehouse (where they were more welcome these days), they paraded through Boston, met their Charlestown counterparts halfway across the Charles River Bridge, and celebrated upon the historic ground at Bunker Hill. The Young Republicans (who changed their name to the Washington Society in 1811) joined the procession in a show of party solidarity but continued to hold their own meetings in Boston, perhaps as much to spite the Federalists as for convenience.[28] But while Federalists could claim victory in driving their enemies out of Boston on Independence Day, the Republicans were clearly ascendent elsewhere. Formerly staunch Federalists defected to the enemy. John Quincy Adams "converted" to the

Republicans in 1808, and a year later his ex-president father gave the endorsement of his august presence to the 1809 Republican celebrations on Bunker Hill.[29]

Despite their self-exile, the Republicans could occasionally tweak Federalist noses on Independence Day. The gubernatorial election of 1807 brought James Sullivan to the statehouse, the first Republican governor in ten years. Although Massachusetts governors had regularly attended the town orations in the past, they were only required by legislative resolve to hear divine worship on Independence Day. So when a committee from the Federalist selectmen called upon Governor Sullivan to request his presence at the town ceremonies, Sullivan replied that "he feared from the number of his engagements for that day he should not be able to attend."[30] The next year brought the same result. On that occasion, John Pierce of Brookline accompanied the morning procession of the governor and legislators to the Brattle Street Church. "This exercise," he confided to his diary, "though recommended by the General Court in 1786 has been disused, or rather united with the exercises accompanying the town oration, til last year, when Gov. Sullivan, expecting to hear some unwelcome truths in the town oration, appointed this exercise, as a substitute for the other. Last year, Dr. Baldwin, in addition to the prayer, gave him an address, in unison with the political sentiments he has chosen to adopt." A staunch Federalist, Pierce chafed at his obligatory attendance. After fulfilling his duty at Brattle Street, he hurried to the Old South Meeting House for the town oration.[31]

Another Republican, Elbridge Gerry, succeeded Sullivan to the governor's seat, and he had no more intention of attending the Federalist ceremonies than had his predecessor. In reply to the selectmen's invitation, Gerry declared that he "had determined to pursue the same mode for that occasion which had been adopted by Gov. Sullivan, and in conformity with the resolve of the Legislature directing religious services to be performed by the chaplains."[32] The absence of the governor from the town oration ceremonies was a quiet but eloquent snub of Boston's Federalists, and an uncomfortable reminder of deep social and political hostilities on the anniversary of national unity.

Once committed to a physical parting of ways on Independence Day, both parties threw themselves into orchestrating the most sensational, noisy, and well-attended Independence Day festivities that

Boston had ever seen. The Republicans turned their processions to Charlestown into Exodus-like spectacles reminiscent of parades promoting the Constitution two decades before. The *Independent Chronicle* on July 3, 1809, desired that all work not indispensable be put aside on the following day, "so as to enable our young men to enjoy the day, by participating in the amusements." The plea was apparently successful, for an observer later reported, "the shops and stores were closed, and all business suspended." The freed shopworkers helped swell the ranks of the procession to about six hundred, making the Republican parade that year the largest yet. The procession wound through the principal streets of the town, beginning at the statehouse, noisily passing the Old South itself, then passing through the commercial district and into the North End. At the head of the parade, youths representing "the Rising Generation" carried flags, plows, sheaves, looms, and other "mechanic" instruments. The centerpiece of the parade was a huge model ship, the *United States,* that was mounted upon wheels and pulled through the town by thirteen white horses. The model proved too large to fit easily through some of the streets, but was accommodated "by cutting away a few impediments" along the route. The entire parade route was decorated, not least, the *Independent Chronicle* reported, with "the beauty of the ladies exhibited from the windows." Even the *Columbian Centinel* noted the parade with some admiration, although the editors could not resist observing that, since Jefferson's embargo the year before had left Boston's merchant fleet "rotting at our wharves," any moving ship—even one on dry land— was a welcome sight.[33]

The next year's Republican parade was equally grand. Sporting the same "emblems of agriculture, manufacture and commerce," the procession drew hundreds of artisans and shopkeepers (formerly allied with the predominantly Federalist merchants) out of Boston for the day. When the celebrants came to the bridge over the Charles River, they were saluted by a revenue cutter anchored nearby. The *United States,* armed with its own miniature cannon, returned the salute. Governor Gerry again excused himself from the town ceremonies, and instead attended the festivities of the Bunker Hill Association, as the Boston/Charlestown Republican coalition now styled themselves. Even some of Boston's children got into the act in 1811, forming their own parade and marching through town in emulation of their fathers' militia companies. Their "little marine company" even towed their own model ship, the *Boston*.[34]

Fearing that the carnival-like processions out of town might further alienate voters, Federalists finally broke with their tradition of subdued celebrations. Partly this was due to the urging of the "rising generation" of Federalists who took up their elders' torch after 1800. Still elitist but more subtle, the new Federalists were willing to abandon their fathers' stuffy style in favor of more popular approaches. Typical of this junior set's attitude is that of a young Federalist who had the audacity to lecture the venerable Robert Treat Paine in 1810, "Let us have men who can relax their principles of morality as occasion may require and adapt themselves to circumstances."[35]

From the Republicans the young Federalists learned the value of historic association, popular rhetoric, and showmanship, and were not afraid to borrow a few leaves from their rivals' book. Conceding the success of Republican processions, the Federalists staged elaborate displays of their own. After the town oration in 1811, Federalists gathered at the still visible roots of the original "Liberty Tree" (cut down by British soldiers during the occupation of Boston) to form a procession. The six hundred or so participants included seventy youths carrying flags, banners, and shields with patriotic mottoes such as "AGRICULTURE," "NAVAL DEFENSE," and even "DECLARATION OF INDEPENDENCE." Eight men in white suits carried a large bust of George Washington, surrounded by seventeen more youths bearing shields with the names of the states emblazoned on them. As the parade passed by the Common on the way to Faneuil Hall, artillerymen fired an unprecedented one-hundred-gun salute.[36]

The Federalists certainly outdid the Republicans in their use of Faneuil Hall. In 1810 they erected three thirty-foot-high decorated columns near the entrance, with several large floats and tableaux nearby. In the two days of July 3–4, 1810, an estimated 20,000 people—almost two-thirds of Boston's population—visited just to view the decorations. A large proportion of these, the *Centinel* proudly noted, were members of "the most amiable, intelligent, and interesting Sex," who bestowed their approval upon the masculine efforts. The decorations committee saw to it that symbols of commerce were not monopolized by the Republicans. In an obvious lampoon of the Republicans' *United States*, the Federalists displayed "a dismantled ship, indicating the present state of commerce."[37] The public dinner filled the Hall to capacity and beyond. Seven hundred people crammed into the Hall; one hundred more were accommodated at tables hastily provided in the gallery below. In recognition of their exertions in the July heat, the sweating cannoneers received their own holiday repast. Even with so many mouths to feed, there was considerable surplus. On the day following the celebration, more than six hundred additional people, allegedly "without any distinction of parties," were invited to the Hall to finish off several leftover barrels of punch and lemonade—the sort of populist appeal unthinkable to elitist Federalists a decade before.[38]

From the beginning of the decade, both parties were fully aware that their annual competition on the Fourth of July compromised the message of unity and harmony that Independence Day was supposed to promote. Certainly some Bostonians were concerned; one wrote a rather sanguine letter to the *Columbian Centinel*, hoping that "on this occasion, our joy will be mingled with no reproaches to the mother country, no servile oraisons for the French benefactors." Proposing that the nation eschew all foreign associations and "retire within itself," the writer continued, "this day, ALL WILL BE AMERICAN, and every honest man in the nation will breathe one sentiment."[39] Curiously, both Federalists and Republicans joined in making frequent appeals for reconciliation on Independence Day. The editors of the *Columbian Centinel* hoped that "a perfect unity of sentiment will pervade every class of citizen," so that the world could see that, "at least on *one day* of the year," Americans were united.[40] The Republicans agreed, at least in theory. The *Independent Chronicle* printed an opinion that "it is on these occasions that efforts should be made for doing away with that hostility and want of social intercourse, which party spirit has heretofore kept alive."[41]

It is easy to dismiss these appeals as blatant hypocrisy, rhetorical smoke screens for selfish political ends. Such a view, however, ignores a fundamental assumption of early nineteenth-century American political culture. Neither Republicans nor Federalists initially envisioned or desired a future that included party politics; each faction hoped for the ultimate triumph of its own political values and the ultimate eclipse of the other's. No one wanted an institutionalized party system that would sanction, and indeed ensure, conflict without end. Despite evidence to the contrary, most Americans who had any cultural stake in the matter undoubtedly wanted to believe that they were "one people," united in purpose and possessed of one political creed. Such, at least, was the message inherent in Independence Day celebrations. As Boston's separate celebrations made dramatically clear, however, such was not the case. Nevertheless, the opposing parties still hoped—sincerely—for a restoration of harmony in a discordant political atmosphere. In much the same way, at Christmastime, did they hope for universal "peace and good will" in spite of perpetual disappointment in that regard. The antagonists simply could not help themselves; sincere as such hopes doubtless were, neither side was willing to surrender its political vision, merely for the sake of harmony.

PHILADELPHIA: THE REPUBLICANS TRIUMPHANT

In contrast to Boston's situation, the collapse of Philadelphia's Federalist party came quickly. Federalist margins of victory in state and local elections had been shrinking gradually throughout the 1790s, until in 1799 the Republicans captured the governor's seat and a majority in the state assembly's lower house. Heavy and successive blows from 1800 to 1802 finished the Federalists' period of dominance in the state and in the city. When John Adams terminated the pointless quasi-war with France in 1800, he defied his own party and precipitated a fatal rift among Federalists. Adams's refusal to be bullied sank his own career and helped bring Thomas Jefferson to the presidency. Months before that fateful election, Philadelphia's Republicans had finally succeeded, by the slimmest of margins, in sending one of their own to represent the city in Congress. They also won seats on the city council.

Adding to Federalist woes, Philadelphia lost its place as the national capital that year when the federal government, as scheduled, moved to its new site on the Potomac River. Without federal patronage to compensate for losses in local offices, the Federalist party in Philadelphia could not rally against the Republican momentum. In the 1801 elections, vigorous Republican campaigning encouraged a turnout of more than 50 percent of the eligible voters. A particularly high proportion of these came from the peripheral wards containing large numbers of the city's artisans and laborers. Republicans achieved further progress in both houses of the state legislature, and for the first time exercised control of the city government of Philadelphia. In 1802 they finally wrested from the Federalists the majority in the state senate, and polled almost three times as many votes for their gubernatorial candidate as their opponents. In 1803, Federalists could not even find enough candidates for the offices available.[42]

Coming only a couple of weeks after the state and local elections, Independence Day in 1800 was virtually a Republican victory celebration. As with Republican newspapers elsewhere, the Philadelphia *Aurora* sported the Declaration of Independence on its front page, with particularly appropriate passages highlighted (referring to self-evident truths and the right to alter or abolish government).[43] The Republican Militia Legion marched in a triumphal procession through traditionally Federalist wards before dispersing for their afternoon entertainments. The Republicans were feeling their new strength and flaunting it; the *Aurora* reported that the legion "never appeared to so great an advantage, nor in greater numbers." Recalling the omens of heavenly favor that Federalists had noticed in 1788, a reporter noted that "the day was calm and cool, and the sky tempered with a refreshing moisture, as if providence seemed to favor the festive day under the happy return of this nation from the delusion under which it has so long labored." The Republicans gave credit for their electoral victory where it was due, and praised "the happy union of the descendants of the Germans and Irish—in spite of the arts employed to divide them." A decade of courting the ethnic and immigrant communities had finally paid off.[44]

If Republicans acted the part of winners, the Federalists played out their roles as losers. No Federalist procession competed with that of the Republicans; "sorrow and disappointment" had reportedly deflated their patriotic spirit. "Among other indications of the returning reign of truth, liberty, and national happiness," the *Aurora* even claimed, "several of the most distinguished supporters of the autocratic system have announced their determination to retire to private life." Federalists could only grumble and protest symbolically at the reversal of fortune. For the first time on July 4 since the British occupation, the bells of Christ Church were silent. At the nearby Marine barracks, the commandant ordered the flag hauled down when the Republican Legion's procession commenced. And at a Federalist oration delivered at the University of Pennsylvania, one of the professors spurned a suggestion that the Declaration of Independence be read,

since "it might offend some who would be present." These actions
fueled Republican taunts that it was now the Federalists who wished
to turn the Fourth of July into a "day of general mourning."[45]

More sour grapes came the next year, as Republicans clinched
more political offices. "Those who call themselves federalists were
invisible," reported their rivals, as the Federalists' passive protests
continued. Christ Church bells were silent again, but this time Republican legalists were ready. Christ Church's charter, reissued after
the Revolution, required the bells to be rung from sunrise to sunset on
the Fourth of July. Even when faced with this irrefutable mandate, it
took "the special interference of the governor" to compel the sexton to
ring the bells in accordance with custom and contract.[46]

With little to celebrate on the political scene, Federalists shunned
the ritual dining that had once been such a part of the day's pleasures
for them as well as for Republicans. Instead, "Ephraim" chided "Democrats" for persisting in a custom that merely fed gluttony and debauchery. "You intend, my friends, to celebrate on the fourth of July,
the triumph you have obtained over Federalists in the election of
Thomas Jefferson";

> and by your celebration you mean, no doubt, to transmit to pos-
> terity a character of your manners. . . . What, then is the mode
> which you have adopted? Verily I am told that you are all
> agreed . . . that it shall be by feats of eating and drinking! . . .
> [W]hat do you hope to achieve by it? What, to show your respect
> for Thomas Jefferson by the costly provisions of your fare, and so
> do honor to yourselves by the quantities which you intend to
> demolish?

What were once "convivial feasts" for Federalists and Republicans
alike, "Ephraim" now dismissed as "the brutalizing amusements of
our western savages."

Nor did the writer stop there; parades were "vain flourishes . . .
useless"; singing and toasting were "the mere effusions of unmanly
intemperance."[47] Like their opponents, the Federalists recognized the
source of the Republicans' new strength, but were obviously disinclined to praise or woo them: one Federalist group reportedly declined
to celebrate because they refused to share the festivities with "the
scum of Europe."[48] For embittered Federalists, the traditional forms of

Independence Day celebration only reminded them of how far and how fast their rising sun had set.

Each year there were fewer who listened to the Federalist jeremiads. The editors of the *Gazette of the United States* found their readership sharply declining; on the day before July 4, 1801, a notice in that paper informed readers that a proposed *Gazette* "for the country" (outside Philadelphia) would have to wait, as subscriptions fell far short of a profitable margin. A short extension for subscriptions was offered, after which time "if . . . sufficient encouragement should not be offered, we shall, with good reason, conclude, that a Federal Gazette for the Country, is not, in the public estimation, a thing worth labouring for, or that such a one as we propose . . . would not be likely to meet with approbation."[49] Encouragement never came, and three years later the *Gazette* closed its offices in the city as well. After fifteen years, the most eloquent Federalist newspaper in Philadelphia no longer had enough readers to sustain it.

Republicans made the most of their enemies' political demise. To replace pictures of former president Adams, new full-length prints of Thomas Jefferson appeared just in time for his first Independence Day as president, as did the lyrics for "Jefferson and Liberty"—a new song to be sung to the tune of the President's March.[50] The traditional cannon firing that year held a fitting irony for Republican gunners: for the first time their artillery was fed with gunpowder from federal stockpiles.[51]

But perhaps the greatest measure of Republican confidence in their victory was the rapid change in their public image and public rhetoric. No longer the minority party, the Republicans quickly dropped their former radical profile and adopted a more mainstream image. For a few years, instead of denouncing and competing with Federalists on Independence Day, Republicans softened both their verbal and their symbolic language. After the 1801 elections they assumed an air of magnanimity and condescending forbearance toward Federalists:

> It will be amusing to perceive how sorely the Declaration of Independence will be read today by the Old Tories—the republicans cannot amuse themselves more harmlessly or effectually, than by touching upon this subject when they meet any of their Tory acquaintance; like genuine republicans *good humoredly*, but not persecutingly, nor with the insolence which we endured from them

so honorably and patiently for some years—bear with them, and let them be convinced as well by our reason as our practice.[52]

As they consolidated their control, Republicans sounded remarkably like their complacent competitors of a few years before.

Time and European politics also removed one of the issues that had identified Republicans with radicalism. When Napoleon proclaimed himself first consul in 1800 and, four years later, emperor of the French, that budding republic seemed forever dead. Further philosophical attachment was pointless, so the triumphant Republicans publicly disowned their former attachment to France, with whose imperial government "we have nothing to do—there is nothing in it congenial with ours nor entitled to our praise."[53] With no international brotherhood of republics left to argue about, republican evangelists adopted a nativistic rhetoric, placing the American union in a divinely favored position without encumbering associations with "the scum of Europe." "However we may be divided on subsequent measures," the *Aurora* gushed, "let us, with united hearts, hail the anniversary of a day, that having conferred liberty on one empire, promises it to the whole world."[54]

With their competition withering, Philadelphia's Republicans also chose to downplay the confrontational character of symbols that had proved so effective for them in the past. The "Liberty Tree" symbol perhaps best represents the process of symbolic metamorphosis after 1800. Although the original Boston elm had been cut down by British troops in 1775, the Liberty Tree as a symbol of resistance to tyranny took root in all of the other colonies. Patriots designated certain trees as Liberty Trees or planted new ones on landmark dates, such as July 4 or at the news of the Yorktown victory. After the Revolution, dissatisfied Shaysites, whiskey tax resisters, and Fries Rebels raised Liberty Trees and Liberty Poles again, this time to protest economic measures of the new United State government.[55] Federalists loathed the symbols as radical and anarchistic, and destroyed these "wooden gods of sedition" wherever they could.[56] On the other hand, law-abiding Republicans rallied around Liberty Trees to signify their discontent with Federalist policies. Against more peaceful, less outwardly seditious meetings the Federalists could do little openly, but they found unofficial ways to attack the hated symbols all the same. In 1799 at North

A Case Something, Extraordinary.
Died by Bleeding of the nose, the Children of Michael Eurich.
his Son henry. and John. and Danial. and his — daughter — Elisa;
the have been bleeding from the beginning of there birth
by the nose, every week. one or the other. their age from
six to Seventeen years, old and died, Except william and
Casandra; william was Shot in mexican war. and michael
by Accident.

1824.   Liberty Tree.

in 1812.

on the East hill in the Borough
of York in main Street.

Musket fire

old mrs. Blaß—
1836. and died 1860.

John König. or
hannes. and the
Execution. by law
for his goods. a cow
is allowet. ha da
muß die law mir eine
gelben law mir eine

the following persons were
Jacob mantel, Jacob nell, Jacob Buser,
Nicholas Huber, old mr. Ferdinand.
Peter wilt, Jacob Ruß, Lourence Shultz.

1812.

mrs Cathr Weiser. frying a Sausage, & A Hound came
and Stole it out the pan. for his Breakfast.
woman Guard   your Kitchen.

the dog devoured with much greedineß,
While mrs. weiser was out for a
Dish & fork to Serve it on the table,
teach a dog and put him in a way to fulfill
its demands, and you make him a moral Agent.

4. Lewis Miller, "Liberty Tree in 1821." This probably depicts an Independence Day
gathering. Note the apparent firearms mishap. (The Historical Society of York County,
Pennsylvania.)

Farms, a suburb of Philadelphia, "some infernal Federal incendiary or incendiaries . . . disgracefully sawed down" a Liberty Tree that had been the focus for the community's July 4 celebrations.[57]

After the victories of Jefferson and other Republicans in 1800, Liberty Trees quickly lost their agitative resonances. Since the pole and tree symbols had been "the recourse of prodemocratic minorities," and the party espousing popular rights now dominated, their former message of resistance to authority was clearly no longer appropriate. Liberty Trees were still popular spots for celebration of Independence Day, as when a group of "Democrats" in 1803 dined under a tree planted by Benjamin Franklin's daughter in 1776. But the purpose and message of the meeting had changed considerably from what it would have been just a few years earlier. People gathered under the sacred boughs not to protest but to commemorate.[58] In the "language of signs," what had once been a *signal* for action had softened to the status of a nostalgic *symbol* (Fig. 4).

Instead of continuing to focus on Federalist scapegoats on Independence Day, the Republican *Aurora* directed public anger outward, at targets that everyone could combine in detesting. Such was the case in 1803, when the irritating and controversial vice president, Aaron Burr, was "honored" with a toast ritual that was more a Bronx cheer: "Aaron Burr, Vice President of the United States—to the right about face, three flashes in the pan, Rogue's March."[59] In like manner the United States's showdown with the Barbary pirates in 1804 and 1805 united public anger against a common enemy, and produced a new crop of enduring heroes for the republic. Virtually every company's toasts included panegyrics to the dash and bravery of Stephen Decatur and American armed forces. The popularity of these new gallants was no mere flash in the pan; even years later the praise bestowed on them on Independence Day rivaled that given to "immortal" Washington. Huge panoramic paintings of the American bombardment of Tripoli went on display at the Chestnut Street Theater in 1806. Outside, an "Allegorical Transparency, called, American Heroes" lit the street, featuring representations of naval officers Edward Preble, Stephen Decatur, and William Eaton, who led his little Marine detachment "to the shores of Tripoli."[60]

But the lions were not yet ready to lie down with the lambs. Old scores were not completely forgotten, nor did partisan attachments disappear. Federalism in Philadelphia was surely down, but not completely out. Federalist candidates still ran, and plenty of influential people still held onto their familiar political beliefs. Republicans could not afford to become too complacent: Had not this been the Federalists' fatal mistake? Republicans still watched, sometimes nervously, for any sign of "aristocratic" resurgence.

Federalists gave them reason to keep looking over their shoulders. Once a term possessing almost magical powers, "Federalist" was rapidly becoming a dirty word.[61] To overcome this liability, the Philadelphia Federalists sought to change their public image, as their Boston brethren had done, by appearing in new forms that avoided the now-pejorative term. Like the Republicans, the Federalists formed social groups with names like "Men of '76" or the "Sons of St. George" (which should have given them away immediately). Even more infuriating to Republicans, one of these neo-Federalist groups took the misleading name of the American Republican Society, "formed on those true Whig principle which led Washington into the field and actuated him in the cabinet." Their Independence Day celebration on the banks of the Schuylkill featured large busts of Washington and the old Republican nemesis, Alexander Hamilton.[62]

Accustomed to spotting political villains, Republicans were quick to alert Philadelphians to the danger of these wolves in sheep's clothing. "Chronologos" warned readers in 1806 that there was plenty still to worry about on Independence Day. He imagined a "hoary-headed patriot" reviewing the past three decades of independence "with joy mingled with melancholy reflection." Among the melancholia were "former Tories enjoying peace and plenty in the land," "the song of 'Hail Columbia' sung in concert with 'God Save the King'—and at a *celebration of the 4th of July* . . . expressions of loyalty to 'his majesty' and determined hostility to the *rebel states* made use of." Forgetting that it was Republicans like himself who first vilified the nearly sainted first president, "Chronologos"'s patriot heard with shock "the name of Washington prostituted to the basest purposes—made the *sheet anchor* of wicked men, and sullied by the praise of political swindlers." By whatever name, the discredited Federalists were nothing more than "Tories" and "apostates."[63]

"Vindicator-Morum" also found the Fourth of July a time for serious reflection. The nation had passed through trying times in the past thirty years, according to this writer, times that were almost fatal to the American experiment in government. Recalling the turbulent 1790s as a period of political terror, "Vindicator" recalled that "it was then sufficient ground for seizing upon a peaceable citizen in the street, and committing him to gaol, that he wore in his hat a flower called the snow ball, or a green branch plucked from a tree. . . . [From 1797 to 1799] riot, outrage and persecution were the order of that day." "Vindicator" went on to chronicle a distinctively Republican interpretation of the recent past, in which the proper observance of Independence Day separated the virtuous from the conniving:

> For several year after the war, the 4th of July was celebrated by all parties professing republicanism in America—nay even those who leaned towards "the mother country" were forced by popular sentiment to give in more or less to the measure.
>
> But as the *black cockade,* of *Women scaring memory,* came into vogue, the ceremonies of the day were neglected or miserably performed. . . . Those in power believed a notice of the day had a "tendency to excite old animosities," and went no further in its observance than the prejudices of the people of the country compelled them. . . .
>
> The *rabble* continued to celebrate the day with enthusiasm— they read the declaration of independence—they sung old war songs, and new liberty ones, danced to the tune of Yankee doodle, and told of queer adventures which took place during the revolution. They ate, drank, and made merry, for their hearts were glad.
>
> By and by the "rabble" got the upper hand. They hurled the *well-born* from their seats of authority, and reduced the chief who then commanded to the rank of an humble citizen, *to be heard of men no more!*—they destroyed his midnight labors, dismounted the black cockade—wouldn't let the old women be frightened by boys in regimentals any longer—made many reformations, and still celebrated the fourth of July.

"Vindicator" concluded with an admonition not to be taken in by the old emperors' new clothes, lest the unhappy days return.[64]

Interpretations such as these were more than simple propaganda. Many Americans in 1806 agreed that before the "revolution of 1800" their nation's ideological future hung in the balance.[65] Federalists may have been out of Philadelphia's political picture at that moment, but

there was nothing (apart from the Republicans) to prevent their returning in a disguise, to trick the people into once again voting away
their rights. In part, the jeremiads of "Chronologos" and "Vindicator-
Morum" resulted from their own party's triumph. Republicans had
first come together to resist Federalist visions of America's future.
With the Republicans in power and their traditional foes fading from
the political stage, the Republicans lost their former role as a crusading party of opposition. Republican writers found old habits hard to
break, old ways of thinking difficult to adjust. For them, Federalists
remained a threat, even though each year brought more evidence of
their political mortality. Independence Day was a supremely appropriate time for serious reflection of the nation's hairsbreadth escape
from despotism, and of the political cleansing that still needed to be
done. The *Aurora* continued to refer to Federalists as "Tories" and
worse, while Fenno's *Gazette,* while it lasted, hurled "insolence and
indecency" at Republicans in return.[66] Elizabeth Drinker felt the anger
still latent in her native city in 1805: "It has been a very quiet day for
the fourth of July, consedering the different parties and dispositions of
the people."[67]

Still, old animosities might have been forgiven, if not forgotten,
and Philadelphia's Independence Day celebrations might have become rituals of healing and accommodation had not politics again
intervened. Britain was still locked in a protracted war with Napoleon's France and its allies. Without an army large enough to challenge
that of the French, the British ministry gave its navy a major role to
play. British warships blockaded French ports in an effort to strangle
trade, and destroyed France's high seas fleet whenever the opportunity appeared. The Royal Navy took a dim view toward anyone
attempting to break the blockade, and navy vessels forcefully turned
away American ships seeking entry to French ports. Ravenous for
seamen, British captains frequently pressed American sailors into
forced service in their ships. Lacking the naval strength to challenge
the mightiest fleet in the world, the United States was helpless to
retaliate forcibly, and Americans could do little more than fume at
British "piracy."

In this atmosphere of increasing international tension, relations
with Britain took a sudden and dramatic turn for the worse. In June
1807, the British warship *Leopard* stopped the American frigate *Chesa-*

peake and demanded that the American captain allow a search for British "deserters" on board. Captain Barron of the *Chesapeake* indignantly declined, certain that no British captain would dare insist on pursuing the matter in American waters against a government vessel. Barron was wrong. The *Leopard* fired several broadsides into the American ship, killing or wounding more than two dozen of the crew. Resistance was useless; in the time it would take Barron to clear his ship for action the *Chesapeake* would be a dismasted wreck. Down came the American colors, and a British boarding party claimed several "deserters" from the *Chesapeake*'s crew before leaving.

The howls of outrage from American throats echoed loudly on the following Fourth of July. Although cooler heads ultimately prevailed, many openly called for war with Britain. The assault on the *Chesapeake* had an electric effect on Philadelphia's Independence Day observances that year, turning the traditional rites into a call to arms, and making any vestigial Anglophilia dangerous. The young men of the Republican Legion seized the opportunity to emulate their Revolutionary fathers, and recruited volunteers to meet the "crisis," observing that "there never was a time, when the youth of our country could more honorably evince their patriotism and spirit, than at present."[68] Philadelphians less inclined toward active service found other ways of showing their patriotic spirit. Mobs surrounded the house of British consul Phineas Bond for several nights, shouting threats and "beatting the rogues march." A British merchant vessel that was unlucky enough to be in port when the news arrived had its rudder sawn off by waterfront residents, who also "quarrl'd" with the ship's captain. The night before July 4, one observer wrote: "tomorrow being the Anniversary of Independence, I am fearful of some noise or hubbub, as handbills are put up, and much noise of the British outrage & c. —inflammatory doings."[69] The *Aurora* did its best to fan the flames, following its customary July 4 printing of the Declaration of Independence with a plea for war, concluding: "The example of the patriots and heroes of '76, is held up to their posterity."[70]

In their frustration and rage, Philadelphians even turned on each other. Although some Republicans welcomed what the *Aurora* termed a "revived . . . enthusiasm spirit," for Joseph Crosby, Independence Day promised only terror and mayhem. Perhaps Crosby had uttered some careless words; perhaps he was locally known as one of the "new Tories" Republicans had so railed against in the past. Whatever the reason, Crosby felt compelled to include a desperate July Fourth notice in the Republican *Aurora:*

TO THE CITIZENS
OF PHILADELPHIA

WHEREAS it has been industriously circulated in different companies, that I am an enemy to this country, and by my neighbor threatened with being torn to pieces.

I wish to inform the public, that it is entirely through a private quarrel, that my neighbor is thus so spiteful.

I declare before God and the citizens of the country, that now gives me bread, that I am not prejudiced against this country, but under the present circumstance of insult, am ready to join with the good American to avenge the cause of an injured country.

JOSEPH CROSBY
No.50, north Fourth street.[71]

Everyone who expected the worst to happen on this Independence Day must have been amazed when the worst did not occur. "The Fourth passed without any act of violence or outrage," reported an obviously relieved Thomas Cope. "It being the anniversary of American Independence, fears were entertained that when the fumes of liquor were added to the effervescence already induced by the recent transactions [the *Leopard* affair], mischief would be the consequence."[72] "Notwithstanding the warmth of public feeling, at late transactions," seconded the *Aurora*, "there was not one instance of disorder, in any part of the city."[73] Joseph Crosby's house was not attacked. Even Elizabeth Drinker, who rarely had anything good to say about the Fourth of July, admitted: "It is as quiet tonight as any night for years past on the 4th of July."[74]

CONFRONTATION AND ACCOMMODATION ON INDEPENDENCE DAY

Boston and Philadelphia especially displayed a pattern of threatened, but unrealized, violent behavior on Independence Day that demands exploration at this point. Passions and provocations intensified on July 4, and violent crowd actions frequently threatened the celebrations. And yet, instances of actual crowd violence were rare and remarkably restrained when they occurred. Just as the centrifugal force exerted on celestial satellites is counteracted by planetary gravity, human impulses for emotional release had to struggle against powerful cultural standards of emotional restraint. It remains to explore how "cultural gravity" kept centrifugal social forces from spinning American political society violently out of control every July 4.

As the preceding chapters have shown, an undercurrent of tension permeated the celebration of Independence Day, tension that occasionally burst forth in violent confrontation. Harmony was always the implied objective of Independence Day observances, but in such politically stressful times, glaring dissonances could not always be adequately camouflaged. When this occurred, the rites of Independence Day produced divisive effects instead. Social tensions, combined with the inherent danger, the consciously cultivated excitement, and the inevitable application of large quantities of alcohol, provided the Fourth of July with all the ingredients for widespread disorder. From the mid-1790s to the War of 1812, July 4 served to focus political and social anxiety; many feared the day as much as they welcomed it. Newspaper and private accounts overwhelmingly betray a sense of relief when, each year, another Independence Day passed (with some exaggeration) "as it ought to . . . in well-regulated and rational festivity." Many dreaded the converse: "irregularity [and] turbulence."[75] What troubled them was the haunting fear that Independence Day had not only failed to promote American nationalism, but was in fact an annual opportunity for the social and political fabric to tear itself apart.

Certainly many contemporaries saw it that way. Clergyman Timothy Dwight observed Bostonians and thought them exceptionally prone to public disturbances. Writing in about the year 1808, Dwight declared that the people of Boston possessed "an ardor easily kindled, a sensibility soon felt and strongly expressed. They admire where graver people would only approve, detest where cooler minds would only dislike, applaud a performance where others would listen in silence, and hiss where a less susceptible audience would only frown."[76] Volatile tendencies could become particularly dangerous on Independence Day. Many diarists agreed in associating July 4 with "hubbub," "great to do," or, more menacingly, "riot" and "debauchery." Newspapers on one day reported harmony and good order on the Fourth, and on the next admitted assaults, drunkenness, and partisan rabble-rousing. At one point, Boston was allegedly "a vast pile of combustibles" by the Fourth of July, only awaiting a spark to precipitate "blood and destruction."

Fueling fears of potential disorder was the knowledge that there was no reliable way to stop it once begun. The constabularies of Boston and Philadelphia were too small to stop a determined crowd action (Charleston's City Guard was a far more effective deterrent). With its rapidly growing and ethnically diverse population, Philadelphia was particularly ripe for public disorder. Philadelphia's Federalists and Republicans deliberately taunted each other with flags, cockades, parades, bells, guns, and orations, daring the other to "start first." Federalists reportedly attempted to "excite hostility even to blood" on Independence Day, which the *Aurora* reported was only avoided (naturally) by the "moderation of republicans." On another such occasion, partisans heckled a company of armed militiamen, "and much more rudeness and insolence were borne by the citizens under arms, than they would without arms have suffered patiently."[77] As the *Aurora* later freely admitted, the Republican militias which formed in the late 1790s were a response to "the unhappy state of society, and the sense of danger" that prevailed. The purpose of these private military cadres was, bluntly, "to prevent the exercise of inordinate power by one or a particular number of persons"—by force of arms, if necessary.[78] The hostility between these groups of armed men was well known. In such a charged atmosphere, one jibe too many, one man angered past endurance, might well have precipitated a bloody melee.

The legacy of the young nation's revolutionary culture added to the possibility of violent encounters on July 4. The significance of Independence Day and America's Revolution was still an open question, despite the efforts of contending parties to resolve it in their favor. Americans shared a language of politically charged words. Terms like *republicanism*, *liberty*, and *independence* were bandied about in contemporary literature and rhetoric as though their definitions were common knowledge. But people understood these words differently. Indeed, such abstract terms are almost impossible to comprehend verbally; hence their tendency to become encoded in visible symbols. But in the volatile 1790s and early 1800s, the resolution of these definitions was of vital importance to the young republic.[79] Republicans and Federalists were not comparing opposed political systems; their ideological conflict took place within the same "cultural frame" of republican political culture. Their struggles were more refined; they argued over divergent *strains* of republicanism. But as James Epstein demonstrates in the case of early nineteenth-century Britain, conflict over alternate definitions within a political culture could be no less passionate or deadly.[80]

The activities of Independence Day provided dozens of opportunities to debate ideological ambiguities, and not merely on the symbolic level. When the ritual time and space of competing groups coincide or overlap, violence is always a real possibility.[81] Neither Federalists nor Republicans were able to eliminate the other and direct the rites of July 4 without hindrance. As a result, patriotic rituals that were supposed to unify had instead a "de-structuring" effect as political partisans were "pressed into an intimacy they would as soon avoid, where the incongruity between the social assumptions of the ritual ('we are all culturally homogeneous . . . together') and what is in fact the case ('we are several different kinds of people who must perforce live together despite our serious value disagreements') leads to deep uneasiness."[82]

Axiomatically, times of radical political transition are rife with tension and filled with violent potential.[83] Before 1800, and for long afterward in the case of Boston, Republicans were a minority party struggling for a place in the existing power structure. At the same time, Federalists were steadily losing influence in that structure. Lewis Coser points out that in such circumstances, anger is commonly directed first at political rivals, rather than at outsiders who challenge the legitimacy of the power structure itself. Indeed, it was because of their enforced intimacy within the political system, combined with the incongruity of message-versus-reality, that the conflict between Federalists and Republicans was so passionate. Individuals who might feel twinges of conscience with their hard feelings on Independence Day could take comfort by justifying their actions with the best of intentions. It was not for personal advantage that citizens turned the Fourth of July into partisan rallies, but for the benefit of the cause they felt they represented. Extremes of behavior are far more justifiable if committed for selfless reasons; the more selfless the end, the more ruthless the means may be.[84] Under the right conditions, republican ideology (however conceived) may not only survive but actually be reaffirmed by occasional violent behavior.

On top of all this, the political tradition of the American Revolution validated violent resistance to "oppression" as a republican hallmark. Before their 1800 victory, Republicans employed revolutionary rhetoric to stigmatize the Federalist-dominated national government as high-handed, tyrannous, aristocratic, and corrupt—the same adjectives that had described the British government to American revolutionaries. The text of the Declaration of Independence contained just such inflammatory rhetoric, and Republicans revived its language every Fourth of July to inflame people against the "Tories" they claimed were still in power, or waiting to seize it. Small wonder that Federalists abhorred the practice of reading the Declaration aloud on Independence Day.[85]

And yet, for all the preconditions, opportunities, and provocations for large-scale partisan violence on "the brightest day in our calendar," nothing of the sort actually materialized. Although always a possibility, violence was clearly not inevitable. For every condition that seemed to encourage violent confrontation, there were subtle but powerful factors working against it.

First, although the rites of Independence Day deliberately excited passions, several also carried within them a means of relieving that excitement. For most political partisans, symbolic and rhetorical violence substituted adequately for the real thing, satisfying their choler while rededicating their allegiance to party. Songs, toasts, parades, symbol manipulation, and vitriolic letters to newspapers were all vehicles for public, but safe, expressions of political and social aggression. So long as Federalists and Republicans attacked each other and not the power structure itself, so long as they remained rivals for place in the same system, they were mutually bound to the rules of play governing that system. Violent rhetoric took the place of actual mayhem, and served as an acceptable outlet for aggression that maintained the political fabric intact. As was the case in the decade before the War of Independence, formulaic expressions "enabled struggle to continue without endangering the state."[86]

The private associations formed by Republicans and Federalists, including the partisan militia, provided participatory outlets for the discontented. A consciousness of belonging to a group, whatever that group's actual prestige and influence, transmitted a feeling of comfort and empowerment to individual members. Group membership and a perception of strength were hedges against despair, which might more readily have found expression in violence. Members of these associations meeting on July 4 participated in group rituals and ceremonies emphasizing harmony and continuity—at least within the group— stabilizing the disintegrating tendencies of increasingly vitriolic disputes. By themselves, ritual forms and group associations are constraints upon the style of ritual behavior.[87]

Second, the political situation was progressive enough to suppress a sense of desperation on the part of Republicans, demonstrably the more aggressive of the two parties. In Philadelphia their influence grew throughout the second half of the 1790s, culminating in their victories of 1800 and 1801 at the local, state, and national level. Had there been no such steady progress in the political arena, frustrated Republicans might well have confronted Federalists more belligerently on Independence Day than they did. After 1800, the aggressive party was in power, and the Federalists deflated and demoralized. From that point onward, Republicans tended to direct public aggression on July 4, when it occurred, at political outsiders like "Tories" and foreign villains.

Dangerously high tensions, and confrontational styles, persisted longer in Boston, where the collapse of Federalism did not follow the national pattern. But even there, Republicans could look to gains outside the town and hope for better times. Jefferson carried the state in 1804; two years later Republicans gained the majority in the state legislature. In 1807, 1808, and 1810, Massachusetts had Republican governors. There was every reason for Republicans to feel sanguine about the political future. They simply could not know how long and how firm the Federalist grip on town politics would be.

But "safety valve" theories and the alleged ability of time to heal all wounds are not by themselves sufficient to explain why Americans did not resort "even to blood" to wrest the rites of Independence Day from their adversaries. Ritual actions could not always resolve the incongruities they generated, and politically committed people are not always content to let time take its course. Something else helped check the passions called forth by ceremony and celebration. Despite the confrontational rhetoric and emotional investment in their respective causes, the political combatants demonstrated a decided tendency to draw back from engaging in physical force as an acceptable policy toward a legitimate end. That reluctance derived from a shared set of values concerning the practical application of republican philosophy: individual virtue and enlightened self-restraint. "Virtue and good manners" were essential qualities for the citizens of a republic. Ideally, self-interest was subordinate to the public good. Lacking a government of compulsion, public order depended upon voluntary restraint and rational self-control. Both Federalists and Republicans professed to be the "real friends of order." With thousands of uncommitted voters to woo each year, they were compelled to confine their energies to the symbolic realm on "the brightest day in our calendar," and to avoid any breach of conduct that might discredit their claims. Both parties interpreted the Revolution as a triumph of republican virtues. Renouncing those virtues through violence could disinherit either party from its political birthright.[88]

The actions of Federalists and Republicans on Independence Day, or the lack of them, speak louder than their bold and defiant words. If there was any determinable "policy" that guided both antagonists on the Fourth of July, it was a policy of restraint. In Philadelphia, partisans simply continued the city's tradition of decentralized observances. Whether meeting in their favorite tavern or picnic spot along the Schuylkill and Delaware Rivers, Philadelphia's celebrants tended to flock with birds of similar feather. Physical distance between differently aligned groups kept the peace. Even when political rivalry was at its height, neither Republicans nor Federalists abandoned their familiar pattern of small, convivial, and dispersed observances in favor of mass rallies that would dominate the city's celebrations of the Fourth of July.

Bostonians clung to their tradition of a unified civic celebration, and it was this impulse that made control of the town's ceremonies such a prize for Federalists and Republicans. Here the idea of separate celebrations was accepted only grudgingly, and as a necessary alternative to meek surrender or escalation. Republicans organized physically separated observances to protest Federalist dominance of what they so obviously craved: control of the town oration. Republicans were careful, however, to perform their processions and other activities at different times, and in different physical spaces, than those of their rivals. For their part, the Federalists refused to reschedule their programs, as they might have done, to compete directly with Republicans. They inconvenienced their opponents whenever they could, as when they denied Faneuil Hall to the Republicans, but neither side was willing to challenge physically the other's July 4 celebrations. Unlike what had habitually transpired on Guy Fawkes Day, rival processions never met (or even tried to meet) on Independence Day to turn Boston's streets into battlefields. No mobs of Republican vigilantes attempted to take over Faneuil Hall and dare Federalists to do something about it. Instead, the Republicans chose to leave town to celebrate elsewhere, rather than fight the town fathers for space, or force themselves upon Boston's inadequate constabulary.

Although unofficial, the truce between Federalists and Republicans on Independence Day was mutually understood. They could compete for the "rites of power," but they could not physically fight for them.[89] Rather than battle concurrently for the same audience on the Fourth of July, Republicans and Federalists carefully kept their distances. Their separate celebrations were always far enough apart to discourage any unwanted physical contact.

Their actions were not simply intended to conceal their true natures from their audiences. Republicans as well as Federalists regarded crowd actions as destructive and anarchistic, the last resort of desperate people. Partisans of both groups feared the results of violent conflict, feared that once begun it would prove impossible to control. Catherine Albanese noticed that both parties' loudest assertions of oneness and appeals for reconciliation occurred "when the greatest threats of division and fragmentation were present," and no wonder.[90] Neither side stood to gain from division and fragmentation, which violence would surely have encouraged.

Certainly the great majority of citizens in both Boston and Philadelphia desired no such thing. Although this analysis has focused upon the actions of committed Federalists and Republicans, most people in Boston and Philadelphia fit neither category. As discussed in Chapter 4, there were many alternatives to spending July 4 as a representative of either party. Partisan processions numbered in the hundreds, but not in the thousands; most residents were content with their relatively passive but all-important role as spectators. It was to this great body of uncommitted potential voters that the parties had to appeal, and to a great degree it was the silent pressure of the uncommitted that prevented political conflict from degenerating into violence, destroying normal relations, and wrecking the social order. As Jeremy Boissevain discovered in modern Malta, "the most important of the factors that inhibit the spread of conflict is the existence of persons whose loyalties are divided between the conflicting sides:

> Such persons have a vested interest in the maintenance of peace and limitation of the area of conflict. . . . What keeps the conflict from becoming more violent are the thousands of persons who have their loyalties divided between [the contending groups]. All these people work to keep the conflict from spreading, if not actually to make peace. Who are they? They are the countless persons whose families have been divided by the conflict, the office-holders who have laid politics aside to preserve the unity of the clubs for which they are responsible, the many who have sought to avoid open commitments to either side, and to remain in contact with both.[91]

Such a person was "Peter Pencil," whose letter in the *Boston Gazette* chastised those " 'glowing hot' with the spirit of liquor and party," and advised each reader "notwithstanding that he may hear of his liberty being at stake, that he is the principle arbiter of his own independence." As for patriotism, he admonished, "do not think it grows only in the hot-bed of opposition."[92] Such also were the people that Republicans had in mind when they restrained themselves from using symbols that might "irritate the public mind."

So despite the very real potential of ritual performance to spotlight contradictions, focus tensions, and divide the people it should unite, the rites of Independence Day remained positive, structuring activities overall. Whether or not consensus best characterizes American politics in the early republic, consensus was the ideal, the theoretical goal of American politics. In that faith in consensus lay Americans' consciousness of being "one people," of possessing a national identity. Broad acceptance of the idea of diversity-within-nationality had to wait for another time; for now, failure to celebrate Independence Day in the proper spirit of unity suggested the failure of the American Revolution—a suggestion too horrible to contemplate. So they did not contemplate it. Instead, Americans celebrated their national identity

as if it were universal, reaffirming their belief in it *because* they celebrated it. And they exercised self-restraint on the Fourth of July because to do so identified them as truly republican and truly American.

Nevertheless, many contemporaries viewed the conflict and tensions generated on the Fourth as dangerous foreboding, and on Independence Day in the years before the War of 1812 they looked back to a
supposedly happier past for clues to future events. The reflections of
both Federalists and Republicans evince more than a trace of nostalgia
and dissatisfaction with the present. In Philadelphia, continued success at the polls did not completely satisfy Republicans. Two days
before one July 4, a pensive correspondent gloomily surveyed the
nation's domestic and international situation, especially America's apparent inability to affect British trade restrictions. "Greene" considered the Fourth of July a particularly appropriate time for citizens "to
consider *the real state of the nation*, and whether he is a democrat or a
federalist, let him express his sentiments honestly, looking to *measures*
and not men:

> The great question for discussion on the 4th of July will be—
> whether with all the wealth and immense resources of our coun-
> try, which will on that day be displayed to the world as in our pos-
> session, the United States is really an *independent* nation—or
> whether the celebration of that glorious achievement of our fore-
> fathers is not turned into perfect mockery. . . . On the 4th of July,
> there will be no wanting for patriotic toasts, and songs and
> speeches. But whilst the Declaration of Independence is read, the
> *independence* of the United States toasted, and "Hail Columbia" is
> sung in full chorus, let us contrast our present with our former
> condition, and seriously reflect whether our meeting this year
> may not more properly be considered the funeral procession of
> our independence than the celebration of its birth day.[93]

Federalist musings were no cheerier. Leverett Saltonstall of Salem
brooded over the changes wrought by time as he anticipated the festivals in his hometown and in Boston:

> Tho' the 4th of July will be celebrated with noise and pomp and
> every demonstration of joy, still the aged patriot of N. England
> must sigh when he looks back to '76. When he considers thro'
> what toils, and perils we passed to effect our independence, and
> to establish a government, which might long continue and protect

the nation, his breast will alternately swell with grief and burn with indignation, that the government has so soon fallen into hands, who treat it so irreverently.[94]

People did not only look to 1776 for comfort. In 1811 the Apollo Theater in Philadelphia featured for that years's Independence Day an "Optical and Mechanical representation of the FEDERAL PROCESSION, as taken on the spot of that glorious and memorable epoch, the fourth of July, 1788." Apparently a scrolling panoramic canvas, the attraction included "figures . . . nearly as large as life, and are seen in passing, extending nearly 1300 feet in length." The great procession of 1788 was legendary in Philadelphia, never equaled or even approached in succeeding years. Folks who remembered it came to the Apollo to relive one of the most amazing sights in the short history of the United States, wondering perhaps why such a spectacular outpouring of political and community spirit had never recurred, or whether it could ever happen again. Probably many of them brought the younger members of their families, hoping somehow to impart to them from the two-dimensional representation a sense of what was truly a multi-dimensional experience. At least, that was the hope of the theater managers, who displayed the panorama "not only to please, but to give information to a rising generation who have heard their parents mention the glorious sight."[95]

The days of gloomy ruminations and nostalgia for a halcyon past were numbered, however. Independence Day, and American political culture, were both poised for a sudden change.

6

MAKING OVER THE FOURTH

The history of our own day . . . especially serves to
exemplify the astonishing influence which this
practice [Independence Day] exercises over the
minds of men, and to evince to us that it is a source,
from which a nation may draw courage, and energy,
in moments of difficulty and of danger.

HENRY M. RUTLEDGE, *AN ORATION DELIVERED IN*
ST. PHILIP'S CHURCH

After our country has been so long agitated by
divisions, and parties mutually exasperated against
each other, it is grateful to find, that there is still one
day in the American calendar, on which all parties
profess at least to rejoice and be exceeding glad. This
may perhaps be still a rallying point of union, around
which all may assemble, after being driven in
various directions by the violence of faction.

COLUMBIAN CENTINEL, July 4, 1805

The War of 1812 was the catalyst for major shifts in political, social, and cultural trends in America. The "Second War of Independence" with Britain marked the climax of the long ideological
struggle between Federalists and Republicans. Federalists were certain that the Republicans who dominated national policy had doomed
the country to a ruinous war that could not be won. Republicans
generally welcomed the conflict as an unequivocal separation from

191

the influence of haughty and conniving enemies. For them, the show-down with Britain cleansed America from its former dependence on British economic policies, and ensured the free trade upon which the Republican vision for America depended.

When the war ended, both parties had changed forever. The fortunes of war virtually finished off the lingering Federalists, while Republicans were forced by their experiences to reassess and sub-stantially alter their political philosophy. In the years immediately following the war, familiar party distinctions blurred to the point of inconsequence. After more than twenty years, Americans received a respite from the splenetic style that had dominated their political culture.

The war also affected the less tangible realm of values and percep-tions. It accelerated the democratization of American society and the rise of "the self-made man" conceit, personified by the volatile war hero Andrew Jackson.[1] For early nineteenth-century Americans, Jack-son was a living vindication of the democratic ethos that rejected lead-ership by a privileged elite. The resurgent democratic impulse that grew out of the war dealt deferential politics a severe blow, and defer-ential political culture as well.

INDEPENDENCE DAY AND "THE FOOLISH WAR"

During the war years, Independence Day was observed very dif-ferently in Federalist-dominated Boston on the one hand, and in Republican Philadelphia and Charleston on the other. Philadelphia's celebrations were somewhat curtailed by circumstances. The hard economic times caused by the interruption of trade, the absence of some militia companies who went to the war, and the disappointment over persistent American military disasters robbed July 4 of much of its wonted gaiety. Nevertheless, many Philadelphians continued to honor the day as best they could. Charlestonians rallied even more wholeheartedly in support of the war effort. On the other hand, the celebration of Independence Day in Boston came virtually to a halt, as Federalists inverted the customary activities to protest the controversial war.

On June 18, 1812, Congress declared war against Great Britain. Years of Republican-sponsored trade embargo had had no appreciable effect on British determination to control European trade, especially since the struggle with Napoleon's empire continued. Too late, the British ministry relaxed its stand on American neutrality privileges, and the two nations blundered once again into war. The bad news reached Boston days before the Fourth of July, and put the Federalists in no mood to celebrate. Instead, two days before the Fourth, Governor Caleb Strong ordered a Puritan-style day of fast, humiliation, and prayer to be observed later in the month, to repent "the foolish war." When Independence Day arrived, bells and cannons still greeted the day (there were yet some Republican gunners and sextons in town), but the Federalist town fathers encouraged nothing beyond the obligatory public oration to entertain the public or to rouse patriotic spirit. The town orations, the centerpiece of the Federalists' celebrations for almost thirty years, occurred "agreeably to the law of 1786," but had little to do with Independence Day. The 1812 speaker made "only a rapid glance" at the events of the Revolution, then launched into a blistering attack on President Madison's administration.[2]

The 1813 observances were little better. The Young Republicans, who remained in town while their elders left, claimed that "fraternity, hilarity, and glee universally predominated" at their meeting at the Exchange Coffee House, but if so, theirs may have been the only gathering in town that could so boast.[3] A single illumination was the only evening event noted in the newspapers. To make matters worse, the uncanny propensity of ill tidings to arrive just before the Fourth of July persisted. The spectacular loss of the USS *Chesapeake* (the same ship that was mauled by the *Leopard* six years before) just outside of Boston Harbor the previous month dampened local spirits considerably, and news of the military disaster at Queenstown arrived just in time to douse them thoroughly.[4] Only too happy to report bad news about "Mr. Madison's War," the *Boston Gazette* related a "Remarkable Incident" calculated to make this Independence Day as bitter as possible. According to the report, an American general named Chandler had toasted the Fourth of July the previous year with a prophecy: "The 4th of July, 1813—may we on this day drink wine within the walls of Quebec." Chandler saw part of his wish come true. He was captured within the year, and sent to Quebec a prisoner. The editor of the *Boston Gazette* hoped that the rest of Chandler's wish was gratified as well.[5]

The comparative gloom that pervaded Boston's Fourths in this critically divisive period illustrates the extent to which the Federalists dominated the town's celebrations. The absence of Federalist-sponsored

public dinners, fireworks, illuminations, entertainments—of everything, in fact, beyond what was required by law or decency—is a
measure of their utter disaffection with the war and its impact on
Boston's commerce. In the years preceding the conflict, flamboyant
display characterized the celebrations of Republicans and Federalists
alike. Now, Federalists protested the war by withholding their celebrations. Since most Republicans were celebrating elsewhere, the usual
"hilarity" of the Fourth was replaced by a few "marks of respect" for
the day. The Republican *Independent Chronicle* lamented that the Fourth
of July had become "a solemn festival" in Boston.[6]

Despite the humiliation of Americans on the battlefield, hopes for a
negotiated peace restored some of the festive forms to Boston's Independence Day in 1814. "Several exhibitions of fireworks" and the illumination of the new Washington Gardens brightened the evening
somewhat, but even these traditional expressions of joy were reported
with a distinct lack of élan.[7] "We have little left to enjoy," the *Boston
Gazette* glumly concluded, "but the remembrance of what our fathers
did."[8] A scathing editorial in that same paper's July 4 issue flailed the
Republicans, "who will endeavor by their vociferations and feasts, to
hide the scenes of misery, of which their profligate conduct has already been the cause." This was no day to sing the praises of those
"political weather-cocks Adams and Jefferson," the writer continued;
the disastrous policies of the Republican government were "enough to
cause the very bones of the prophetic Washington to shake with horror."[9] In nearby Dorchester, the Federal Republicans "celebrated" the
day sunk in dismal melancholy. Their toasts and ceremonies composed a whining litany of complaint, despair, bitterness, and self-pity.
After toasts to the war ("its results will be as disgraceful to its authors,
as 1775 was glorious to our country") and to "the illegitimate brat,
Democracy," they concluded with an ironic rendition of "Hail Columbia! Happy Land!"[10]

For their part, the Republicans removed their Independence Day
activities even farther from Boston, joining in the regional celebrations
recently organized in more hospitable Concord. Federalist hints at
secession widened the gulf between the two parties, alarming some
and leading to renewed appeals for reconciliation. "The times call on
us to unite," the *Independent Chronicle* observed in its 1814 Fourth of
July issue. "At this present crisis, UNION is the great object to be ac-

quired. We cannot but view with indignation the attempts to dissolve this bond of our national security."[11]

Federalists could not have their way in Philadelphia as they had in Boston. If they chose not to celebrate, that hardly affected the rest of the city, as Philadelphians had never relied upon officially ordered observances. Philadelphia's Republicans responded to the declaration of war with enthusiasm, and made the ensuing Independence Day little more than a citywide demonstration of support for the war. Republicans castigated Governor Strong's day of fasting as cowardly and treacherous, and determined to present as great a contrast with Massachusetts reticence as possible. Republicans wanted people to regard July 4, 1812, as the date for a new "declaration of independence."[12]

Republicans mustered all of the symbolic arts, and the performing arts, at their disposal to rally public support for the war, and to dispel doubts of the nation's ability to take on its old adversary again. One citizen composed a poem, "The Battle of Trenton," that recounted that glorious gamble against long odds, and concluded:

> Such were the feats our sires display'd,
> When Britain first dared our right invade—
> Again we've drawn th' American blade,
>   That strikes for death or liberty.
>
> Comrades, to arms! the war trump's blown,
> Think of the deeds your sires have done,
> Think that Washington looks on—
>   Then charge for death or victory![13]

The Olympic Theater presented the Fourth of July favorite *Bunker Hill*, now subtitled "*What We Have Done, and What We Can Do.*" Patrons entered the theater under a large transparent painting depicting the "Immortal Washington," with a "goddess of Liberty" on his left. To Washington's right was "a naval engagement, the ships almost enveloped in fire and smoke ... the eagle above is darting the lightnings of his vengeance upon the affrighted foe." While stagehands changed sets after the death of General Warren, the audience heard a song and recitation piece called "The Spirit of Independence." This was followed by "a new musical entertainment, in two acts, called the AMERICAN NAVAL PILLAR, OR, A TRIBUTE OF RESPECT TO THE TARS OF COLUMBIA." The subject matter reflected coastal Americans' fixation with the

Atlantic theater of the war. The performance featured the presentation of a triumphal pillar inscribed with the names of naval officers who had distinguished themselves in the Barbary war—Rogers, Decatur, and Hull—and were shortly to do so again. After some interpretive dance, "Columbia" descended to the stage supported by "Liberty" and "Justice," who then addressed the audience. War fever must have packed the house as never before; the theater managers admitted that the performance on this anniversary was especially "lucrative."[14]

According to the Republican press, the Fourth of July reunited people who had been inveterate enemies shortly before: "The volunteer associations, composed of the men of the hitherto opposed political sects, were seen united, and rallying around the standard of their country." Philadelphians reportedly marked the day with "an unanimity of spirit of general concord, that have not been before displayed since the *federal procession*"—an ironic comparison for the ultra-Republican *Aurora* to make.[15]

By the following year, Philadelphians had become less sanguine about the progress of the war. The British had learned of the state of hostilities too late in 1812 to mount an American campaign. In the spring of 1813, however, the British ministry sent reinforcements to Canada and imposed a blockade of American ports. Philadelphia was effectively shut off from the Atlantic world until the war's end. As in the Revolution, the war brought hard times to the city, and the celebrations of Independence Day that year were subdued. There were fewer private dinners and little indication of public spirit, although the *Aurora* continued to vilify "Massachusetts drawing her goose quill for her enemies" while Pennsylvania drew its sword against them.[16]

A renewed sense of urgency gripped Philadelphians in 1814 as they anticipated a full-scale invasion by British troops. As both the Fourth of July and the expected attack approached, a correspondent urged his fellow citizens: "Let next Monday not be a day of idle parade and dissipation, but a day of solemn resolves and manly decision. . . . The emergency is great, pressing, and all important—Not a day, not an hour, should be lost."[17] Another observed that

> To drink toasts at convivial entertainments, is one thing; to make
> ourselves formidable to an unrelenting enemy, who come 3000
> miles from their homes, prepared and equipped to destroy and

murder, is quite a different affair. . . . Every man in the country
should be aroused from his lethargy, and prepare himself without
delay to defend, with fortitude and courage, our sacred soil. . . .
The enjoyment of peace, for the last 30 years, is the cause we are
so little acquainted with the art and science of war. . . . It is time we
rally around the standard of our country, and shew ourselves the
legitimate descendants of our immortal ancestors.

The volunteer militias turned out again on the Fourth, and formed a
procession to rally patriotic citizens to the defense of their homes and
country.[18]

In Charleston also, Independence Day whipped up enthusiasm for
the war. One observer noticed that although he saw nothing beyond
the usual July 4 activities in town, these were attended "with increased
enthusiasm." Anticipation fueled the celebrations; for the previous
week Charlestonians had been taking precautions against another
British invasion by sea by rebuilding old Fort Moultrie. Enlisting local
tradition and historical memory, the call went out for "600 PALMETTO
Logs, best quality" to restore the venerable battery. As they labored,
the people of Charleston must have hoped the Royal Navy would
make a second try at forcing the harbor entrance, and allow them to
repeat the victory of 1776. On the Fourth itself, citizens put aside their
ideological animosities, at least publicly. The American Revolution
Society and the '76 Association, formerly representing opposite political poles, paraded together for the first time in a goodwill gesture
brokered by the Society of Cincinnati, "which should evince to their
citizens that they were equally united in heart." Even the *Charleston
Courier,* the last Federalist newspaper in the state, got behind the public war fever, praising "the beauty and holiness of patriotism," and
echoing "the wishes of every good citizen, that all party feeling should
be forgotten in the contest in which we are now engaged."[19]

The contrast between the celebrations of Independence Day in
Boston and in the more southern cities could hardly have been greater.
Boston's Federalist control of key ceremonies enabled them effectively
to kill the Fourth of July in that town during the conflict with Britain.
For fifteen years they had seen the "mobocracy" dominate national,
state, and local politics, until it must have seemed to them that Boston
was the last bastion of rational men. With so few political weapons left
to their disposal, the Federalists used Independence Day to strike out

at their opponents. They may not have wished to destroy Independence Day itself, but by crippling its accustomed observance they hoped to awaken people to the imminent danger of losing all to foreign invaders and Republican mismanagement. By sabotaging the rites of Independence Day, Federalists proved persuasively how significant those rites had become. On the other hand, Philadelphians and Charlestonians used the Fourth to gather public support for the conflict, and to promote spiritual renewal during the darkest period of the war. During those years, Independence Day possessed an immediacy—in Philadelphia especially—that it had lacked since the Revolution. As in that first war for independence, July 4 called the people to arms in a desperate cause.

"WITHOUT DISTINCTION OF PARTY"

Both parties welcomed the conclusion of hostilities in 1815. The Federalists were glad to see normal commerce restored, and the Republicans crowed about "triumphing" over John Bull. But the end of the war did not bring a return to politics as usual in the coastal towns. Former political lines blurred as both Federalists and Republicans responded to new circumstances.

As the Federalists' hostility to the war had grown, so had their isolation from mainstream opinion. For many Americans, the litany of Federalist protest and abuse crossed a line that bordered on disloyalty. When the British attacked the Chesapeake area in the summer of 1814, Federalists were forced to choose between their principle of opposition to the war and resistance to the invaders. Their party was split when some Federalist leaders rushed to arms to defend against the attack, and Federalist congressmen agreed to support measures to repel the British troops. This division only made the Federalist delegates and supporters of the ill-fated Hartford Convention look foolish and treasonous by comparison. The meeting was organized by New England Federalists to draft constitutional amendments that would check Republican policies and restore a larger share of New England's waning political power. As the tide of public opinion turned against opponents of the war, the Federalists' enemies accused the convention delegates of being secessionists and traitors. When Americans received the almost simultaneous news of the Treaty of Ghent ending the war and Andrew Jackson's stunning victory at New Orleans, the Federalists and their obstructionist policies were utterly discredited.[20] Federalists who could not or would not adapt their principles soon lost what few political offices remained to them. The die-hards retired from public life.

As for the Republicans, the demise of the Federalists as a going political concern left them without their traditional foils. The Republicans had always defined themselves in opposition to their enemies; without these, the Republicans lost a measure of their primal vitality. In addition to the need to remake their platform, Republicans reassessed their traditional economic philosophy as a result of the war. When foreign trade was choked off by the blockade, American manufactures received new attention and an accepted place in Republican ideology. This "liberalization" of Republican political economy obscured the lines that had traditionally separated Federalists and Republicans. Long-standing political distinctions diminished, making reconciliation possible for all but the most adamant partisans.[21] Assessing the sweeping changes in the political atmosphere, one July 4 correspondent declared that "the notion that there exists among those formerly called federalists, the least expectation of regaining power and holding it as a federal party, is preposterous. . . . No, there is no hope, there is no effort, to reinstate the old federal party in power; the elements of all old parties have been scattered."[22]

Postwar Independence Day celebrations reflected and reaffirmed the changes in American political culture. In Philadelphia and Charleston, where Federalism had long since ceased to be the dominant persuasion, the reconciliation of the parties was an easier matter than in Boston. Just before July 4 in 1814, one Republican correspondent confided that he had "long considered the federalists in some degree an injured party—a few, who are distracted or bought, are editors of their papers; and a solitary few, who wished to govern the country, have exhibited the character of insanity. Most of them will defend their country, or perish in the attempt."[23]

Three days after these soothing words appeared in print, and while the British invasion was still imminent, Philadelphian Samuel Breck attended a July 4 oration at the New Theater. Breck considered the oration too long and "imperfectly committed to memory," but more irksome to Breck was the now-inappropriate political stance of the speaker:

> One thing was dwelt upon by Dr. Caldwell, which can have none but a bad effect, and that was a comparison drawn in strong colours between the Army and the Navy. The first has been unsuccessful and he made it the property of the Democrats—the second has covered itself with glory, and he claimed it all for the Federalists. . . . Upon this topick the orator used inflammatory and irritating language. Surely it cannot be good policy to foster a jealousy between the Army and the Navy.[24]

In the years following the cessation of hostilities, Philadelphians attempted to sort out and comprehend the sudden changes in the intellectual demeanor of Americans. Independence Day in 1815 brought a return of the familiar festive modes to the city, but there was hardly a vestige of the factional bitterness that Samuel Breck had witnessed the year before. As usual, the Fourth of July was a befitting time to examine the progress of the nation, particularly in the light of the recent conflict. "It is curious," one analyst wrote, "to remark the political calm, which now prevails throughout the United States. It is attributable to various causes—the ratification of the peace with England snatched from the grasp of faction many a pretext for clamor; . . . The scope for speculation is another cause for the calm. . . . Another cause is the remoteness of the time for important elections—So that apparently the people at large are contented and united."[25]

As party distinctions melted away, even the terms "Federalist" and "Republican" required reexamination. One writer recognized the ability of these words to comprehend a wealth of symbolic associations that could make or break a political party. He concluded that "of the two terms it was soon evident that *republican* was the most popular, not because it was less popular to approve the federal form of government, but because the term republican conveyed a meaning better understood."[26]

With the restored peace, the Fourth of July celebrations regained their former luster in Boston. Federalists played down the disastrous effects of the Hartford Convention, instead reminding citizens in 1815 of "the enjoyment of Peace, and business, and returning Prosperity," that "will give a zest to the occasion."[27] The editors of the *Boston Gazette* expected "a very general and brilliant display of patriotic ardor and festivity" upon the Fourth in 1815, "particularly among the disciples of Washington."[28] These prophets were not mistaken; great public enthusiasm greeted the fireworks and illuminations, patriotic tableaux, plays, and other diversions that reappeared throughout the town after a three-year moratorium. While Federalists welcomed the return of normal commerce, Republicans chose to interpret the war as a moral victory for the United States. An editor for the *Independent Chronicle* exulted: "the recent conflict with the Nation from whom we emancipated ourselves when in infancy, has placed us on higher independent ground than we ever stood before."[29]

The rival newspapers avoided the traditional verbal swipes taken at one another in past years. Before the war, each party had studiously avoided reporting the other's Independence Day activities, except when an opportunity for acidulous commentary presented itself. In 1815 the papers expressed a less combative mood. The town celebrated "in the customary manner," reported the *Independent Chronicle*, and "the bells rang merry peals at times through the day."[30] The *Columbian Centinel* also exercised restraint, even when admitting that "a great number of citizens" from Boston attended "the [Republican] rural celebrations in Dorchester and Lexington."[31]

Although Boston's Federalists and Republicans were less willing to forgive and forget than their Philadelphia counterparts, their journalistic détente continued into the next Independence Day celebration in 1816. The *Columbian Centinel* reported a festive air pervading Boston and all the towns nearby. The Federalist newspaper also noted with satisfaction that John Adams had resumed his attendance at the town oration after his long estrangement from the Federalists. The Old South Meeting House that day was "full to overflowing."[32] Two successive Fourths without the traditional, galling rhetoric was a considerable accomplishment that was not lost on Bostonians. Reflecting upon the restored festivity and conciliatory mood, a correspondent to the *Independent Chronicle* observed:

> this display of joy and hilarity does not consist in pageantry or in noisy acclamations, but in reverting to the glorious achievements of our Revolutionary patriots. . . . We have had two wars on this

question, and thank God we have triumphed over our enemies in both. . . . We now know our enemies. Let us guard against them. . . . On this day, while we bury the hatchet of discord, let us erect the BEACON by which we may avoid the quicksands of perfidious friendship.[33]

The Boston Republicans were back in town for the 1816 celebration, and apparently glad to be. The *Independent Chronicle* reversed its former policy and detailed the still-Federalist-dominated town celebrations; if the Republicans felt that Adams's presence at the Old South was a defection, their toasts to him that day did not betray it. Instead, their newspaper proudly announced that "from the number, elegance and variety of the uniforms, the [town] Procession is considered one of the most brilliant witnessed here."[34]

Not all party bitterness dissolved with the conclusion of the War of 1812, but the reports of Boston's Independence Day celebrations reflected the changing political situation in town. When Republicans returned to celebrate the Fourth of July in Boston after the War of 1812, they found their adversaries already beaten. Federalists had little stomach for further ritual combat. Some, like Leverett Saltonstall, never recovered a fondness for politics, nor for Independence Day:

> Why did they not stop jingling the bells on Saty.? I could never see the necessity of disturbing all sober people to celebrate the independence of the Nation. I have sometimes become a perfect Tory, and wished the rebellion had been smothered before the 4th of July '76. It is horrible at the first dawning of the day, when you are enjoying a morning slumber to be disturbed by that confused sound—and to have your sleep afterwards murdered.[35]

Before the war and during its first year, Federalists had enjoyed a brief revival, but the peace negotiations at Ghent, the victory at New Orleans, and the disaster of the Hartford Convention embarrassed and dismayed them; the very name "Federalist" became an epithet.[36] The last vestiges of Federalism slowly crumbled. When Governor John Brooks refused to stand for reelection in 1823, no avowed Federalist again sat in the state executive's chair.

Two years after the war's end, President James Monroe toured the northeastern states as part of his campaign to subdue Federalist holdouts and to cement the "good feeling" that temporarily replaced the party warfare of thirty years. His schedule brought him to Boston for the Fourth of July. In his honor, the town bedecked itself as never before; the statehouse and every building near it displayed flags, wreaths, garlands, pictures of Washington, and the "naval heroes" of the late war. The military display and parade were splendid. The people of Boston turned out "without distinction of party" in the largest crowds since the visit of the "sainted Washington."[37] The Old South was once again filled to capacity, especially since the president attended the town oration. The newspapers carried no discouraging words of party spirit; the *Independent Chronicle* even ended its fifteen-year tradition of printing the Declaration of Independence on the front page of its July 4 issue. Only the Washington Society could not resist breaking the truce. At its annual Independence Day meeting, someone offered a toast to "The Hartford Convention—an old sore that flattery cannot heal."[38]

The editors of the *Independent Chronicle* were sure, however, that old sores were indeed being healed. A few days after Monroe's departure, an editorial appeared in that newspaper that simply could not have been written a few years before. Noting how much the president's presence in Boston had contributed to the "unusual éclat" of the Fourth, the writer continued:

> The easy and affable manners of the President charmed all hearts. . . . The visit of the President seems wholly to have allayed the storms of party. People now meet in the same room who would before scarcely pass [in] the same street, and move in concert, where before the most jarring discord was the consequence of an accidental encounter. . . . It is found that citizens in opposite parties are not so unworthy [of] reciprocal respect as before they were thought to be, and that each have qualifications which entitle them to the esteem of the other. The spirit of exclusive self-love wears away, and intercourse with each other shews even to prejudiced minds, that the virulence of party spirit . . . is not so strong or immovable as has been suspected. This harmony is a harbinger of a better order of things, and we trust it will continue beyond the cause which produced it.[39]

A year after the president's visit, William Tudor described the character of the people of Boston in his *Letters on the Eastern States*. Tudor had cause to know his subject: he had once delivered an Independence

Day oration in Boston, and had kept abreast of political matters there. The town was, he reported,

> an orderly, quiet place, which effect is produced more by the character of the people, than by the vigour of the police, of which there is very little. There are two or three festival days in the course of the year, when there are military parades, and a great concourse of people are collected; yet there is no riot, no disorder; even drunkenness is rarely seen, and the streets are as quiet on the evening of such a day, as on any other. A great improvement has taken place in these respects, within the period of the present generation.[40]

The pattern of Independence Day celebrations in Boston following the War of 1812 supports Tudor's observation. There had indeed been a major change in the public comportment and behavior of Bostonians since the days when Timothy Dwight had stressed the disturbing volatility of the people of Boston. Boisterous partisan celebrations in Boston had reached their zenith in the years just before 1812. With the restoration of peace, the partisan cast of celebrations rapidly diminished. Without partisan parades, dinners, and fireworks displays, Bostonians no longer felt pulled between the hostile camps at Bunker Hill and the Old South. Independence Day celebrations in Boston took on a more orderly routine. Parades, speeches, and fireworks continued to supply the pomp and festive air required for the day, but the factious tensions that had both marred and embellished previous Fourths were gone. A South Carolinian visiting Boston on Independence Day in 1822 confirmed the leveling of ideological creeds when he attended two orations, "the Democratic and the Federal; and as far as my judgement goes in politics, they were both Republican."[41] Independence Day had once driven Americans apart; after the War of 1812 it seemed to be a means of reconciling them.

Something may have been lost in the process, for there were those who actually missed the bad old days. In describing the celebrations in 1815, the editor of the *Boston Gazette* sounded positively bored with all the peacemaking. "Our limits," he claimed, "will not permit the insertion of the numerous accounts of the late national celebration; nor perhaps is it of consequence to repeat their publicity, as they exhibit nothing but what is familiar to every mind—and in their toasts, as a natural consequence of returning peace, there is little of that 'fire of the flint' which is requisite to elicit wit, or awaken enthusiasm."[42]

INDEPENDENCE DAY AND THE "NATIONAL CHARACTER"

"What a day!" exclaimed the editor of Charleston's *Southern Patriot* in an 1815 article entitled "The Fourth of July." "What happiness, what emotion, what virtuous triumph must fill the bosoms of Americans!" Despite America's lack of preparedness in the late war, despite the superior war machine of the British enemy, despite a war fought on several fronts, and the burning of the national capital, he maintained, "The foe is discomfitted and fled. We have triumphed." In the past, the writer continued, Independence Day orators had invoked the patriotic sentiments attached to events of the Revolution, forty years before. "To what feelings will the orator *now* appeal?" he asked, and, answering his own question, "To those of manly pride, and pious gratitude to Heaven, and confidence in ourselves and our resources." Most of all, he declared, Americans could feel proud and rejoice on this day, "because you have established a NATIONAL CHARACTER."[43]

In the wave of resurgent nationalism that followed the War of 1812, rhetoricians increasingly spoke of a "national character" that was forged from the shared trials and triumphs of the conflict. No less a personage than Speaker of the House Henry Clay declared before Congress that "a great object of the war has been attained in the firm establishment of the national character." To insinuations that the war had accomplished nothing material, Clay retorted, "Have we gained nothing by the war? Let any man look at the degraded condition of the country before the war. The scorn of the universe, the contempt of ourselves; and tell me we have gained nothing by the war? What is our present situation? Respectability and character abroad—security and defense at home. . . . Our character and our constitution are placed on a solid basis never to be shaken."[44]

The idea of a "national character" was nothing new, but previous attempts to define it had run afoul of party politics over the previous decades. What was new in 1815 was a widespread confidence that the recent war had brought about the realization of an authentic American archetype—virile, confident, progressive. On that first July 4 after the peace, Charleston revelers raised their glasses to "The Late War . . . it has brightened the character of the nation, and made every American feel he had a country."[45] This national character supposedly transcended political and sectional identities. With the long European wars at an end, normal trade with the world reestablished, and internecine political warfare on the wane at home, Americans embarked upon a new phase of ideological development. After a long period of national dissonance, the war and its aftermath inspired a "renewal of collective identity."[46]

Much of the enthusiasm was generated by what Revolutionary veterans had once called "the rising generation." Now fully risen to young maturity, raised in a political tradition that had always invoked Revolutionary precedents, the 1812 generation could finally point to their own efforts, their own sacrifices, in protecting and perpetuating the Revolution. They conceived the War of 1812 as a kind of reenactment of the conflict that had so shaped their parents' lives. So many Independence Day activities had sought to connect the new generation spiritually with the Revolution, and now that generation demonstrated how well they had learned their lesson. Like their forebears, the 1812 generation validated the sacrifice of so many of their lives by the heroic result: "Before they retired to their honorable graves," the *Southern Patriot* averred, "they had made free eight millions of their countrymen." Perhaps even more revealing is the acknowledgment of another writer that many of the younger generation "may have thou't the 18th of June [the date of Congress's declaration of war on Britain] almost as propitious a day for America as the 4th of July."[47]

The new national character had appropriately new, or appropriately revised, icons to represent it. As in the past, these fresh symbols received maximum exposure on the Fourth of July. Also as in previous years, the language of signs employed on Independence Day both reflected and affected the belief in the Revolutionary continuum and the final attainment of a definitive national character. No longer the private property of Republicans, the Declaration of Independence enjoyed a second, more popular revival as a result of America's "Second War of Independence." Readings of the Declaration on Independence Day remained popular activities, but the document's defiant rhetoric spoke with new meaning and vigor to a generation sensible of having survived a conflict with the same enemies their parents had faced.[48] New heroes, worthy inheritors of the Revolutionary tradition, took their places with George Washington and Thomas Jefferson in the pantheon of American patriots. In all of the port cities, Americans hung transparencies of, and drank toasts to, the naval heroes of the war: Stephen Decatur, Isaac Hull, Oliver Hazard Perry, and Thomas MacDonough.

More than to any other, however, Americans drank to the "Hero of New Orleans," Andrew Jackson, a new American hero in more than one sense. To admirers he was "the intrepid soldier of his country," "the scourge of foreign foes," and "the envy and terror of domestic courtiers."[49] Four and a half years after Jackson's victory, people still wrote new patriotic songs like "Jackson and New Orleans" for Independence Day celebrations.[50] More than merely the man of the hour, Jackson's lasting appeal and fame indicated a public readiness for new heroes, new patriotic paragons that reflected the "bumptious nationalism and the defiant abandonment of Europe" that characterized American political culture after 1812.[51] Just as Washington had embodied the virtues of American republicanism during the Revolutionary age, Jackson represented what Americans wanted to be in the age of democratic revival. Symbolically speaking, Jackson was the new Washington.[52]

Orators, newspaper editors, and politicians were rarely very clear about just what "the national character" was; its qualities, imperatives, and its extent. As with many such terms, its strength lay in its ambiguity. Any attempt to define a national character would soon run up against regional distinctions. What all proponents of the national character agreed upon, however, was its origin not in the first American Revolution of 1776, but in the "second" of 1812. The "national character" of the 1812 generation was a conceit of their own making, at once an attempt to identify with the Revolutionary generation, and to proclaim their own autonomy, even superiority: Had they not just completed the process which their parents had only begun? If their military prowess would not stand close scrutiny, the 1812 generation could point with pride to their achievement of what the older generation had for so long sought but never realized. "National character" was a symbol for the 1812 generation, no less than "liberty" had been for their elders. Equally ambiguous, the terms nevertheless held power to unite the generations that had produced them. That power would prove as mortal as the generations themselves.

FESTIVAL FOR A NEW AMERICA

By this time, the July 4 holiday had spread to smaller towns, villages, and settlements all over the United States, so that a newspaper correspondent in 1815 could confidently declare that "eight millions of people united in one festive celebration of the National Birth Day."[53] But it was the very word "festive" that troubled some Americans; they sensed that the character of July 4 celebrations was changing, and wondered what the change signified. Days after the 1811 celebrations in Philadelphia, Benjamin Rush wrote to his old friend John Adams to describe the scene. Despite Adams's praise of "games, sports, guns, bells" and bonfires thirty-five years ago, both he and Rush now shared a distaste for the growing dominance of celebratory forms over "pomp and parade." Rush ruefully described the events of July 4 as running "in the manner I expected":

> The military men . . . ran away with the glory of the day. Scarcely a word was said of the solicitude and labors and fears and sorrows and sleepless nights of the men who projected, composed, defended, and subscribed the Declaration of Independence. Do you recollect your memorable speech upon the day on which the vote was taken? Do you recollect the pensive and awful silence which pervaded the house when we were called up, one after another, to the table of the President of Congress to subscribe what was believed by many to be our own death warrants?[54]

In Massachusetts, Leverett Saltonstall also found something wanting on Independence Day. "It is a day which ought to be observed, tho' we have but little of the spirit left, which actuated that immortal body of sages in congress . . . [in] '76."[55]

Aging patriots and disgruntled Federalists were not the only ones to sense that times had changed, and not necessarily for the better. Just before Independence Day in 1820, an article in *Niles' Weekly Register* observed that with the passage of time, "nearly all the great actors in 1776 have made their exit to 'another and better world.'" But something else, something less tangible, seemed to be passing also. Ironically, the author continued, the success and much-vaunted prosperity of the United States was eroding some of the finer qualities of the "national character":

> we have made some aberrations from the republican simplicity and honest zeal for the welfare of the nation, which existed in those days, chiefly, perhaps, by the acquisition of wealth and consequent growth of luxury and extravagance. . . . We have had days of prosperity and seasons of adversity; we have borne the latter much better than the former. When dangers pressed, the people were alive to their interests and surmounted every difficulty: but in a state of ease and seeming security, these interests were neglected.[56]

Another writer, reflecting on the activities of a recent July 4, agreed that Americans suffered from political apathy. "As to the mass of the people," he lamented, "it must be confessed that a pernicious indifference reigns among them"; they were too "occupied with private concerns" to give the significance of Independence Day serious thought. "The memorable days of our Revolutionary history," sighed a Charlestonian, "do not now bring with them . . . those lively feelings which they formerly did."[57] As if to support this last assertion, even Independence Day orations seemed to turn from their venerable Revolutionary texts and forms. The *Charleston Courier* praised an oration of 1823 for its "new and pleasing style" and for being "in great measure novel in its arrangement." Significantly, the reported admitted, "the allusions to Revolutionary events" were "not numerous, nor long dwelt upon."[58]

A noticeable increase in the emphasis given to celebration activities on Independence Day in the decade following the War of 1812 supports those who felt they detected a shift in ritual accent. Popularization of the Fourth of July had freed virtually everyone in Boston and Philadelphia, and at least half of the population of Charleston, to participate in the festivities in some form. Left to themselves, people found their own ways to relieve their "festival deprivation." Along with the demise of recognizable political parties went their colorful and well-attended Fourth of July rallies. With partisan celebrations no longer providing an outlet for public involvement, and without new popular ceremonies to take their places, people filled the gaps with "festival."

The new festive pattern was particularly evident in Philadelphia. Its burgeoning population fed an increasingly carnival-like atmosphere surrounding the Fourth of July. The Circus Theater in 1817 promised its public songs, recitations, and comedy, but virtually nothing in the way of patriotic edification, unless one counts a "pantomime" called "The Sailor's Lady."[59] Other theaters advertised similar content. Fourth of July theatrical offerings had always included a mix of patriotic themes and lighter fare, but soon after the War of 1812, the playbills were dominated by vapid farces and acrobatic acts. Likewise, the city's museums succumbed to the public's perennial hunger for entertainment and sensationalism. To honor Independence Day in 1821, the Philadelphia Museum featured "Signor Helene . . . the celebrated musician who plays on six different musical instruments at the same time, and produces a most singular whistling with his mouth, as an accompaniment."[60] Two years later, the Washington Museum's July 4 attractions included a wax tableau of the shocking duel in which the heroic Stephen Decatur was killed by James Barron, the man who had surrendered the *Chesapeake* to the *Leopard* so many years before.[61] In 1824, a "Large Saloon" in Fifth Street offered a Fourth of July showing of "Picturesque, Philosophical, Mechanical, Dextrous and Illusive Recreations." Balloon ascensions that once kindled Enlightenment-style fascination in the sciences, and that signified the rising American empire, now served as a stage for gymnasts and daredevils: one July 4 ascension near Center Square featured an acrobat who stood on his head atop the balloon.[62]

Center Square was becoming a problem on Independence Day. The square was one of five public areas laid out in William Penn's original design for the city. As Philadelphia's population grew in the early nineteenth century, surveyors marked out the entire area between the Delaware and Schuylkill Rivers in the planned pattern of straight streets and square blocks for which the city is still famous. Placed midway between the rivers, Center Square was the logical place for Philadelphia's new Pump House that brought water from the Schuylkill into the city. The square and its steam-operated marvel of engineering became a focus of municipal pride. Militia companies and other Independence Day celebrants took to using the parklike area for their celebrations (Fig. 5). The square's distance from the crowded waterfront and commercial areas also made it a preferable location for

5. Lewis Krimmel, "Fourth of July in Centre Square." Philadelphia's famous Pump House is the backdrop of the artist's genre painting (ca. 1812). Compare this relatively sedate scene with Krimmel's rendering of the same subject in 1819. (Courtesy of the Museum of American Art of the Pennsylvania Academy of Fine Arts, Philadelphia. Pennsylvania Academy purchase [from the estate of Paul Beck, Jr.])

fireworks displays. Increasingly, Center Square became the focus for the people who stayed in town to celebrate July 4.

Some of the celebrations there raised loud objections. "The vicinity of Center Square," wrote one outraged citizen in 1821, "has, too often, been disreputably distinguished." "Petty gambling establishments" abounded at the square on July 4, "to which apprentice boys and others are enticed."[63] The situation was apparently no better the next year. Lashing out at the drunkenness and gambling that accompanied Independence Day at Center Square, "Truth" pronounced:

> These celebrations, notwithstanding it may be considered by some as almost treason to say so, are uniformly attended in this quarter of the union, with pernicious results. . . . Intemperance and riot are generally witnessed in many directions before the end of the day, reeling to and fro in dreadful unison. . . . The suburbs of the city, are at this day, selected as the scene of open and bare faced violations of the liquor laws.[64]

The day was being polluted, according to "Truth" and other protesters; there was "no opportunity for profitable reflection," and no inducement to "exalt moral feelings, or strengthen political principles." One newspaper advised its readers to leave their children at home on the Fourth.[65] Petitioned by private citizens and municipal authorities, Mayor Robert Wharton banned vendors' stalls and booths from Center Square in 1823. The gamblers, hucksters, and unscrupulous liquor merchants simply moved their operations to "the hill opposite Fairmont" at the edge of the city (probably near the location of the Philadelphia Museum of Art).[66]

If Philadelphia would not tolerate such amusements on the Fourth, there were plenty of other places that did. A revolution in transportation enabled more people than ever to leave the city for the day. Steamboats plied the Delaware, ferrying people to the Jersey Shore and back, and even ran to New York. In 1826 the Washington Greys took advantage of this new mobility to celebrate Independence Day in New York rather than in their own city. An estimated twelve thousand of their fellow citizens—nearly 10 percent of the city's population—took boats to Camden across the river. Some of them could not get back until the next day, despite the fact that the steamers ran until 11:30 on the night of July 4.[67]

A wonderfully rich document of 1819 complements all the written accounts describing the changing nature of Independence Day celebrations. In that year, John Lewis Krimmel of Philadelphia painted *Independence Day in Center Square* (Fig. 6). The artist obviously knew his subject well: in the crowded scene Krimmel brought together a world of human activity and sentiment that collectively made up Independence Day. In the center background looms the famous Pump House, before which march two companies of militia. Two officers, one representing the navy and one the army, occupy the center foreground. Arm in arm, they point proudly to pictures adorning the fronts of two tents at either side of the painting. The naval officer points to a print of the 1813 *Chesapeake/Shannon* battle headed with the motto "Don't Give Up the Ship."[68] In turn, the Army officer indicates a print illustrating the battle of New Orleans.

The patriotic allegory ends there, for behind the embracing officers transpire all the (by then) familiar activities of July 4. Under the tent at left, a militia officer offers a toast to a private party of men and women enjoying a holiday picnic. The men, all holding glasses, appear to be quite merry already, as does a fiddler at the near end of the table. Through the back flap of the tent, the viewer can just make out a man in civilian dress, arms upraised and mouth opened wide in speech. If He is making an impromptu oration, he does not appear to be drawing much attention. To the right of the tent, a female vendor sells fruit and bottles of liquor. A knot of cigar-smoking men stands just beyond her, engaged in conversation over a recently purchased bottle and a meal of oysters. One man is expostulating on a subject the viewer can only imagine. Just visible beyond them, two young strollers seem preoccupied with each other, while to the right of center middle ground, two men stripped to shirt sleeves appear ready to begin a boxing or wrestling match—whether prizefight or spontaneous brawl is unclear. More vendors occupy the right middle ground. At the right foreground, a seated woman is selling or giving out pamphlets on what seems an assortment of subjects: patriotic odes perhaps, or temperance pamphlets. One young man has his hand over his heart as he reads, as though he were singing, or taking a pledge. Almost within arm's reach of the woman, two children play with fireworks, one about to set off a small cannon. And behind them, almost lost in the crowd, an elderly Revolutionary War veteran bares

6. Lewis Krimmel, "Independence Day at Center Square" [1819]. (The Historical Society of Pennsylvania.)

his honorable scars to some young men and women who look decidedly indifferent.

Krimmel's painting captures much of the excitement, fun, and humor of Independence Day in the years following the War of 1812. He has also caught much of the change, ambiguity, and irony surrounding the activities in Center Square. Celebration clearly dominates the space; the militia march virtually unheeded, and the orator (if that is what he is—he could be a raving drunkard) is unheard. Intoxication in the left tent competes with temperance on the right of the painting. In turn, the enterprising pamphlet seller (or crusading temperance woman) contrasts with the women in the painting who have come only as spectators. Denied an immediate role in the rites of Independence Day, the determined-looking matron is nonetheless involved, whether she is selling patriotism in print or attacking the social evil that July 4 encourages. Blacks appear in the painting, as they probably did in actuality, only as children. One dances to the fiddler's tune while a second surreptitiously gulps the liquor vendor's profits under the table. Finally, aside from the icon of Washington over the tent at left, only the aging and crippled veteran reminds the viewer of the Revolutionary roots of the occasion. Significantly, the two (young) officers in front direct the viewer, not to memorials of the Revolution, but to symbols of their own (probably vicarious) achievements in the more recent war. In Krimmel's painting, the Revolution is a fading memory, an epic increasingly relegated to history books. Only one man in the crowd seems to know what Independence Day is supposed to be about, and nearly everyone is ignoring him.

When Krimmel painted his now-famous canvas, Independence Day signified something far different from what it had been when it was first created, different even from what it had been before the War of 1812. "By 1820," wrote Gordon Wood, "Americans had moved into another century, not only in time but in thought, in the way they perceived themselves and the world."[69] They had gone from a republican ideology based on subordination to the public good, to one that glorified individual initiative. They had passed from a political culture based upon government by the republic's elites to the verge of a democratic revival in which elitism was despised. The "rising generation" reshaped Independence Day to reflect and to serve its own needs, reinterpreting the rituals and symbols of national identity (or fashioning new ones) to fit the times. In this way, both generations honored July 4, though for reasons that were literally a generation apart.

For decades, younger Americans had read or heard stories about the Revolution and the pivotal moment of July 4, 1776. Every year they celebrated that glorious moment in the past and the heroes of that moment. The day and the heroes had become legendary, their virtue a paragon of republican principles and behavior. But legendary virtues are difficult to live up to. The "rising generation" had been annually subjected to nagging and intrinsically unfair comparisons between themselves and their famous forebears. Introspective letters and editorials, in which younger writers argued their worthiness of the Revolutionary legacy, regularly accompanied Independence Day reports. Boastful militia toasts betrayed young men's longing to realize their own identities by proving a military skill and ardor equal to those of Washington's men. Americans may also have sensed an uneasiness over a realization that some of the broader social promises of the Declaration of Independence had not been kept. In 1819, the same year that John Krimmel painted *Independence Day at Center Square,* a pensive correspondent wrote a letter that was printed in Philadelphia's *Aurora,* and that might have been the caption for Krimmel's painting:

> Forty three years have elapsed since American independence was declared, and nearly all the actors in the scenes of that period have descended to the grave. While our citizens are celebrating the day, it may not be unprofitable for them to . . . inquire whether the flame of devotion to liberty and their country that animated the patriots of 1776 glows in the breasts of the generation of 1819. . . . We cannot take to ourselves the merit of our ancestors and vaunt of our devotion to liberty, on their account; we must give evidence of it in our own conduct, else we run into the absurdity with which we reproach others. . . . If there be any such, they are unworthy of being covered with the mantle of the men of 1776, for they possess none of their principles; they may shout and huzza, when the Declaration of Independence, and the patriots of the revolution are toasted; but it will be as idle as for a worthless and degenerate son to attempt to attach virtue and patriotism to his own person, by vaunting of the virtuous and patriotic deeds of his ancestor.[70]

Increasingly, however, Americans of the post-Revolutionary generation refused to compare themselves unfavorably with their parents.

The War of 1812 gave them a new datum point for mapping out their destinies. They believed they had triumphed over Great Britain, and selected new heroes to represent their victory. The earthy Andrew Jackson represented the new generation better than the godlike Washington. For young Americans, the war had been a "Second War of Independence" not only from Britain, but from the tyranny of old models of patriotism. After 1815, they stopped trying to measure up to impossible standards of virtue. Krimmel's painting contains few references to the Revolution because by 1819, Americans celebrated not their past, but themselves.

7

JUBILEE

And thou shalt number seven sabbaths of years unto
thee, seven time seven years; and the space of the
seven sabbaths of years shall be unto thee forty and
nine years.

And ye shall hallow the fiftieth year, and proclaim
liberty throughout all the land unto all the
inhabitants thereof.

A jubilee shall that fiftieth year be unto you. . . . It
shall be holy unto you.

LEVITICUS 25:8, 10–12

It will, no doubt, as it is the anniversary that answers
to the ancient Jubilee among the Hebrews, be
celebrated with extraordinary zeal . . . and many
commemorative orations will be spoken. . . . It will be
often found a difficult one to bring to its ornament
any flowers of poesy or modes of eloquence that
have not been used before.

DEBORAH NORRIS LOGAN, *DIARY,* July 4, 1826

In 1826 the nation celebrated the fiftieth anniversary of the
Declaration of Independence. The "Jubilee" birthday inspired a number of personal reflections as well as public celebrations. Deborah
Norris Logan of Philadelphia remembered when the Declaration was
read in the statehouse yard for the first time in 1776. "It was a time of

fearful doubt and anxiety with the people," she recalled. "Many were appalled at the boldness of the measure, and the first audience of the Declaration was neither very numerous, nor composed of the most respectable class of citizens." Fifty years to the day later, Logan found it "impossible on this remarkable day not to fall into a chain of thoughts inspired by its recollections." Her thoughts were somber:

> Setting aside the grand and almost overwhelming remembrances which the anniversary of the Independence of our country never fails to introduce to the mind, with all the train of events . . . and thinking only of the tide of human beings that at that period lived, and acted, and looked forward, as we do now, but have since dropped into the sea of oblivion, a melancholy would be too apt to take possession of the mind.

Almost parenthetically, Logan added that "by an odd coincidence" she found herself that day "employed in the same work that I was, on this day 50 years ago—clearstarching."[1]

Samuel Breck was only a few years younger than Deborah Norris, but his outlook more reflected that of the post-Revolutionary generation. Writing in his diary on the same day, Breck was untroubled by the nagging gloom that plagued Logan:

> It is fifty years this day since our bold and right worthy fathers declared this great country independent of Great Britain. And whatever may have been the anticipations of the most enthusiastic patriot that day, in relation to our growth in numbers, wealth and political importance, they have been more—greatly more than realized. This, my beloved Country, presents on this 50th anniversary of its birth as a nation, a picture of prosperity, tranquility, happiness and good fellowship, from one end of the Empire to the other, which every citizen must love to contemplate, and strive to perpetuate.[2]

The meditations of Samuel Breck and Deborah Logan represent coexisting—and competing—moods of Americans who had lived to see a symbolic milestone passed. Breck chose to succumb entirely to July 4's patriotic allure. He cast aside all doubt, all the paradoxes and uncertainties accumulated in a half-century of American political culture. His is the voice of an irrepressibly self-confident generation in an age of democratic reform. Deborah Logan's voice is more bittersweet. Looking past the "overwhelming remembrances . . . with all the train of events" with which Independence Day inevitably bombarded people, Logan found ambiguity and contradiction in the event Americans celebrated. Like many in the "tide of human beings" that walked in procession before her mind's eye, Logan could not share Breck's hyperbolic acclaim of what "our bold and worthy fathers" had accomplished: fifty years later, Logan was still clearstarching. In some fundamental ways, for her and for millions of other Americans, male and female, little seemed to have changed.

Within days of their Jubilee entries, Breck, Logan, and the rest of America learned of the nearly simultaneous deaths that July 4 of Thomas Jefferson, who had penned the Declaration, and of John Adams, who had talked him into doing it. "It seems too strange a coincidence to be true," mused Deborah Logan. "According to the doctrine of chances, what an odds would have been against its so occurring!" "This is a very singular coincidence," agreed Samuel Breck.[3] Many Americans became convinced that there was more than mere coincidence involved. There was something supremely fitting and symbolic in the occurrence: "Whose death," the *Aurora* inquired, "was ever so graced by such a funeral oration, thus delivered!" It was "as if Providence had spared [them]" to reach this puissant liminal moment.[4] Some even believed that Adams and Jefferson had chosen their time to die, and gave up their ghosts on the Jubilee day by force of will.[5] By dying when they did, Adams and Jefferson seemed to reveal "a mysterious agreement between mankind, nature, and the gods." Their "timely deaths" helped define their lives, and seemed to signify a final blessing on their country's history and progress. At the same time, they symbolized for Americans the close of one age and the dawning of another.[6]

The wide acceptance of this epochal interpretation of two deaths indicates a general contemporary awareness that a new phase of American society and political culture had indeed begun. From the 1820s onward, Independence Day activities acquired a wealth of new associations resulting from the rapid democratization of American society. As the impulse for moral reform gathered force, evangelical preachers seized upon July 4 gatherings to promote national righteousness.[7] In New England, mill girls and women formed their own

"Sabbath School Unions" that met on July 4 for picnics and feminine fellowship.[8] Women also found active roles in the reform movement, particularly in temperance work. There they claimed their long-
denied place in the rites of Independence Day by staging July 4 rallies
against the hearty drinking that was so much a part of the occasion.[9]
The 1820s also witnessed the commencement of a new period in labor-
class consciousness and activity. As the social and economic gulf between employers and wage-earners widened, trade unions and labor
associations regarded Independence Day as a powerfully symbolic
time to march in processions or to schedule strikes and demonstrations.[10] Additionally, a new and ugly phase in urban race relations was
already under way, in which whites increasingly excluded blacks from
participation in any of the rites of white society. The ensuing decades
saw deadly and destructive race riots erupt in several northern cities.[11]

    Independence Day had always contained ceremonial and celebra-
tional characteristics—John Adams originally thought that there was
room for both—but inexorably the festive elements of Independence
Day dominated. By the middle of the nineteenth century, Independence Day was much more of a working-class holiday than it had been
during its first fifty years, and the unstructured style preferred by
working people was apparent to all observers.[12] In 1837 the British
author Frederick Marryat witnessed his first July 4 celebration in New
York. "The Americans may have great reason to be proud of this day,
and of the deeds of their forefathers," he admitted, "but why do they
get so confoundedly drunk?" Marryat watched as the "respectable or
timorous" citizens made a "precipitate escape" from the city at daybreak. For the rest of the day and night the streets belonged to the
crowds, who utterly ignored the old municipal ban on fireworks.[13] In
Philadelphia, Sidney George Fisher regularly fled to a friend's house
in the country "to escape the noise, the vulgarity and various abom-
inations of 4th of July patriotism. On that day all laws seem suspended
and riot, incendiarism, drunkenness and uproar form an appropriate
celebration of the anniversary of democratic triumph."[14]

    More than ever, variety was the keynote of Independence Day
activities. A New Hampshire diarist in 1839 noted "how different the
American people celebrate this day, some for dinners, some tem[per-
ence] meetings, Abolition, [African] colonization, peace &c., some
fishing, gunning, swimming, riding and many other things . . . whilst

many work all day."[15] The observations of chroniclers after 1830 indicate an important trend in Fourth of July celebrations. As Americans approached the middle of the nineteenth century, Independence Day increasingly revealed not so much what they held in common as what separated them.

This was especially so in Charleston. Regional and national events from 1819 onward progressively convinced white Charlestonians that their distinctiveness from the rest of the nation was perhaps more important than the bond of "national character." The panic of 1819, followed by a decade of economic decline in the city, stung the residents smartly. The more industrialized and capital-rich northern states were able to recover relatively quickly, partly, as in the case of New York, by taking over Charleston's shipping needs. The Missouri Compromise debates of 1820 served notice to Charlestonians, as to Southerners everywhere, that their political economy, based on slavery, was anathema to many northern Americans. Adding still more to the growing sense of isolation and distinctiveness, the Denmark Vesey insurrection of 1822 remained white Charlestonians of the dangers inherent in their "peculiar institution"—an institution that forced them to be constantly on guard against the black majority within while combating antislavery assaults from without. The defensiveness and insecurity bred by these events, falling in succession like hammer blows, accelerated Charleston's transformation to an inward-looking, "closed society" that regarded "national interest" as interpreted by Northerners with instant suspicion.[16]

In the years immediately following the War of 1812, Charlestonians had proclaimed and celebrated a universal "national character" on Independence Day. Increasingly, however, July 4 in that city seemed to highlight disturbances in the nationalist ethos, and even introduced a return to emphasis on regional loyalties. During the 1821 celebrations of the Charleston Rifle Corps, the usual transparency of George Washington was replaced by two new displays, one an effigy of the American eagle and the "National Standard," and the other a large transparency of the South Carolina arms. This dual motif became instantly popular, even adorning the front of Charleston's Theater Company building for its 1823 Fourth of July program.[17] Subtle changes, these, but in their symbolic blurring of national preeminence over the states, they spoke volumes in the "language of signs."

Equally significant, the long-ignored Palmetto Day showed strong signs of making a comeback. At the height of the transports over the "national character," one old patriot who remembered the attack on Fort Moultrie so long ago could "scarce realize the apathy that is now manifested at its anniversary. It is numbered with the days before the flood." Another asked: "Can it be possible that Carolinians should ever forget a Victory, which was no less important to the general success of the Revolution, than it was highly favorable to the patriotism and valor of their Native State?"[18] Interest in the old Revolutionary holiday revived as Charlestonians turned to their past for inspiration and reassurance in the troubling times after 1819. Feeding the public need for local heroes, Alexander Garden's *Anecdotes of the Revolutionary War* appeared in 1822. This "key work in South Carolina hagiography" brought back to heroic life the memories of General Moultrie, Francis Marion, and the intrepid Sergeant Jasper of Fort Moultrie fame.[19] Within a few years, a "Native genius" thrilled Charlestonians with a re-creation of the battle in miniature, complete with floating, firing models of the British ships of the line, in the harbor waters just off the popular Bathing House. During the Jubilee celebrations, promoters of regional patriotism used Independence Day to drum up donations for a fitting monument to Charleston's proudest moment.[20]

Thus, within a few years of the heady post-1815 days, Charlestonians' trust in the validity of a "national character" showed signs of coming apart in favor of a more familiar, traditional, local identity. Years before, Charleston's Independence Day orators had called July 4 "the proudest day in the Calendar of the Republic." They had wondered at the "novel and sublime . . . spectacle of ten millions of people" celebrating as one. "We know," one speaker told his audience,

> That at this moment the temples of the Most High are crowded by thousands of our countrymen, who are offering up ascriptions of praise, or listening to the spirited effusions of patriotic eloquence. Though unallied to us by the ties of friendship, though unknown to us by the kindred relations of domestic life, their breasts are vibrating in unison with ours, for they boast the same name, the same country, and the same aera of national liberty.[21]

But by 1826 they could not boast of having the same understanding of what Independence Day was supposed to represent. There was in-

deed something powerful in the idea of a shared set of goals and
ideals, whether encoded in terms of "liberty," "independence," or "national character," but simply invoking the words could not make such
ideals universal, nor universally comprehended.

"Other nations have burst their chains," conceded the editor of the
Southern Patriot in 1817, "and placed themselves in the rank of independent empires: but what other nation has established a yearly Sabbath and jubilee to freedom?" The assumption of legitimacy via ritual
could hardly have been better expressed. At the same time, the editor's rhetorical question suggests his uncertainty as to the nature and
quality of early American nationalism. In the young United States,
conceptions of the "nation-state" competed constantly with more familiar "communities of allegiance."[22] While the first was primarily
territorial, the latter was personal. While nationalism was relatively
novel, localism was ancient. While "the nation" was an abstraction,
every person's community was real. The framers of the Constitution
were right to worry about the ability of the states and the regions to
unite and to cooperate; by the time Jefferson and Adams were in their
graves, the nation had weathered several sectional storms already, and
its greatest test was little more than thirty years away. South Carolina's
attachment to a federal government may have been conditional from
the beginning, as one historian has argued.[23] On Independence Day,
Americans celebrated an ideal of national union that had never been
truly realized, as if by celebrating the ideal they could make it fact. The
Fourth of July helped both to craft and to promulgate the master
"cultural fiction" of nationalism, a notion born initially not from long
awareness of common identity, but from an immediate practical imperative for collective resistance to Britain.[24] Ironically, as the United
States approached the sectional crises of the mid-nineteenth century,
two of July 4's most outstanding characteristics—its toleration of new
interpretations and its ability to cloak disharmony—worked against
any consensus of vision concerning the nation's past. The growing
plurality of messages communicated on Independence Day diffused
the original message of an American national identity, and the holiday's capacity for masking tensions and contradictions within the political culture abetted a mass self-deception that mistook form for
substance.

Not everyone was deceived. Musing on the nature of political holidays in 1818, a correspondent to the *Charleston Courier* recognized how
national fetes could steer the public into ways of thinking that would
ultimately put them on a collision course with each other. "The recollections of the past," he wrote, "must, in great measure be absorbed in
the feelings and interests of the present, or the prospects of the future.
New connections arise, and new views display themselves, identified
with interests for which we are more zealous, and therefore occupy
our liveliest sensibilities."[25] In the second quarter of the nineteenth
century, Charleston's "interests" diverged dramatically from those of
Boston and Philadelphia, and from what Charlestonians perceived as
an increasingly intrusive federal government. The Jubilee celebration
of 1826 was perhaps the last high point of federal nationalism in
Charleston and the rest of the state in the century; only six years later
came the showdown with Andrew Jackson and the national government over nullification, and "southern nationalists" began to argue for
secession more seriously than ever before. As the unresolved issues of
the Revolution neared their bloody solution in the 1860s, Independence Day lost nearly all relevance for the people of Charleston.[26]

The rites of Independence Day were never merely the "trimmings" of
nationalist political culture.[27] The observance of Independence Day
had to a significant degree succeeded in fostering national consciousness in the Revolutionary and Confederation periods, a time when
real political union among the thirteen states was tenuous at best. It
was a task for which public ritual was well suited. Such "performances
of culture" have the power to plant and propagate the "myths" that
bind societies together: the myths of cultural unity, of social continuity,
of unchanging tradition, of shared belief—in short, of nationhood. Ritual performances of the kind examined in these pages are, as John
MacAloon argues, more than entertainment, more than didactic or
persuasive formulations, and more than cathartic indulgences; they
are "occasions in which as a culture or society we reflect upon and
define ourselves, dramatize our collective myths and history, present
ourselves with alternatives, and eventually change in some ways
while remaining the same in others."[28] On July 4, Americans declared
that they held certain fundamental outlooks and interests in common

in spite of often formidable social, ideological, and eventually sectional characteristics to the contrary. For a time they believed the myth they created, but in the early American republic nationalism was always, and perhaps is still, as much aspiration as fact. Depending as it did upon recently invented traditions, American nationalism was a fragile construct. Its maintenance required a powerful application of faith in a mystic homogeneity that embraced but superseded a broad range of backgrounds, beliefs, and regional loyalties. Independence Day rituals articulated and reinforced that critical faith, temporarily extending the "community of allegiance" beyond state and regional boundaries—*communitas* on a national scale.

But the myth had to contend with political realities. There is irony in the realization that, if the United States in 1783, 1798, or 1812, had in fact been a contented, complacent federation of like-minded communities, Independence Day might well have fallen into disuse and been "numbered with the days before the flood," as had Palmetto Day before the 1820s. Ideological turmoil in the post-Revolutionary decades saw to it that that did not happen, and the Fourth of July became instead a vigorous patriotic festival, in which Federalists and Republicans interpreted and reinterpreted America's past and tried to shape its future. Independence Day was, and is, a testament to the power of the myth *e pluribus unum,* and to the ability to translate the myth afresh through public commemoration and festival. The very public and politically charged dissonances displayed by Republicans and Federalists on Independence Day alerted Americans to the difficulty of achieving a truly national identity in an ideologically pluralistic society. Nevertheless, the myth survived the War of 1812 stronger than ever, whereas the contending political parties did not.

Astute Americans quickly learned the power of Independence Day to communicate and to shape public opinion, as the proliferation of partisan July 4 activities throughout the antebellum period attests. Americans embraced the celebration of the Fourth of July wholeheartedly, but for a catalogue of reasons that diffused the original message of *communitas* and substituted narrower agendas that took on a sacredness of their own. As July 4 became increasingly politicized, privatized, and democratic, the old rites lost their power to reconcile and reaffirm. The message of harmony that was originally so central to Independence Day dissolved during the middle of the nineteenth century; the rites simply could not function "properly" when the very nature of nationalism was being challenged. When the breakdown (or polarization) of American national identity climaxed in civil war, the need to make sense out of the disaster demanded a revised mythos of nationhood, one with new heroes, villains, symbols, and rites; one in which the victors could unblushingly rationalize the war as an unavoidable "rite of passage" that ushered in a "new birth" of freedom.[29]

NOTES

INTRODUCTION

1. Charles William Janson, *The Stranger in America, 1793–1806* (New York, 1935), 23–26. The orator to whom Janson took exception was young John Quincy Adams, giving his first major public speech.

2. Janson, *The Stranger in America*, 25.

3. Paul Friedrich, "Revolutionary Politics and Communal Ritual," in *Political Anthropology*, ed. Marc J. Swartz, Victor W. Turner, and Arthur Tuden (Chicago, 1966), 192.

4. *Gazette of the United States* (Philadelphia), July 7, 1794; *Boston Gazette*, July 5, 1815.

5. Barry Schwartz, *George Washington: The Making of an American Symbol* (New York, 1987), 78.

6. In the last few decades, historians, anthropologists, and sociologists have borrowed creatively from one another to produce a new body of literature on ritual studies. See, for example, Susan G. Davis, *Parades and Power: Street Theater in Nineteenth-Century Philadelphia* (Berkeley and Los Angeles, 1986); Peter Shaw, *American Patriots and the Rituals of Revolution* (Cambridge, Mass., 1981); Charles S. Sydnor, *American Revolutionaries in the Making: Political Practice in Washington's Virginia* (New York, 1965); the essays in *"We Gather Together": Food and Festival in American Life*, ed. Theodore C. Humphrey and Lin T. Humphrey (Ann Arbor, 1988); Sally F. Moore and Barbara G. Myerhoff, *Secular Ritual* (Amsterdam, 1977); and in Sean Wilentz, ed., *Rites of Power: Ritual and Politics Since the Middle Ages* (Philadelphia, 1985).

7. Proctor, *Enacting Political Culture: Rhetorical Transformations of Liberty Weekend 1986* (New York, 1991), 1.

8. Lynn Hunt, *Politics, Culture, and Class in the French Revolution* (Berkeley and Los Angeles, 1984), 54. See also Clifford Geertz, "Centers, Kings, and Charisma: Reflections on the Symbolics of Power," in *Culture and Its Creators: Essays in Honor of Edward Shils*, ed. Joseph Ben-David and Terry Nichols Clark (Chicago, 1977), 167–68.

9. For a thoughtful survey of the interrelation of religion and politics in America, see Gary Wills, *Under God: Religion and American Politics* (New York, 1990).

10. Catherine L. Albanese, *Sons of the Fathers: The Civil Religion of the American Revolution* (Philadelphia, 1976), 17.

11. Ronald L. Grimes, *Beginnings in Ritual Studies* (Lanham, Md., 1982), introduction, n.p.

12. Two fine examples of ritual studies of this period, and exemplary of "macro-" and "micro-" approaches, are Rhys Isaac, *The Transformation of Virginia, 1740–1790* (Chapel Hill, N.C., 1982), and Rodris Roth, "Tea-Drinking in Eighteenth-Century America: Its Etiquette and Equipage," in *Material Life in America, 1600–1860*, ed. Robert Blair St. George (Boston, 1988), 439–62.

13. See for example Cedric Lawson, "Patriotism in Carmine: 162 Years of July 4th Oratory," *Quarterly Journal of Speech* 26 (February 1940): 12–25; A. V. Huff Jr., "The Eagle and the Vulture: Changing Attitudes Toward Nationalism in Fourth of July Orations Delivered in Charleston, 1788–1860," *South Atlantic Quarterly* 73, no. 1 (Winter 1974): 10–22; Fletcher M. Green, "Listen to the Eagle Scream: One Hundred Years of the Fourth of July in North Carolina," in *Democracy in the Old South and Other Essays* (Nashville, 1969), 111–56.

14. Merle Curti, *The Roots of American Loyalty* (New York, 1946), 140–41.

15. Kurt W. Ritter and James R. Andrews, *The American Ideology: Reflections of the Revolution in American Rhetoric* (Falls Church, Va., 1978), 16–17.

16. Robert P. Hay, "The Liberty Tree: A Symbol for American Patriots," *Quarterly Journal of Speech* 55 (1969): 415.

17. I shall use the term "Revolution" throughout this study as it was generally used by contemporaries: the period of the War for Independence, 1775–83.

18. Gordon S. Wood, ed., *The Rising Glory of America, 1760–1820* (New York, 1971), 1. Catherine Albanese characterizes the period as one of "self-confident uncertainty"; *Sons of the Fathers*, 221.

19. Gordon Wood, *The Creation of the American Republic, 1776–1787* (New York, 1969), 354.

20. Wood, *Creation of the American Republic*, 355.

21. John M. Murrin, "A Roof without Walls: The Dilemma of American National Identity," in *Beyond Confederation: Origins of the Constitution and American National Identity*, ed. Richard Beeman, Stephen Botein, and Edward C. Carter II (Chapel Hill, N.C., 1987), 343, 344.

22. Joyce Appleby, *Capitalism and a New Social Order: The Republican Vision of the 1790s* (New York, 1984), 15.

23. Gordon Wood, "Interests and Disinterestedness in the Making of the Constitution," in *Beyond Confederation*, ed. Richard Beeman, Stephen Botein, and Edward C. Carter II, 103. Wood asserts virtually the same sentiments in *The Rising Glory of America*, 8.

24. John R. Howe Jr., "Republican Thought and the Political Violence of the 1790s," *American Quarterly* 19 (1967): 147–65.

25. Wood, *The Rising Glory of America*, 9.

26. For some thoughtful discussions on the nature of nationalism, see Benedict Anderson, *Imagined Communities: Reflections on the Origin and Spread of Nationalism* (London, 1983).

27. A term borrowed from James H. Kettner, *The Development of American Citizenship, 1608–1870* (Chapel Hill, N.C., 1978), 3.

28. John Hellmann offers a succinct and, for this study, appropriate definition of "myth" as "the stories containing a people's image of themselves in history." John Hellmann, *American Myth and the Legacy of Vietnam* (New York, 1986), ix.

29. Eric Hobsbawm, "Introduction: Inventing Traditions" in *The Invention of Tradition*, ed. Eric Hobsbawm and Terrence Ranger (Cambridge, 1983), 4.

30. Daniel J. Boorstin, *The Americans: The National Experience* (New York, 1965), 373.

31. Clifford Geertz uses the metaphor of a spider's web to explain the dynamism of "culture." Humans spin "webs of significance" to make sense of their world, and these "webs" support in turn the humans who create them. Together, the strands form "an ordered system of meaning and of symbols, in terms of which social interaction takes place." Since the cultural web is constantly being spun as people interact, however, its pattern never remains uniform over time. Geertz quoted in David E. Proctor, *Enacting Political Culture*, 3–4; see also Clifford Geertz, "Ritual and Social Change: A Javanese Example," *American Anthropologist* 59, no. 1 (February 1957): 33.

32. Lynn Hunt, *Politics, Culture, and Class in the French Revolution*, 10–11. Richard L. Bushman employs a similar definition in Bushman, *King and People in Provincial Massachusetts* (Chapel Hill, N.C., 1985), 3–4.

33. William Rueckert, *Kenneth Burke and the Drama of Human Relations* (Berkeley and Los Angeles, 1982), quoted in Proctor, *Enacting Political Culture*, 2.

34. Definitions of "symbol" range from the simplistic to the positively arcane. An example of the former is David Zarefsky, *President Johnson's War on Poverty: Rhetoric and History* (Tuscaloosa, 1986), 2, which defines "symbol" as "anything which stands for something else."

    On words as symbols: "Liberty" is one of the "god-words" studied by David Proctor in *Enacting Political Culture*. Richard L. Merritt explicates the significance of the increasing frequency of the term "American" in colonial newspapers up to the Revolution in his *Symbols of American Community, 1735–1775* (New Haven, 1966).

    For examples of persons as symbols, see Richard Lentz, *Symbols, the News Magazines, and Martin Luther King* (Baton Rouge, La., 1990); Barry Schwartz, *George Washington: The Making of an American Symbol* (New York, 1987); Peter Shaw's profiles of Thomas Hutchinson, John Wilkes, and Lord Bute in Shaw, *American*

Patriots and the Rituals of Revolution (Cambridge, Mass., 1981), 26–73; John William Ward, *Andrew Jackson: Symbol for an Age* (New York, 1955).

35. Victor Turner's "conventional" understanding of ritual refers to "formal behavior for occasions not given over to technological routine, having references to beliefs in mystical powers or sources." Sally F. Moore and Barbara G. Myerhoff, eds., *Secular Ritual*, 21. See also Ralph Beals and Harry Hoijer, *An Introduction to Anthropology* (New York, 1956), 496. For an overview of the evolution of ritual studies over the past century, see the introductory chapter to Moore and Myerhoff, *Secular Ritual*.

36. Moore and Myerhoff, *Secular Ritual*, 199. Edward Leach calls ritual simply "any expression of cultural form," but clearly this is not specific enough for the purpose of this study; included in such a definition would be such prosaic forms as an alphabet, or shaking hands by way of greeting. Edmund R. Leach, *Political Systems of Highland Burma* (Cambridge, Mass., 1954), 4. Note also that the rites of Independence Day generally do not serve any immediate "practical" or "technical" purpose (as does, for example, Christian baptism). Indeed, according to Ronald Grimes, ritualization occurs "when meaning, communication, or performance become *more* important than function and pragmatic end" (my emphasis). If a ritual not only has meaning, but "works" (baptism), it possesses a *magical* dimension. Grimes, *Beginnings in Ritual Studies*, 36, 45.

37. Victor Turner, *The Ritual Process: Structure and Anti-Structure* (Chicago, 1969).

38. Geertz, "Ritual and Social Change," 32.

39. Proctor, *Enacting Political Culture*, 1.

40. See Chapter 4.

1
"EXCELLENT POLITICAL MOVES"

1. Ronald L. Grimes, *Beginnings in Ritual Studies* (Lanham, Md., 1982), 41–42.

2. Grimes, *Beginnings in Ritual Studies*, 48–49. At this point I must distinguish between my general use of the terms "celebrate" or "celebration" with reference to the overall observance of Independence Day, from ritual celebratory types; that is, the yearly celebration (observance) of July 4 included both ceremonial and celebratory ritual styles, as defined above.

3. Richard L. Bushman, *King and People in Provincial Massachusetts* (Chapel Hill, N.C., 1985), 14–17.

4. For an instance of less-than-proper comportment on the king's birthday, see Peter Shaw, *American Patriots and the Rituals of Revolution* (Cambridge, Mass., 1981), 104.

5. See Shaw, *American Patriots and the Rituals of Revolution*, 15–18, and Gary Nash, *Urban Crucible: The Northern Seaports and the Origins of the American Revolution* (Cambridge, Mass., 1986), 164–65, for descriptions of Pope's Day in pre-Revolutionary Boston.

6. Shaw, *American Patriots and the Rituals of Revolution*, 199. Dirk Hoerder compiles a list of colonial holidays in *Crowd Action in Revolutionary Massachusetts, 1765–1780* (New York, 1977), 46.

7. The Scripture reads: "Wherefore the king hearkened not unto the people. . . . So when all Israel saw that the king hearkened not unto them, the people answered the king, saying, What portion have we in David? . . . To your tents, O Israel: now see to thine own house, David."

8. *Boston Gazette,* July 7, 1777; *Independent Chronicle,* July 10, 1777.

9. This description of the 1777 celebration is assembled from the *Pennsylvania Evening Post,* July 3 and 5, 1777; John Adams to Abigail Adams, July 5, 1777, quoted in Charles Warren, "Fourth of July Myths," *William and Mary Quarterly* 2, no. 3 (July 1945): 256; and a report from Capt. —— Parker to Gen. Anthony Wayne, Philadelphia, July 5, 1777, Wayne Papers 3:109, Historical Society of Pennsylvania.

10. See *Gazette of the State of South Carolina,* June 30, 1777; and Elmer Douglas Johnson, trans., "A Frenchman Visits Charleston in 1777," *South Carolina Historical and Genealogical Magazine* 52, no. 2 (April 1951): 88–92, for first Palmetto Day exercises. On the makeup of Palmetto Society, see Richard Walsh, *Charleston's Sons of Liberty: A Study of the Artisans, 1763–1789* (Columbia, S.C., 1968), 116.

11. *Gazette of the State of South Carolina,* July 7, 1777.

12. Shaw, *American Patriots and the Rituals of Revolution,* 199, 221; George C. Rogers Jr., *Charleston in the Age of the Pinckneys* (Norman, Okla., 1969), xi.

13. Grimes, *Beginnings in Ritual Studies,* 40; Barbara G. Myerhoff, "We Don't Wrap Herring in a Printed Page: Fusion, Fictions and Continuity in Secular Ritual," *Secular Ritual* (Amsterdam, 1977), 199–200.

14. Catherine L. Albanese, *Sons of the Fathers: The Civil Religion of the American Revolution* (Philadelphia, 1976), 71.

15. Warren, "Fourth of July Myths," 255–56.

16. See Charles Warren, "Fourth of July Myths," and Daniel Boorstin, *The Americans: The National Experience* (New York, 1965), 373–80; "mystery": Boorstin, *The National Experience,* 377.

17. For example, William Loughton Smith of Charleston was aware of the July 2 vote, but insisted that the Declaration was the true "instrument" of independence. William Smith, *An Oration in St. Phillip's Church, before the Inhabitants of Charleston, South Carolina, on the Fourth of July, 1796, in Commemoration of American Independence* (Charleston, 1796), 21.

18. Albanese, *Sons of the Fathers,* 185.

19. *Common Sense* (Penguin ed., 1986), 82.

20. *Pennsylvania Evening Post,* July 3, 1777.

21. Grimes, *Beginnings in Ritual Studies,* 44.

22. Albanese, *Sons of the Fathers,* 9.

23. Roberto Da Matta, "Constraint and License: A Preliminary Study of Two Brazilian National Rituals" in Moore and Myerhoff, eds., *Secular Ritual,* 245.

24. Steven Rosswurm, *Arms, Country, and Class: The Philadelphia Militia and the "Lower Sort" During the American Revolution* (New Brunswick, N.J., 1987), 46, 160.

25. *Pennsylvania Evening Post,* July 3, 1777.

26. *Pennsylvania Evening Post,* July 5, 1777.

27. Charles Warren, "Fourth of July Myths," 255–56.

28. Parker to Wayne, July 5, 1777, Wayne Papers 3:109.

29. Elaine Forman Crane, ed., *The Diary of Elizabeth Drinker* (Boston, 1991), 1:225. Boston was apparently spared this sort of rowdiness, as the British evacuation in March of 1776 had all but cleared that town of Tory elements. I have turned up no evidence of Independence Day intimidation in Charleston in 1777, but it would be surprising if there was none.

30. Charles Warren, "Fourth of July Myths," 255.

31. *Pennsylvania Evening Post,* July 5, 1777. Hannah Griffith, whose friends were on the receiving end of the evening's activities, had still another view:

> The unarmed Quakers—& the Tories
> Sustained the Honors of the night
> And still, the poor unshuttered stories
>   Hang zig zag Trophies of their might.

"The Glorious 4th of July 1777 A Satirical Poem by Hannah Griffiths (Fidelia)," Pemberton Papers 30:58, Historical Society of Pennsylvania.

32. The 1778 observances are pieced together from Warren, "Fourth of July Myths," 256–57; Crane, *Diary of Elizabeth Drinker,* 1:314; "Diary of Grace Growden Galloway," *Pennsylvania Magazine of History and Biography* 55 (1931): 38; *Pennsylvania Packet,* July 4, 1778.

33. Warren, "Fourth of July Myths," 257. Elizabeth Drinker reported some fireworks, but apparently these were not judged worthy of comment elsewhere. Crane, *Diary of Elizabeth Drinker,* 1:355.

34. The only reference to the 1781 anniversary was an account in the July 12 issue of the *Pennsylvania Gazette* that described the university commencement held on that day. The trustees and faculty invited army and navy officers to a cold luncheon at the State House afterward.

35. *The Independent Gazetteer* (Philadelphia), July 5, 1783; Crane, *Diary of Elizabeth Drinker,* 1:411.

36. *Boston Gazette,* July 6, 1778. The next French visit, two months later, was less cordially received. After the near-disastrous Rhode Island campaign, the battered fleet put into Boston for repairs. Accused of ruining the chance for a major victory, the French were jeered and mobbed; two Frenchmen, one a naval officer, were killed in anti-French riots.

37. *Boston Gazette,* July 12, 1779; July 10, 1780; July 9, 1781; July 8, 1782.

38. Louisa Susannah Wells, *The Journal of a Voyage from Charleston, S.C. to London Undertaken During the American Revolution by a Daughter of an Eminent American Loyalist in the Year 1778 and Written from Memory Only* (New York, 1906), 2.

39. *Gazette of the State of South Carolina,* July 8, 1778.

40. *Gazette of the State of South Carolina,* July 8, 1778; George C. Rogers, Jr., *Evolution of a Federalist: William Loughton Smith of Charleston, 1758–1812* (Columbia, S.C., 1962), 164.

41. *Gazette of the State of South Carolina,* July 21, 1779.

42. An interesting dustup occurred, however, when the American prisoners of the capitulation, barracked at nearby Haddrell's Point, celebrated the Fourth of July with music, dancing, and an illumination of their barracks. The British considered this a "gross outrage" and an "indecent abuse" of the terms of capitulation, especially as the American officers, who according to those same terms had been allowed to keep their pistols, used them to fire salutes in honor of the occasion. See William Moultrie, *Memoirs of the American Revolution* (New York, 1968), 2:130–36.

43. Johnson, "A Frenchman Visits Charleston," 89.

44. Nash, *Urban Crucible,* 243–44; Shaw, *American Patriots and the Rituals of Revolution,* 223.

45. David E. Proctor, *Enacting Political Culture: Rhetorical Transformations of Liberty Weekend 1986* (New York, 1991), 4.

46. David Cannadine, "The Context, Performance, and Meaning of Ritual: The British Monarchy and the 'Invention of Tradition'" in *The Invention of Tradition,* ed. Eric Hobsbawm and Terrence Ranger (Cambridge, 1983), 160.

47. Johnson, "A Frenchman Visits Charleston," 91.

48. Victor Turner, *The Ritual Process: Structure and Anti-Structure* (Chicago, 1969), 94–96. For a recent critique and refinement of Turner's theories see Caroline Walker Bynum, "Women's Stories, Women's Symbols: A Critique of Victor Turner's Theory of Liminality" in Bynum, *Fragmentation and Redemption: Essays on Gender and the Human Body in Medieval Religion* (New York, 1991).

49. Richard Handler, *Nationalism and the Politics of Culture in Quebec* (Madison, Wis., 1988), 4.

50. See, for example, Charles Royster, *A Revolutionary People at War: The Continental Army and American Character, 1775–1783* (New York, 1979).

51. Barry Schwartz, *George Washington: The Making of an American Symbol* (New York, 1987), 102. Schwartz is referring to Washington's funeral and mock-funerals throughout the nation, but his observation is appropriate to Independence Day as well. See Catherine Albanese's comments on "sacred time" in *Sons of the Fathers,* 9.

2

SPIRITUAL BLOOD

1. *Boston Town Records, 1778–1783,* Report of the Record Commissioners of the City of Boston (Boston, 1895), 26:289–91.

2. *Boston Town Records, 1778–1783,* 291.

3. *Boston Town Records, 1778–1783,* 305.

4. *Boston Town Records, 1778–1783,* 219.

5. *Boston Town Records, 1778–1783,* 291.

6. *Boston Town Records, 1778–1783,* 305.

7. Gordon Wood, *The Creation of the American Republic, 1776–1787* (Chapel Hill, N.C., 1969), 367.

8. Clifford Geertz notes that "puritanical" pretensions often accompany radical nationalism. "Deep Play: Notes on the Balinese Cockfight," in *Myth, Symbol, and Culture*, ed. Clifford Geertz (New York, 1971), 2.

9. Wood, *Creation of the American Republic*, 427, 571.

10. Dirk Hoerder, *Crowd Action in Revolutionary Massachusetts* (New York, 1977), 386.

11. *Boston Gazette*, July 6, 1778.

12. *Independent Chronicle*, July 10, 1783. Warren's trendsetting oration is reprinted in Gordon Wood, *The Rising Glory of America* (New York, 1971), 56–69.

13. *Independent Gazetteer*, July 10, 1784.

14. Wood, *Creation of the American Republic*, 426–27.

15. *Independent Gazetteer*, July 9, 1785.

16. Johann David Schoepf, *Travels in the Confederation*, trans. Alfred J. Morrison (1911; reprint, New York, 1968), 97.

17. This account of the 1786 Philadelphia celebration, except where otherwise indicated, is taken from the *Independent Gazetteer*, July 8, 1786, and the *Pennsylvania Gazette*, July 12, 1786.

18. Charles Warren, "Fourth of July Myths," *William and Mary Quarterly* 2, no. 3 (July 1945): 259.

19. *Independent Gazetteer*, July 8, 1786.

20. Julien Dwight Martin, "The Letters of Charles Caleb Cotton, 1798–1802," *South Carolina Historical and Genealogical Magazine* 51, no. 4 (October 1950): 222. See Jerome Nadelhaft, *The Disorders of War: The Revolution in South Carolina* (Orono, Maine, 1981).

21. A major fire in January 1778 destroyed 252 houses in Charlestown. Occupation put a virtual stop rebuilding efforts until well after the war. Richard Walsh, *Charleston's Sons of Liberty: A Study of the Artisans, 1763–1789* (Columbia, S.C., 1968), 80.

22. George C. Rogers Jr., *Charleston in the Age of the Pinckneys* (Norman, Okla., 1969), 132.

23. Schoepf, *Travels in the Confederation* (1968 ed.), 2:166.

24. Ulrich B. Phillips, "The South Carolina Federalists, I," *American Historical Review* 14, no. 3 (April 1909): 532–33.

25. Phillips, "South Carolina Federalists," 533–34.

26. This "lower and rougher class" actually included some well-off artisans, merchants lacking British contacts, and many "discontented officers," former planters who had been forced to sell their slaves to get through the war. Schoepf, *Travels in the Confederation*, 203–4, 205.

27. Phillips, "South Carolina Federalists," 533.

28. *South Carolina Gazette and General Advertiser*, July 5, 1783; George W. Williams, *Saint Michael's, Charleston, 1751–1951* (Columbia, S.C., 1951), 257–60. The British left only one set of bells, those of Saint Phillip's Church, so that the town would not be without some way of sounding an alarm.

29. *South Carolina Gazette and General Advertiser*, July 5, 1783.

30. *South Carolina Gazette and General Advertiser*, July 12, 1783; Walsh, *Charleston's Sons of Liberty*, 117.

31. Walsh, *Charleston's Sons of Liberty*, 120; *South Carolina Gazette and General Advertiser*, July 10, 1784.

32. *Independent Chronicle*, July 8, 1784; *Boston Gazette*, July 4, 1816; *Independent Gazetteer*, July 11, 1789.

33. Catherine Albanese, *Sons of the Fathers: The Civil Religion of the American Revolution* (Philadelphia, 1976), 189.

34. David Cressy, *Bonfires and Bells: National Memory and the Protestant Calendar in Elizabethan and Stuart England* (Berkeley and Los Angeles, 1989), 1.

35. *Independent Gazetteer*, July 8, 1786.

36. "Boyle's Journal of Occurrences in Boston, 1759–1778," *New England Historical and Geneological Register* 85 (1931): 128. There was apparently little change in the situation by 1793, when a foreign visitor observed that "of the military, about five hundred infantry made a fine appearance, and as many more, without regimentals, formed a perfect contrast." Charles William Janson, *The Stranger in America, 1793–1806* (New York, 1935), 25–26. Unsurprisingly, newspaper accounts consistently ignore the appearance and performance of the regular militia units. On distinctions between regular and voluntary militias in Philadelphia, see Steven Rosswurm, "The Philadelphia Militia, 1775–1783: Active Duty and Active Radicalism," in *Arms and Independence: The Military Character of the American Revolution*, ed. Ronald Hoffman and Peter J. Albert (Charlottesville, N.C., 1984), 75–118, esp. 78–79. For Charleston see Michael Stauffer, "Volunteer or Uniform Companies in the Antebellum Militia: A Checklist of Independent Companies, 1790–1899," *South Carolina Historical Magazine* 88, no. 2 (April 1987): 108–16.

37. *Independent Chronicle*, July 5, 12, 1787.

38. Charles Royster traces the persistent image of the Revolutionary citizen-soldier in *A Revolutionary People at War: The Continental Army and American Character, 1775–1783* (New York, 1979).

39. On the theory and practice of American militia in post-Revolutionary America, see Lawrence Delbert Cress, *Citizens in Arms: The Army and Militia in American Society to the War of 1812* (Chapel Hill, N.C., 1982).

40. Charles Pythian-Adams, "Ceremony and the Citizen: The Communal Year at Coventry, 1450–1550," in *Crisis and Order in English Towns 1500–1700: Essays in Urban History*, ed. Peter Clark and Paul Slack (London, 1972), 58.

41. The focal point of Brazilian Independence Day is a military parade, and here too "one of the main streets is made ready, marking out the places where the participants in the ritual (the soldiers) are to be, where the public is permitted, and where the authorities are to be." Da Matta, "Constraint and Licence: A Preliminary Study of Two Brazilian National Rituals," in *Secular Ritual*, ed. Sally Moore and Barbara G. Myerhoff (Amsterdam: Van Gorcum, Assen, 1977), 246. I would argue that in the above example, the public are "participants" also.

42. Ronald L. Grimes, *Beginnings in Ritual Studies* (Lanham, Md., 1982), 44. Even Boston's Pope's Day, with its semi-orderly processions mocking social hierarchy, required a degree of order, and an audience. One great difference between processions sponsored by authority, and rituals of inversion, like Pope's Day, is in the degree and kind of audience participation tolerated.

43. *Independent Chronicle,* July 5, 1787.

44. *Pennsylvania Gazette,* July 12, 1786.

45. After joining in a rendition of John Dickinson's "liberty Song" in 1769, John Adams reflected that the exercise was "an excellent mode of 'cultivating the sensations of freedom.' " Albanese, *Sons of the Fathers,* 58.

46. *Boston Town Records, 1778–1783,* 291. "Virtue" was indeed the theme of the first Boston Independence Day oration. See the printed text in Gordon Wood, *The Rising Glory of America, 1760–1820* (New York, 1971), 25–35.

47. William Read to Jacob Read, Charleston, July 8, 1796, C. E. French Papers, Massachusetts Historical Society.

48. Kurt W. Ritter and James R. Andrews, *The American Ideology: Reflections of the Revolution in American Rhetoric* (Falls Church, Va., 1978), 2. Significantly, the same witness who complained of the length and predictability of William Smith's Charleston oration admitted that overall it was "an elegant thing & spoken with neat oratory . . . his allegories stupendous & elegantly contrived."

49. A British traveler reported from Boston in 1793 that "we could barely get within the doors" of the Old South to hear the oration. Janson, *The Stranger in America,* 24.

50. Diary of Nathan Webb, July 5, 1790. Massachusetts Historical Society.

51. As did Elizabeth Cranch of Braintree in 1786 and John Pierce of Brookline in 1808. Diary of Elizabeth Cranch, Massachusetts Historical Society; Memoirs of John Pierce, Massachusetts Historical Society.

52. Gabriel referred to the traditional Fourth of July oration as "ritual performance." Ralph Henry Gabriel, *The Course of American Democratic Thought,* 3d ed. (New York, 1986), 98–100.

53. Grimes, *Beginnings in Ritual Studies,* 42.

54. *State Gazette of South Carolina,* July 6, 1793.

55. Gillian Feeley-Harnik, *The Lord's Table: Eucharist and Passover in Early Christianity* (Philadelphia, 1981).

56. See *Independent Chronicle,* July 6, 1786; *Independent Gazetteer,* July 6, 1787, for examples; the rhetoric of harmony in connection with public or private dining on the Fourth of July is found passim.

57. James Griffith, "We Call it 'Tucson Eat Yourself': The Role of Food at a Constructed Festival" in *"We Gather Together": Food and Festival in American Life,* ed. Theodore C. Humphrey and Lin T. Humphrey (Ann Arbor, Mich., 1988), 219–33.

58. *Independent Chronicle,* July 6, 1786.

59. Quoted in Charles H. Sherril, ed., *French Memoirs of Eighteenth-Century America* (1915; reprint, Freeport, N.Y., 1971), 89–90.

60. *Independent Chronicle,* July 8, 1784.

61. On oath-taking as a social as well as a religious rite, see Joseph Plescia, *The Oath and Perjury in Ancient Greece* (Tallahassee, Fla., 1970); William Ames, *The Marrow of Theology* (Boston, 1968), 267–68; Keith Thomas, *Religion and the Decline of Magic* (New York, 1971), 44; Christopher Hill, *Society and Puritanism in Pre-Revolutionary England* (New York, 1964), chap. 11, "From Oaths to Interest," 382–419.

62. "In a celebratory moment, the ritual action is a deed in which the symbols do not merely point, mean, or recall, but embody fully and concretely all that is necessary for the moment." Grimes, *Beginnings in Ritual Studies,* 48–49, 230.

63. Da Matta, "Constraint and Licence," 246.

64. *Boston Gazette,* July 8, 1805.

65. *Independent Chronicle,* July 10, 1788.

66. *By-Laws and Orders of the Town of Boston* (Boston, 1801), 8–9.

67. *Report of the Record Commissioners of the City of Boston: Selectmen's Minutes from 1799 to and Including 1810* (Boston, 1904), 305.

68. *Columbian Centinel,* July 3, 1805; *Independent Chronicle,* July 4, 1805. "Several complaints having been made against the practice of firing India Crackers and other small fireworks in the streets; the Chairman was desired to insert an advertisement in the papers, calling upon the citizens to give their aid in stopping these dangerous practices." Significantly, these complaints were delivered to the selectmen in May 1816. No similar complaints are found in connection with the Fourth of July. *Report of the Record Commissioners of the City of Boston: Selectmen's Minutes 1811 to 1817 and part of 1818* (Boston, 1908), 185.

69. *Columbian Centinel,* June 29, 1811.

70. Grimes, *Beginnings in Ritual Studies,* 48. Natalie Davis argues that "carnival" forms can reinforce the existing social order, as well as suggest alternatives to it. Natalie Zemon Davis, *Society and Culture in Early Modern France* (Stanford, Calif., 1975), 123.

71. Victor Turner, *The Ritual Process: Structure and Anti-Structure* (Chicago, 1969), 96.

72. Barry Schwartz, *George Washington: The Making of an American Symbol* (New York, 1987), 107.

73. Many books exist on this topic, but on Boston and Philadelphia particularly, see Marjorie Drake Ross, *The Book of Boston: The Federal Period, 1775 to 1837* (New York, 1961); Russell Frank Weigley, *Philadelphia: A 300-Year History* (New York, 1982), especially 155–223. For an engaging overview of American material culture in this period, see Barbara Clark Smith, *After the Revolution: The Smithsonian History of Everyday Life in the Eighteenth Century* (New York, 1985).

74. *Independent Gazetteer,* July 8, 1786.

75. Albanese, *Sons of the Fathers,* 222.

76. Albanese, *Sons of the Fathers,* 189–90.

77. *Independent Gazetteer,* July 8, 1786.

78. Hugh Duncan, "A Sociological Model of Social Interaction as Determined by Communication," *Communication and Social Order* (New York, 1968), 350, quoted in

David E. Proctor, *Enacting Political Culture: Rhetorical Transformations of Liberty Weekend 1986* (New York, 1991), 4.

79. *Independent Gazetteer,* July 8, 1786.

80. Albanese, *Sons of the Fathers,* 9.

81. *Boston Gazette,* July 6, 1789; [Charleston] *City Gazette,* July 7, 1789 (my emphasis).

82. *Independent Gazetteer,* July 8, 1786 (my emphasis).

83. *Pennsylvania Gazette,* July 12, 1786.

84. *Aurora General Advertiser,* July 6, 1799.

85. Lester H. Cohen, *The Revolutionary Histories: Contemporary Narratives of the American Revolution* (Ithaca, N.Y., 1980), 18, 229.

86. Quoted in Richard Handler, *Nationalism and the Politics of Culture in Quebec* (Madison, Wis., 1988), 17.

87. See Gary B. Nash, *The Urban Crucible: The Northern Seaports and the Origins of the American Revolution* (Cambridge, Mass., 1986).

88. Pope's Day traditions in Boston may not have died out so suddenly or so completely as previously thought, and the town authorities in 1783 may well have feared renascent crowd actions such as those in Charleston. Writing in the 1830s, Samuel Breck vividly recalled an invasion of his father's house by a set of "anticks" in 1782, when he was eleven, on the occasion of a holiday he could not quite recall. He remembered them as "a set of the lowest blackguards" who forced their way into the house, made free with the use of some of its contents, and performed an impromptu death/rebirth pantomime resonant of ancient Mummers' plays. "There was no refusing admittance," declared Breck. "Custom had licensed these vagabonds to enter even by force any place they chose," and "the only way to get rid of them was to give them money." The incident is very much in the tradition of the supposedly defunct Pope's Day activities. H. E. Scudder, ed., *Recollections of Samuel Breck, with Passages from his Note-Books, 1771–1862* (Philadelphia, 1877), 35–36.

89. This statement requires qualifications. Gary Nash's comparative study of colonial seaport towns demonstrates that Philadelphia was spared the severe fluctuations of trade experienced by sister ports as a result of the "French and Indian" wars until the Seven Years' War, 1756–63. After that time, Philadelphia shared in the difficult postwar economic downturn. Nash, *Urban Crucible.* And according to Billy G. Smith, Philadelphia was never a workingman's paradise; see his excellent *"The Lower Sort": Philadelphia's Laboring People, 1750–1800* (Ithaca, N.Y., 1990).

90. John K. Alexander, "The Fort Wilson Incident of 1779: A Case Study of the Revolutionary Crowd," *William and Mary Quarterly,* 3d ser., 31 (1974): 589–612.

91. William Duane, ed., *Extracts from the Diary of Christopher Marshall, Kept in Philadelphia and Lancaster During the American Revolution 1774–1781* (Albany, N.Y., 1877), 224.

92. Weigley, *Philadelphia: A 300-Year History,* 156.

93. Schoepf, *Travels in the Confederation,* 101–2.

94. Sam Bass Warner Jr., *The Private City: Philadelphia in Three Periods of its Growth* (Philadelphia, 1968), 43.

95. Richard G. Miller, *Philadelphia–The Federalist City: A Study of Urban Politics, 1789–1801* (Port Washington, N.Y., 1976), 20–23.

96. Warren, "Fourth of July Myths," 259–60.

97. Rachel N. Klein, *Unification of a Slate State: The Rise of the Planter Class in the South Carolina Backcountry, 1760–1808* (Chapel Hill, N.C., 1990), 125; *South Carolina Gazette and General Advertiser,* July 10, 1784.

98. *South Carolina Gazette and General Advertiser,* July 13, 1784.

99. *South Carolina Gazette and General Advertiser,* July 5, 15, 1783.

100. *Columbian Herald,* July 6, 1785 (my emphasis).

101. John Davis, *Travels of Four Years and a Half in the United States of America, During 1798, 1799, 1800, 1801, and 1802* (New York, 1909), 62; Martin, "Letters of Charles Caleb Cotton," 220, 222.

102. Schoepf, *Travels in the Confederation,* 167; Martin, "Letters of Charles Caleb Cotton," 220.

103. Davis, *Travels,* 102–3.

104. See M. Foster Marley, "Mighty Monarch of the South: Yellow Fever in Charleston and Savannah." *Georgia Review* 27 (1973): 56–70.

105. Raymond A. Mohl, ed., " 'The Grand Fabric of Republicanism': A Scotsman Describes South Carolina," *South Carolina Historical Magazine* 71 (July 1970): 179.

106. Schoepf, *Travels in the Confederation,* 172.

107. On at least one occasion, when a particularly dangerous heat spell led to a number of deaths, the Independence Day military review was canceled altogether. *Charleston Courier,* July 3, 1824.

108. George Fenwick Jones, "The Siege of Charleston as Experienced by a Hessian Officer," *South Carolina Historical Magazine* 88, no. 2 (April 1987): 171; Schoepf, *Travels in the Confederation,* 164; Mohl, " 'The Grand Fabric of Republicanism,' " 171. Apparently the situation was little improved three decades later; see "A Frenchman Visits Charleston, 1817," *South Carolina Historical and Genealogical Magazine* 49, no. 3 (July 1948): 139–40.

109. *Charleston Courier,* July 6, 1809. If only the orator could have taken advantage of a "Life Preservative" advertised in 1823, especially formulated for "Ladies and Gentlemen Who design to join in the hilarities of our national birth day." The seller assured customers that a few drops of this "Cordial" would "restore natural vigor, energy, and cheerfulness; & prevent lassitude & faintness through the most intense heat during the summer months." *Charleston Courier,* July 3, 1823.

110. Grimes, *Beginnings in Ritual Studies,* 36.

111. *Pennsylvania Gazette,* July 12, 1786.

112. Lynn Hunt, *Politics, Culture, and Class in the French Revolution* (Berkeley and Los Angeles, 1984), 60.

113. Grimes, *Beginnings in Ritual Studies,* 223.

114. Albanese, *Sons of the Fathers,* 58.

115. *Pennsylvania Gazette,* July 8, 1788 (my emphasis).

116. *Independent Chronicle,* July 6, 1786.

117. *Aurora General Advertiser,* July 6, 1799 (my emphasis).

3
A PARTISAN HOLIDAY

1. According to Sean Wilentz, processions of tradesmen were unknown in America before the Revolution, although common on European saint's days, holy days and public festivals; see Wilentz, *Chants Democratic: New York City and the Rise of the American Working Class* (New York, 1984), 88–89. However, in 1766, Robert Treat Paine witnessed a procession in Plymouth, Massachusetts, celebrating the repeal of the Stamp Act. The procession included "all orders everyone carrying a Badge of their business & a standard before them with this Inscription, *Stamp Act repeald Liberty restored, all Trades flourishing, GOD save the King & Bless the Parliament.*" It is certainly possible that there were similar processions elsewhere. Diary of Robert Treat Paine, May 19, 1766, Massachusetts Historical Society (MHS). I am indebted to Ed Hanson at the MHS for this citation.

2. [Boston] *Centinel,* February 13, 1788.

3. The following account is based on Francis Hopkinson, *An Account of the Grand Federal Procession, Philadelphia, July 4, 1788. To which is Added, a Letter on the Same Subject* (Philadelphia, 1788), except where otherwise noted.

4. Prior to Pennsylvania's ratification, Hopkinson had published an argument for the Constitution entitled "The New Roof." The procession's "Federal Edifice" was the physical embodiment of Hopkinson's literary image. Russell Frank Weigley, *Philadelphia: A 300-Year History* (New York, 1982), 164–66.

5. Diary of Charles Willson Peale, June 30–July 4, 1788, American Philosophical Society (APS).

6. Benjamin Rush to Elias Boudinot(?) July 9, 1788, L. H. Butterfield, ed., *Letters of Benjamin Rush* (Princeton, N.J., 1951), 1:473. Rush is the author of the "anonymous" letter printed in the Philadelphia newspapers, and subsequently included in Hopkinson's account. Apparently this anonymity was at Rush's request (see letter to Jeremy Belknap, July 15, 1788, ibid., 1:478).

7. Charles Biddle, *The Autobiography of Charles Biddle, Vice-President of the Supreme Executive Council of Pennsylvania* (Philadelphia, 1853), 226.

8. One of these banners, that of the carpenters, is on display at Carpenters Hall, Philadelphia. Another has only recently come to light. In 1988, almost exactly two hundred years after its first use, the white silk banner carried by the tobacconists was discovered in Vermont. Matching Hopkinson's detailed description almost perfectly, the five-foot-square flag, still in good condition, has been professionally conserved and is on display at the Library Company of Philadelphia.

9. Diary of Charles Willson Peale, July 1, 1788.

10. Biddle, *Autobiography,* 227. Many others also found the oration anticlimactic: "Of the enormous multitude which on all sides surrounded the temple of liberty, but few could distinctly hear and understand the speaker. My location was such, that

not many of his words were audible. I therefore did not wait for his peroration; but after looking and listening for some time, followed the example of many others, and made for my home." Ashbel Green, *The Life of Ashbel Green* (New York, 1849), 176.

11. Thomas Clifford Jr. to ——, Philadelphia, July 11, 1788. Clifford Papers 8:280, Historical Society of Pennsylvania (HSP).

12. Rush to Boudinot(?) July 9, 1788, Butterfield, *Letters of Benjamin Rush*, 1:470.

13. Anna Clifford to Sarah Clifford, Philadelphia, July 11, 1788, Clifford Papers, 8:279, HSP.

14. Diary of Nathaniel R. Snowden, July 4, 1788, HSP.

15. Green, *The Life of Ashbel Green*, 175–76.

16. Rush to Boudinot(?) July 9, 1788, Butterfield, *Letters of Benjamin Rush*, 1:470 (my emphasis).

17. The "ship of state" was a popular device in other federal processions as well, featuring prominently in those of Boston and New York.

18. Hopkinson, *Account of the Grand Federal Procession*, 18.

19. Hopkinson, *Account of the Grand Federal Procession*, 17, 18; Rush to Boudinot(?) July 9, 1788, Butterfield, *Letters of Benjamin Rush*, 1:474.

20. Hopkinson, *Account of the Grand Federal Procession*, 9–10; *Independent Chronicle*, July 3, 1788; *Pennsylvania Gazette*, July 9, 1788; Diary of Charles Willson Peale, July 4, 1788.

21. Hopkinson, *Account of the Grand Federal Procession*, 8.

22. Rush to Boudinot(?) July 9, 1788, Butterfield, *Letters of Benjamin Rush*, 1:471.

23. Rush to Boudinot(?) July 9, 1788, Butterfield, *Letters of Benjamin Rush*, 1:470–74.

24. Green, *Life of Ashbel Green*, 176; Diary of Nathaniel R. Snowden, July 4, 1788.

25. Rush to Boudinot(?) July 9, 1788, Butterfield, *Letters of Benjamin Rush*, 1:472.

26. Rush to Boudinot(?) July 9, 1788, Butterfield, *Letters of Benjamin Rush*, 1:474.

27. Sally F. Moore and Barbara G. Myerhoff, introduction to *Secular Ritual*, ed. Sally F. Moore and Barbara G. Myerhoff (Amsterdam, 1977), 5.

28. Rush to Boudinot(?) July 9, 1788, Butterfield, *Letters of Benjamin Rush*, 1:471.

29. Rush to Boudinot(?) July 9, 1788, Butterfield, *Letters of Benjamin Rush*, 1:473. Elizabeth Drinker was one Philadelphia Quaker who thought militia parades, especially on Independence Day, "rediculous." Elaine Forman Crane, ed., *The Diary of Elizabeth Drinker* (Boston, 1991), 2:1050, 1424; 3:1664.

30. Rush to Boudinot(?) July 9, 1788, Butterfield, *Letters of Benjamin Rush*, 1:474.

31. Rush to Boudinot(?) July 9, 1788, Butterfield, *Letters of Benjamin Rush*, 1:476.

32. Proctor, *Enacting Political Culture*, 5.

33. Victor Turner, "Liminality and the Performative Genres," in *Rite, Drama, Festival, Spectacle: Rehearsals Toward a Theory of Cultural Performance*, ed. John J. MacAloon (Philadelphia, 1984), 22.

34. Moore and Myerhoff, introduction to *Secular Ritual*, 24 (my emphasis).

35. Ronald L. Grimes, *Beginnings in Ritual Studies* (Lanham, Md., 1982), 42, 130.

36. Proctor, *Enacting Political Culture*, 6.

37. *Independent Gazetteer*, July 2 and 9, 1791.

38. John R. Howe Jr., "Republican Thought and the Violence of the 1790s," *American Quarterly* 19 (1967): 153.

39. Howe, "Republican Thought and the Violence of the 1790s," 150.

40. Thomas Jefferson to Edward Rutledge, June 24, 1797. Quoted in Howe, "Republican Thought and the Violence of the 1790s," 148.

41. *Independent Chronicle*, July 7, 1791; installments appeared passim through July.

42. *Independent Gazetteer*, July 7, 1792.

43. *Independent Chronicle*, July 7, 1791.

44. *Independent Gazetteer*, July 9, 1791.

45. *Independent Chronicle*, July 4, 1793 (emphasis in original).

46. *State Gazette of South Carolina*, July 8, 1793.

47. *Independent Chronicle*, July 5, 1794. Similar convictions pervade the papers and correspondence of Republicans. See Philip S. Foner, ed., *The Democratic-Republican Societies, 1790–1800: A Documentary Sourcebook of Constitutions, Declarations, Addresses, Resolutions, and Toasts* (Westport, Conn., 1976).

48. David Ramsey, *An Oration, delivered on the Anniversary of American Independence, July 4, 1794, in St. Michael's Church, to the Inhabitants of Charleston, South Carolina* (London, 1795), 27.

49. *Independent Chronicle*, July 5, 1792.

50. *Independent Gazetteer*, July 9, 1794.

51. *Boston Gazette*, July 14, 1794.

52. *Pennsylvania Gazette*, July 10, 1793.

53. *Gazette of the United States*, July 7, 1794.

54. Richard G. Miller analyzes the erosion of Federalist power in Philadelphia in *Philadelphia—The Federalist City: A Study of Urban Politics, 1789–1801* (Port Washington, N.Y., 1976).

55. *Gazette of the United States*, July 8, 1794.

56. George C. Rogers, Jr., *Charleston in the Age of the Pinckneys* (Norman, Okla., 1969), 117–19; Rachel N. Klein, *Unification of a Slave State: The Rise of the Planter Class in the South Carolina Backcountry, 1760–1808* (Chapel Hill, N.C., 1990), 123.

57. The erosion of low-country hegemony and the growth of backcountry political power is the subject of Rachel N. Klein, *Unification of a Slave State*. Mark Kaplanoff agrees that during the early national period the division between the low-country and backcountry interests was "the paramount fact of Carolinian political life." Mark D. Kaplanoff, "How Federalist was South Carolina in 1787–1788?" in *The Meaning of South Carolina History: Essays in Honor of George C. Rogers, Jr*, ed. David R. Chestnutt and Clyde N. Wilson (Columbia, S.C., 1991), 70.

58. On the Democratic-Republican coalition, their composition, and their activity, see Richard Walsh, *Charleston's Sons of Liberty: A Study of the Artisans, 1763–1789* (Columbia, S.C., 1968), 117; Foner, *The Democratic-Republican Societies,* 9, 38, and passim; Klein, *Unification of a Slave State,* 204; Rogers, *Charleston in the Age of the Pinckneys,* 119; and Eugene Perry Link, *The Democratic-Republican Societies, 1790–1800* (Morningside Heights, N.Y., 1942), 70–71, 126. For the Charleston city delegates' stand on debtor relief see Kaplanoff, "How Federalist was South Carolina in 1787–1788?" 71.

59. Catherine L. Albanese, *Sons of the Fathers: The Civil Religion of the American Revolution* (Philadelphia, 1976), 206.

60. Albanese, *Sons of the Fathers,* 210.

61. Rush to Boudinot(?) July 9, 1788, Butterfield, *Letters of Benjamin Rush,* 1:475.

62. For example, see *Gazette of the United States,* July 1, 1789.

63. *Columbian Centinel,* June 28 and July 2, 1794. The editors of the paper were not convinced of the anonymity of the perpetrators. Obviously suspicious of Adams's official outrage, they referred to the disturbances as having been directed by "persons *perhaps* unknown."

64. Frank Monaghan, *John Jay, Defender of Liberty* (New York, 1935), 388.

65. Crane, *The Diary of Elizabeth Drinker,* 1:571.

66. *Independent Gazetteer,* July 8, 1795.

67. Weigley, *Philadelphia: A 300-Year History,* 193.

68. *Gazette of the United States,* July 3, 1795.

69. *Aurora General Advertiser* [hereafter *Aurora*], July 7, 10, 1795. A French agent reported to his Committee of Safety: "It is enough to read the series of toasts proposed in those two cities [Philadelphia and Baltimore] to judge of the impression made on public opinion by the treaty." Quoted in Charles H. Sherril, ed., *French Memoirs of Eighteenth-Century America* (1915; reprint, New York, 1971), 89.

70. *Independent Gazetteer,* July 8, 1795.

71. The preceding account was pieced together from Monaghan, *John Jay,* 391–92; *Independent Gazetteer,* July 8, 1795; Crane, *Diary of Elizabeth Drinker,* 1:699; Weigley, *Philadelphia: A 300-Year History,* 193. For two very different contemporary versions of the same incident, see *Gazette of the United States,* July 7 and 17, 1795.

72. Monaghan, *John Jay,* 392.

73. *Independent Chronicle,* July 8, 1795.

74. *Aurora,* July 10, 1797.

75. *Gazette of the United States,* July 3 and 5, 1798; Charles Warren, "Fourth of July Myths," *William and Mary Quarterly* 2, no. 3 (July 1945): 261.

76. *Independent Chronicle,* July 5, 1796.

77. *Boston Gazette,* July 4, 1796.

78. Lynn Hunt, *Politics, Culture, and Class in the French Revolution* (Berkeley and Los Angeles, 1984), 53.

79. Raymond Firth, *Symbols: Public and Private* (Ithaca, N.Y., 1973), 65–66.

80. Hunt, *Politics, Culture, and Class*, 24.

81. On "liberty caps" see James Epstein's excellent essay "Understanding the Cap of Liberty: Symbolic Practice and Social Conflict in Early Nineteenth-Century England," *Past and Present* 122 (February 1989): 75–118. On "liberty trees" see Arthur Schlesinger, "Liberty Tree: A Genealogy," *New England Quarterly* 26 (December 1952): 435–58; Robert P. Hay, "The Liberty Tree: A Symbol for American Patriots," *Quarterly Journal of Speech* 55 (1969): 414–24; and Peter Shaw, *American Patriots and the Rituals of Revolution* (Cambridge, Mass., 1981).

82. Quoted in Albanese, *Sons of the Fathers*, 200–201.

83. *Pennsylvania Gazette*, July 10, 1793.

84. *Boston Gazette*, July 4, 1796.

85. Hunt, *Politics, Culture, and Class*, 55.

86. *Columbian Centinel,* July 4 and 7, 1798; *Independent Chronicle,* July 2, 5–9, and 7, 1798; emphasis in original.

87. Charleston was apparently also seething over the cockade issue; an appeal in a newspaper on July 4 of that year urged "THE SOUTH CAROLINA YOUTH . . . particularly . . . to mount the American Cockade this day." It was not to be a surrender of principles, explained the obviously concerned writer, but rather "as a token of unanimity in their attachment to the independence purchased for them by the blood of their ancestors." The politics of the writer are unclear, but the purpose of the notice was obviously to avoid the sort of confrontation that occurred in Boston. *State Gazette of South Carolina,* July 4, 1798.

88. Epstein, "Understanding the Cap of Liberty," 81.

89. For the symbolic import of the tricolor cockade in France, see Hunt, *Politics, Culture, and Class*, 57–58.

90. Firth, *Symbols: Public and Private*, 339, 356.

91. Hunt, *Politics, Culture, and Class*, 53.

92. Epstein, "Understanding the Cap of Liberty," 117.

4

OBSERVING THE FOURTH

1. Diary of Thomas F. Pleasant, Historical Society of Pennsylvania (HSP).

2. Kenneth Roberts and Anna B. Roberts, eds. and trans., *Moreau de St. Mery's American Journey* (New York, 1947), 336.

3. *Independent Gazetteer*, July 2, 1791.

4. *Boston Gazette*, July 4, 1796; *Gazette of the United States* July 7, 1792, July 6, 1802; *Aurora*, July 10, 1797.

5. *Gazette of the United States*, July 7, 1794.

6. *City Gazette*, July 1, 1797.

7. William L. Smith, *An Oration, delivered in St. Philip's Church, before the Inhabitants of*

Charleston, South Carolina, on the Fourth of July, 1796, in Commemoration of American Independence (Charleston, 1796), 22; *Aurora*, July 7, 1802.

8. *Boston Gazette*, July 3, 1806.

9. *Independent Chronicle*, July 3, 1803.

10. *Boston Gazette*, July 3, 1806.

11. *Boston Gazette*, July 9, 1801.

12. *Boston Gazette*, July 3, 1806.

13. Roberts and Roberts, *Moreau de St. Mery's American Journey*, 336.

14. Elaine Forman Crane, *The Diary of Elizabeth Drinker* (Boston, 1991), 2:819.

15. Crane, *The Diary of Elizabeth Drinker*, 1:699.

16. *Columbian Centinel*, July 7, 1802.

17. *Gazette of the United States*, July 7, 1792.

18. The *Columbian Herald* for July 7, 1794, reported some 800 men in uniform; the 1790 census returns for Charleston indicate a total of 2,810 free white males residing in the city.

19. "Diary of Edward Hooker, 1805–1808," *Annual Report of the American Historical Association for the year 1896* (Washington, 1897), 890–91. See also *Charleston Courier*, July 3, 1806, for a hilarious lampoon of an Independence Day militia gathering submitted by "Toby Filpot."

20. *Independent Chronicle*, July 2 and 8, 1802.

21. *Boston Gazette*, July 6, 1818; *Independent Chronicle*, July 8, 1818.

22. Susan G. Davis, *Parades and Power: Street Theater in Nineteenth-Century Philadelphia* (Berkeley and Los Angeles, 1986), 126.

23. Diary of George Nelson, July 5, 1790, HSP.

24. Diary of John Frisker, July 4, 1814, HSP.

25. Diary of Elizabeth Cranch, passim, Massachusetts Historical Society (MHS).

26. Diary of Charles Willson Peale, July 4, 1804, American Philosophical Library (APS). It is interesting that Peale should condemn country people for celebrating the Fourth; he seems to have felt that Independence Day was strictly an urban holiday, and that there was something wrong in interrupting the agrarian work cycle.

27. Crane, *The Diary of Elizabeth Drinker*, 2:1530.

28. Focusing on a later period in Philadelphia history, Susan Davis received the impression that the custom of leaving the city on July 4 began in the 1820s. Davis, *Parades and Power*, 44.

29. Diary of George Nelson, July 5, 1790, HSP.

30. *Pennsylvania Gazette*, July 4, 1792.

31. *Pennsylvania Gazette*, July 10, 1793.

32. *Aurora*, July 1, 1806.

33. Diary of Nathaniel Snowden, July 4, 1799; July 4, 1801; July 5, 1802, HSP.

34. "A Frenchman Visits Charleston, 1817," *South Carolina Historical and Geneological Magazine* 49, no. 3 (July 1948): 136, 145.

35. My assessment of Boston's celebration pattern is inferred in part from the *lack* of country entertainments mentioned or advertised in the Boston papers, in contrast with Philadelphia's. Direct evidence is scattered but tends to confirm this impression. For example, a newspaper advertisement offered a reward for the return of a wallet lost on the Fourth "between Chelsea Bridge and the Common." The direction of movement indicated implies that the owner was an out-of-towner, riding or walking into Boston for the festivities. *Boston Gazette,* July 6, 1809. See also the account of the fireworks display in *Boston Gazette,* July 8, 1805.

36. Gary B. Nash, *Forging Freedom: The Formation of Philadelphia's Black Community, 1720–1840* (Cambridge, Mass., 1988), 143.

37. Walter Muir Whitehall, *Boston: A Topographical History* (Cambridge, Mass., 1979), 73–74. Charleston's growth rate was the smallest of the three, from 16,359 to 23,239 to 25,356 in those same years.

38. Benjamin Rush to Mrs. (Julia) Rush, July 7, 1809, L. H. Butterfield, ed., *Letters of Benjamin Rush* (Princeton, N.J., 1951), 2:1006.

39. Crane, *The Diary of Elizabeth Drinker,* 2:1424.

40. Sarah Wister to Owen Jones, July 4, 1797, Kathryn Zabelle Derounian, ed., *The Journal and Occasional Writings of Sarah Wister* (Cranbury, N.J., 1987), n.p.

41. Letter of William Read to Jacob Read, July 8, 1796, G. E. French Papers, MHS.

42. *Independent Chronicle,* July 6, 1795, and July 8, 1818.

43. *Aurora,* July 4, 1808; *Independent Gazetteer,* July 9, 1785.

44. *City Gazette,* July 6, 1797; *Columbian Centinel,* July 4, 1801; *Charleston Courier,* July 4, 1820.

45. *Independent Chronicle,* July 3, 1806; *Boston Gazette,* July 8, 1805.

46. *Independent Chronicle,* July 12, 1791.

47. *Aurora,* July 1, 1801.

48. *Charleston Courier,* July 4, 1820.

49. *Independent Chronicle,* July 12, 1791; *Charleston Courier,* July 4, 1804.

50. *Aurora,* July 4, 1799, July 3, 1800.

51. *Boston Gazette,* July 4, 1814; *City Gazette,* July 1, 1799. An unimpressed French visitor referred to Charleston's Vauxhall on Broad Street as "the pompous name given to an enclosure of half an acre which comprises a cafe, baths and several square fathoms of grass plots forming the public garden." "A Frenchman Visits Charleston, 1817," 147. See also Harold D. Eberlein and Cortlandt V. Hubbard, "The American 'Vauxhall' of the Federalist Era," *Pennsylvania Magazine of History and Biography* 68 (1944): 150–74.

52. For examples see *Independent Chronicle,* July 4, 1799, July 4, 1803.

53. Crane, *Diary of Elizabeth Drinker,* 2:1050.

54. *Southern Patriot*, July 5, 1817.

55. Diary of Nathaniel Snowden, July 4, 1799; *Charleston Courier*, July 1, 1805; Billy G. Smith and Susan E. Clepp, "The Records of Gloria Dei Church: Burials, 1800–1804," *Pennsylvania History* 53 (1986): 65.

56. *Independent Chronicle*, July 2, 1798 (the flavors were strawberry, cherry, raspberry, and apple); *Charleston Courier*, July 4, 1806.

57. *Aurora*, July 3, 1804, and July 4, 1817.

58. *City Gazette*, July 3, 1788; *Charleston Courier*, July 4, 1806, and July 4, 1808. See also *South Carolina State Gazette*, July 3, 1802, for an advertisement offering "GREEN TURTLE For the Festival on Monday next."

59. Instead of attending an oration, for example, young Ralph Izard wrote from Boston to his mother that "We, the officers of the Navy, dined with Commodore Preble on the Fourth of July and afterwards went to the play." Ralph Izard to Alice Izard, July 6, 1803, Ralph Izard Family Letters, in Cheves-Middleton Papers, South Carolina Historical Society.

60. *Boston Gazette*, July 12, 1779.

61. *Pennsylvania Gazette*, July 23, 1794.

62. Thomas Clark Pollock, *The Philadelphia Theater in the Eighteenth Century* (Philadelphia, 1933), 48–49; George C. Rogers Jr., *Charleston in the Age of the Pinckneys* (Norman, Okla., 1969), 110–11. On the subject of theater in the early republic see Susan L. Porter, *With an Air Debonair: Musical Theater in America, 1785–1815* (Washington, D.C., 1991).

63. *Independent Chronicle*, July 4, 1799, and July 3, 1797.

64. "A Frenchman Visits Charleston, 1817," 147, 153.

65. *Aurora*, July 2, 1808.

66. *Aurora*, July 3, 1802. See also the July 4, 1823, issue of the *Charleston Courier* for a description of "The Patriotic Effusion" called "The Standard of Liberty," and "a patriotic piece, never performed here . . . [called] "The Festival, or, The Fourth of July," featuring such characters as "fearnought," "Genius of Columbia," "Peace," "Plenty," and "Commerce."

67. This excerpt from the "production of Mrs Marriott" is printed in the *Columbian Herald*, July 4, 1794. I have been unable to find any other part of the script.

68. John Burke, *Bunker-Hill; or the Death of General Warren. An Historic Tragedy in Five Acts* (New York, 1797). Hereafter, page numbers refer to this edition of the script.

69. In politically charged times, however, orations frequently descended to loud polemic; one listener referred to a Springfield, Massachusetts, event as a "roration." B. Pynchon to Margeret Orne, July 14, 1796, Cushing-Orne Papers, MHS. My thanks to Donna Curtin for this citation.

70. *Boston Gazette*, July 4, 1803.

71. Charles Pythian-Adams, "Ceremony and the Citizen: The Communal Year at Coventry, 1450–1550," in *Crisis and Order in English Towns 1500–1700: Essays in Urban History*, ed. Peter Clark and Paul Slack (London, 1972), 58.

72. Diary of Charles Willson Peale, July 3, 1801, APS.

73. *Independent Gazetteer,* July 9, 1785.

74. *Boston Gazette,* June 30, 1803.

75. *South Carolina Gazette and General Advertiser,* July 5, 1783, and July 3, 1784. A Charlestonian in 1866 remarked that the city's lack of an adequate water supply had still not been addressed, and was responsible for the severity of Charleston's frequent fires since 1796. "The people," he concluded, "are partly to blame for this supineness." J. N. Cardozo, *Reminiscences of Charleston* (Charleston, 1866), 29.

76. *The By-Laws and Orders of the Town of Boston* (Boston, 1801), 52; *Aurora,* July 6, 1803; *Ordinances of the City Council of Charleston, in the State of South Carolina, Passed since the 28th of October, 1801* (Charleston, 1804), 419.

77. *Pennsylvania Gazette,* July 10, 1793.

78. *Boston Gazette,* July 3, 1809, and July 2, 1812.

79. *Reports of the Records Commissioners of the City of Boston: Selectmen's Minutes from 1799 to and Including 1810* (Boston, 1904), 305. Charleston's city council also demanded that "squibs, crackers or other fire-works" be used only in officially designated places, with fines for noncompliance two and a half times greater than Boston's; see *Ordinances . . . Passed since the 28th of October, 1801,* 419.

80. *Columbian Centinel,* July 7, 1810.

81. Records of Old Swedes Church (Gloria Dei): Burial Records, 1750–1831, 349, HSP.

82. Crane, *Diary of Elizabeth Drinker,* 2:1424, 1050.

83. *Aurora,* July 2, 1805.

84. William Duane, ed. *Extracts from the Diary of Christopher Marshall, Kept in Philadelphia and Lancaster During the American Revolution, 1774–1781* (Albany, N.Y., 1877), 251.

85. *Porcupine's Gazette,* July 5, 1798.

86. H. E. Scudder, ed., *Recollections of Samuel Breck with Passages from his Note-Books, 1771–1862* (Philadelphia, 1877), 91.

87. Records of Old Swedes Church (Gloria Dei): Burial Records, 1750–1831, 362, 395, 496, HSP.

88. Crane, *Diary of Elizabeth Drinker,* 2:1051; 3:2052.

89. *Independent Gazetteer,* July 9, 1785.

90. Raymond A. Mohl, ed., " 'The Grand Fabric of Republicanism': A Scotsman Describes South Carolina," *South Carolina Historical Magazine* 71 (July 1970): 183; Johan David Schoepf, *Travels in the Confederation,* trans. Alfred J. Morrison (1911; reprint New York, 1968), 2:217–18; "A Frenchman Visits Charleston, 1817," *South Carolina Historical and Geneological Magazine* 49 (July 1948): 149.

91. "Diary of Edward Hooker, 1805–1808," 890; "Nefarious Wretches, Insidious Villains, and Evil-Minded Persons: Urban Crime in Charleston's *City Gazette,* in 1788," *South Carolina Historical Magazine* 88, no. 3 (July 1987): 161.

92. *Southern Patriot,* July 5, 1816.

93. *Charleston Courier,* July 7, 1807.

94. *Independent Chronicle,* July 11, 1799; July 6 and 7, 1807; July 9, 1810.

95. Crane, *Diary of Elizabeth Drinker,* 2:1050. John Hall concluded that Charleston's pick-pockets were very active on public occasions also; see Hall, "Nefarious Wretches," 164.

96. *Boston Gazette,* July 9, 1798.

97. *Aurora,* July 6 and 7, 1815.

98. *Charleston Courier,* July 7, 1812.

99. *Boston Gazette,* July 7, 1806.

100. *Boston Gazette,* July 4, 1805; *Independent Chronicle,* July 8, 1805.

101. Crane, *Diary of Elizabeth Drinker,* 1:314.

102. *Pennsylvania Gazette,* July 4, 1787; *Aurora,* July 6, 1805, and July 4, 1807. A Charleston slave also used the distractions of July 4 to run away; see *Charleston Courier,* July 6, 1808.

103. *Reports of the Records Commissioners of the City of Boston: Selectmen's Minutes from 1787 through 1798* (Boston, 1896), 333; *Reports of the Records Commissioners of the City of Boston: Selectmen's Minutes from 1799 to and Including 1810* (Boston, 1904), 72, 187; *Independent Chronicle,* July 4, 1805, July 8, 1784, July 6, 1786; *Boston Gazette,* July 8, 1805.

104. Howard O. Sprogle, *The Philadelphia Police, Past and Present* (Philadelphia, 1887), 70–73.

105. Hall, "Nefarious Wretches," 158.

106. David R. Chestnutt et al., eds., *The Papers of Henry Laurens* (Columbia, S.C.), 13:551 and note.

107. *Southern Patriot,* July 5, 1816.

108. Crane, *Diary of Elizabeth Drinker,* 1:459, 699, 3:1664, 1944.

109. Benjamin Rush to son James, July 5, 1810, Butterfield, *Letters of Benjamin Rush,* 2:1056.

110. Christine Stansell, *City of Women: Sex and Class in New York, 1789–1860* (New York, 1986), 22.

111. Davis, *Parades and Power,* 47; Mary P. Ryan, *Women in Public: Between Banners and Ballots, 1825–1880* (Baltimore, Md., 1990), 16; James Epstein, "Understanding the Cap of Liberty: Symbolic Practice and Social Conflict in Early Nineteenth-Century England," *Past and Present* 122 (February 1989): 103.

112. Davis, *Parades and Power,* 119; *Aurora,* July 11, 1800. James Epstein observed similar use of white garments by women in contemporary England. White was "a self-reflective symbol of feminine purity simultaneously alluding to the purity of the radical cause" in which they were engaged. Epstein, "Understanding the Cap of Liberty," 96.

113. *Independent Gazetteer,* July 2, 1791.

114. *Aurora,* July 6, 1805; *Boston Gazette,* July 4, 1796.

115. Davis, *Parades and Power*, 190. David Glassberg deftly puts his finger on the dilemma of women aspiring to anything more than token inclusion in the rites of Independence Day. Referring to the characteristics of modern patriotism in general, he argues that "defining sacrifice in war as the principal patriotic act leaves little space for women in the ritual construction of the nation-state and, by implication, national political life." David Glassberg, "Patriotism from the Ground Up," *Reviews in American History* 22, no. 1 (March 1993): 2.

116. *Boston Gazette*, July 9, 1787; *Independent Chronicle*, July 8, 1805.

117. Janson, *The Stranger in America*, 25.

118. Diary of Charles Willson Peale, July 4, 1804, APS.

119. Crane, *The Diary of Elizabeth Drinker*, 2:1050.

120. Diary of William Wood Thackera, July 4, 1814, HSP.

121. *Charleston Courier*, July 1, 1805.

122. *Independent Gazetteer*, July 3, 1790; *Gazette of the United States*, July 6, 1791.

123. *Aurora*, July 7, 1801.

124. *Columbian Herald*, July 3, 1795.

125. *Aurora*, July 8, 1825.

126. James Epstein noticed similar rituals and ritual import among women supporting reform movements in England. Epstein, "Understanding the Cap of Liberty," 102, 105.

127. *State Gazette of South Carolina*, July 6, 1793.

128. *Independent Chronicle*, July 4, 1805; *Independent Gazetteer*, July 11, 1810.

129. *Independent Chronicle*, July 4, 1805.

130. *Boston Gazette*, July 4, 1808, July 4, 1811, July 3, 1815.

131. *Charleston Courier*, July 2, 1807.

132. *Boston Gazette*, July 9, 1787. Mary Ryan avers that civic authorities did not encourage female participation or set aside specific places for them at public events until after 1840, when such practices coincided with the American nativistic agenda. This is clearly not the case. Ryan, *Women in Public*, 31–32.

133. *Aurora*, July 6, 1805.

134. On misogyny and republican ideology, see Stansell, *City of Women*, 20–24.

135. *Independent Gazetteer*, July 11, 1810; *Independent Chronicle*, July 12, 1787.

136. *Independent Chronicle*, July 8, 1811.

137. *Aurora*, July 7, 1804.

138. *Aurora*, July 5, 1811.

139. William L. Smith, *An Oration*, 9.

140. Nash, *Forging Freedom*, 114, 135. See also Billy G. Smith, *"The Lower Sort": Philadelphia's Laboring Poor, 1750–1800* (Ithaca, N.Y., 1990), 193.

141. For Election Week activities see Shane White, " 'It Was a Proud Day': African

Americans, Festivals, and Parades in the North, 1741–1834," *Journal of American History* 81, no. 1 (June 1994): 13–50.

142. Diary of Nathan Webb, July 5, 1790, MHS.

143. *Boston Gazette*, July 6, 1809; *Independent Chronicle*, July 9, 1810; *Boston Gazette*, July 3, 1809.

144. Terrence Tirowen, His Posthumous Papers, from letter date 1840 by compiler, HSP.

145. Nash, *Forging Freedom*, 157, 173; Smith, *"The Lower Sort,"* 165.

146. Nash, *Forging Freedom*, 176–77. Nash is not certain if the second incident occurred in 1805 or slightly later.

147. Alice Morse Earle, *Customs and Fashions in Old New England* (New York, 1899), 226.

148. Sol Smith quoted in White, " 'It Was a Proud Day,' " 17.

149. Prince Hall, *A Charge, Delivered to the African Lodge at Menotomy* (Boston, 1797). I am indebted to Mike Pardee for this citation.

150. Nash, *Forging Freedom*, 181.

151. Nash, *Forging Freedom*, 165–69, 101.

152. Nash, *Forging Freedom*, 189.

153. *Independent Chronicle*, July 10 and 19, 1808; July 13, 1812; Thomas Gray, *A Sermon Delivered in Boston before the African Society on the Fourteenth Day of July, 1818, the Anniversary of the Abolition of the Slave Trade* (Boston, 1818), frontispiece.

154. "Diary of Edward Hooker, 1805–1808," *Annual Report of the American Historical Association for the Year 1896* (Washington, D.C., 1897), 890. The dinner was in Columbia, S.C.

155. *Charleston Courier*, July 9, 1806.

156. Rachel N. Klein, *Unification of a Slave State: The Rise of the Planter Class in the South Carolina Backcountry, 1760–1808* (Chapel Hill, N.C., 1990), 150.

157. Donald J. Senese, "The Free Negro and the South Carolina Courts, 1790–1860," *South Carolina Historical and Geneological Magazine* 68 (July 1967): 140, 142.

158. Richard Walsh, *Charleston's Sons of Liberty: A Study of the Artisans, 1763–1789* (Columbia, S.C., 1968), 24.

159. Rogers, Jr., *Charleston in the Age of the Pinckneys*, 142; Peter Wood, *Black Majority: Negroes in Colonial South Carolina from 1670 through the Stono Rebellion* (New York, 1974).

160. Rogers, Jr., *Charleston in the Age of the Pinckneys*, 131; Klein, *Unification of a Slave State*, 211.

161. Rogers, Jr., *Charleston in the Age of the Pinckneys*, 28.

162. Cardozo, *Reminiscences of Charleston*, 28.

163. *South Carolina State Gazette*, July 6 and 7, 1798; *Charleston Courier*, July 6, 1820. See also *Charleston Courier*, July 7, 1819; and William Read to Jacob Read, July 8, 1796, French Papers.

164. William L. Smith, *An Oration, . . . 1796*, 39. Smith was referring to the great fire that

had destroyed five hundred houses only three weeks before. That fire may have been the work of thieves using the fire as a distraction from their activities; see William Read to Jacob Read, July 8, 1796, French Papers. It is possible that other incidents of arson on Independence Day were intended to cover similar crimes, but the accounts I have seen do not suggest it. Whatever the motives, I believe that the *effect* of these intentionally set fires was to deepen the white suspicion of city blacks.

165. *Ordinances of the City Council of Charleston, in the State of South Carolina, Passed since the Incorporation of the City* (Charleston, 1802), 67–68, 224; *Ordinances of the City Council of Charleston, in the State of South Carolina, Passed between the 24th Day of September, 1804, and the 1st Day of September, 1807* (Charleston, 1807), 396–97.

166. Mohl, ed., " 'The Grand Fabric of Republicanism,' " 173; "A Frenchman Visits Charleston, 1817," 141 n; For punishments see *Ordinances . . . Passed since the Incorporation of the City*, 224; *Ordinances . . . Passed since the 28th of October, 1801*, 419; *Ordinances . . . 1807*, 405.

167. "Nefarious Wretches, Insidious Villains, and Evil-Minded Persons," 159; Mohl, ed., " 'The Grand Fabric of Republicanism,' " 188.

168. Charleston's court and police records for this period do not survive, but neither the newspapers nor travelers' accounts suggest that the city was unusual in this regard. In fact, one observer felt safe in Charleston at night specifically because blacks were kept off the streets—a testament not only to the effectiveness of the City Guard, but to expectations of where crime was likely to come from. "A Frenchman Visits Charleston, 1817," 141.

169. George Fenwick Jones, "The 1780 Siege of Charleston as Experienced by a Hessian Officer," *South Carolina Historical Magazine* 88, no. 2 (April 1967): 72.

170. *City Gazette*, July 1, 1799.

171. There were, however, a number of private sales that coincided with July 4; see for example *City Gazette*, July 4, 1797.

172. "Diary of Edward Hooker," 904.

173. Nash, *Forging Freedom*, 176.

174. Diary of Thomas F. Pleasant, July 4, 1815, and July 4, 1817, HSP; The Diary of Samuel Breck, July 4, 1815, July 4, 1817, and July 4, 1818, HSP.

175. *Aurora*, July 5, 1811.

176. Pythian-Adams, "Ceremony and the Citizen," 68.

5

"EVEN TO BLOOD"

1. Rachel N. Klein traces the evolution of low-country/backcountry political relations in *Unification of a Slave State: The Rise of the Planter Class in the South Carolina Backcountry, 1760–1808* (Chapel Hill, N.C., 1990); see also George C. Rogers Jr., *Charleston in the Age of the Pinckneys* (Norman, Okla., 1969).

2. *Boston Town Records, 1778–1783*, A Report of the Record Commissioners of the City of Boston (Boston, 1895), 26:305.

3. This was in 1795, when George Blake was hailed as a "truly Republican young gentleman," in whom many thought they recognized "a *Hancock, Warren,* and other patriots of '75." *Independent Chronicle,* July 6, 1795.

4. *Independent Chronicle,* July 7, 1798.

5. *Independent Chronicle,* July 12, 1802.

6. *Independent Chronicle,* July 5 and 8, 1802.

7. *Independent Chronicle,* July 8, 1802.

8. *Independent Chronicle,* July 4, 1803, and July 5, 1804.

9. *Independent Chronicle,* July 8, 1805.

10. Records of the Washington Society, Boston. Massachusetts Historical Society, entry for July 4, 1805; *Independent Chronicle,* July 8, 1805.

11. *Columbian Centinel,* July 7, 1802; *Boston Gazette,* July 8, 1802; emphasis in original.

12. *Independent Chronicle,* July 7, 1803.

13. *Independent Chronicle,* July 3, 1806, and July 8, 1802.

14. Moses Coit Tyler, *Literary History of the American Revolution* (New York, 1897), 1:521.

15. Philip F. Detweiler, "The Changing Reputation of the Declaration of Independence: The First Fifty Years," *William and Mary Quarterly* 19 (October 1962): 568–69.

16. *Boston Gazette,* July 16, 1801.

17. *Columbian Centinel,* June 25, July 6 and 16, 1803.

18. *Independent Chronicle,* July 8, 1802.

19. *Independent Chronicle,* July 7, 1803.

20. *Independent Chronicle,* July 5, 1804.

21. *Columbian Centinel,* July 6, 1811; emphasis in original.

22. See beginning of Chapter 1.

23. *Boston Gazette,* July 4, 1805. This pathetic attempt to compete with the Republicans' appropriation of the Declaration made no appreciable impression on Fourth of July customs, however.

24. *Boston Gazette,* July 7, 1803.

25. Diary of William Plumer, June 5, 1806. Quoted in David Hackett Fisher, *The Revolution of American Conservatism* (New York, 1965), 183.

26. *Independent Chronicle,* June 30, 1806; July 9, 1810.

27. *Independent Chronicle,* July 9, 1810.

28. *Independent Chronicle,* July 4 and 10, 1808.

29. *Independent Chronicle,* July 9, 1810; July 6, 1809.

30. *Selectmen's Minutes, 1799–1810,* 341.

31. Memoirs of John Pierce, 1803–49, entry for July 4, 1808, Massachusetts Historical Society.

32. *Selectmen's Minutes, 1799–1810,* 440.

33. *Independent Chronicle*, July 3 and 6, 1809. *Columbian Centinel*, July 5, 1809.

34. *Independent Chronicle*, July 5 and 9, 1810; July 8, 1811.

35. Quoted in E. Digby Baltzell, *Puritan Boston and Quaker Philadelphia: Two Protestant Ethics and the Spirit of Class Authority and Leadership* (New York, 1979), 199. David Hackett Fischer describes the "new Federalists" of post-1800 in *The Revolution of American Conservatism*.

36. *Columbian Centinel*, July 6, 1811.

37. *Columbian Centinel*, July 3, 1811.

38. *Columbian Centinel*, July 5 and 7, 1810.

39. *Columbian Centinel*, July 5, 1802.

40. *Columbian Centinel*, July 3, 1801.

41. *Independent Chronicle*, July 5, 1802.

42. Russell Frank Weigly, *Philadelphia: A 300-Year History* (New York, 1982), 202–3, 222.

43. *Aurora*, July 4, 1800.

44. *Aurora*, July 7, 1800.

45. *Gazette of the United States*, July 2 and 3, 1800; *Aurora*, July 7, 8, and 9, 1800.

46. *Aurora*, July 7, 1801.

47. *Gazette of the United States*, July 3, 1801.

48. *Aurora*, July 10, 1801.

49. *Gazette of the United States*, July 3, 1801.

50. *Aurora*, July 2 and 7, 1801.

51. *Aurora*, July 7, 1801.

52. *Aurora*, July 4, 1801.

53. *Aurora*, July 7, 1802.

54. *Aurora*, July 9, 1802.

55. Arthur M. Schlesinger, "Liberty Tree: A Genealogy," *New England Quarterly* 26 (December 1952): 454–56.

56. Schlesinger, "Liberty Tree," 455. In his study of the "liberty cap" in early nineteenth-century Britain, James Epstein noted that at the "Peterloo" massacre, the Manchester militia likewise "pursued the banners and caps of liberty with vicious enthusiasm—scores were to be settled, authority restored, definitions reimposed." James Epstein, "Understanding the Cap of Liberty: Symbolic Practice and Social Conflict in Early Nineteenth-Century England," *Past and Present* 122 (February 1989): 99.

57. *Aurora*, July 7 and 11, 1800.

58. *Aurora*, July 8, 1803.

59. *Aurora*, July 11, 1803.

60. *Aurora*, July 6, 1804; July 1, 1806.

61. Catherine Albanese notes that shortly after the ratification of the Constitution, "the word *federal* quickly assumed a symbolic import which made it a standard invocation to bless any project." *Sons of the Fathers: The Civil Religion of the American Revolution* (Philadelphia, 1976), 209. By 1815, writes David Fischer, it was "an epithet, a smear word." *Revolution of American Conservatism*, 180.

62. *Pennsylvania Gazette*, July 11, 1810.

63. *Aurora*, July 1, 1806; emphasis in original.

64. *Aurora*, July 3, 1806; emphasis in original.

65. Joyce Appleby has argued ably that such was indeed the case. Joyce Appleby, *Capitalism and a New Social Order: The Republican Vision of the 1790s* (New York, 1984).

66. *Aurora*, July 10, 1801; July 7, 1802.

67. Elaine Foreman Crane, ed., *The Diary of Elizabeth Drinker* (Boston, 1991), 3:1844.

68. *Aurora*, July 3, 1807.

69. Crane, *The Diary of Elizabeth Drinker*, 3:2051–52. See also the diary of Rebecca Guest, vol. 16, entry for July 4, 1807, Historical Society of Pennsylvania.

70. *Aurora*, July 4, 1807.

71. *Aurora*, July 6 and 4, 1807. The matter apparently ended peaceably; see *Aurora*, July 7, 1807.

72. Eliza Cope Harrison, ed., *Philadelphia Merchant: The Diary of Thomas P. Cope, 1800–1851* (South Bend, Ind., 1978), 213.

73. *Aurora*, July 6, 1807.

74. Crane, *The Diary of Elizabeth Drinker*, 3:2052.

75. *Aurora*, July 6, 1799.

76. Timothy Dwight, *Travels in New England and New York* (Cambridge, Mass., 1969), 1: 366–67.

77. *Aurora*, July 7, 1802; July 6, 1805.

78. *Aurora*, July 3, 1805. "As a matter of fact, many of the democratic clubs were formed around a militia company that made up the nucleus of the organization." Eugene Perry Link, *The Democratic-Republican Societies, 1790–1800* (Morningside Heights, N.Y., 1942), 181. For an example of a similar Federalist association in Charleston, see *City Gazette*, July 9, 1798.

79. David G. Hackett, "The Social Origins of Nationalism: Albany, New York, 1754–1835," *Journal of Social History*, 21, no. 4 (1987–88): 672; Barry Schwartz, *George Washington: The Making of an American Symbol* (New York, 1987), 18; Appleby, *Capitalism and a New Social Order*, 16.

80. James Epstein, "Understanding the Cap of Liberty."

81. Natalie Zemon Davis provides examples from Reformation-era France in "The Reasons of Misrule," in her *Society and Culture in Early Modern France* (Stanford, Calif., 1975), 170.

82. Clifford Geertz, "Ritual and Social Change: A Javanese Example," *American Anthropologist* 59, no. 1 (February 1957): 52.

83. Michael Feldberg, "The Crowd in Philadelphia History: A Comparative Perspective," *Labor History* 15, no. 3 (Summer 1974): 334.

84. Lewis A. Coser, *The Functions of Social Conflict* (Glencoe, Ill., 1964), 70–71, 118.

85. On political and moral traditions as legitimizers of violent behavior see Natalie Davis, "The Rites of Violence" in *Society and Culture,* 152–87.

86. Richard L. Bushman, *King and People in Provincial Massachusetts* (Chapel Hill, N.C., 1985), 25.

87. Appleby, *Capitalism and a New Social Order,* 8, 61; Sean Wilentz, "Artisan Republican Festivals and the Rise of Class Conflict in New York City, 1788–1837," in *Working-Class America: Essays on Labor, Community, and American Society,* ed. Michael H. Frisch and Daniel J. Walkowitz (Urbana, Ill., 1983), 51.

88. Barry Schwartz, *George Washington: The Making of an American Symbol,* 167. See also Joyce Appleby, *Capitalism and a New Social Order,* for her insightful discussion of the evolution of republican philosophy during this period.

89. The phrase is from Sean Wilentz, *Rites of Power: Ritual and Politics Since the Middle Ages* (Philadelphia, 1985).

90. Albanese, *Sons of the Fathers,* 208.

91. Jeremy Boissevain, *Saints and Fireworks: Religion and Politics in Rural Malta* (New York, 1965), 138–39.

92. *Boston Gazette,* July 9, 1801.

93. "Greene," *Aurora,* July 2, 1810; emphasis in original.

94. Diary of Leverett Saltonstall, *Saltonstall Papers,* 2:206.

95. *Aurora* ("for the country" series), July 3, 1811.

6

MAKING OVER THE FOURTH

1. Steven Watts, *The Republic Reborn: War and the Making of Liberal America, 1790–1820* (Baltimore, Md., 1987), 291, 296; Gordon S. Wood, *The Rising Glory of America, 1760–1820* (New York, 1971), 13.

2. *Boston Gazette,* July 2 and 6, 1812.

3. *Independent Chronicle,* July 8, 1813.

4. *Columbian Centinel,* July 3 and 7, 1813; *Boston Gazette,* July 8, 1813.

5. *Boston Gazette,* July 8, 1813.

6. *Columbian Centinel,* July 6, 1814; *Independent Chronicle,* July 4, 1815.

7. *Columbian Centinel,* July 6, 1814.

8. *Boston Gazette,* June 30, 1814.

9. *Boston Gazette,* July 4, 1814.

10. *Boston Gazette,* July 7, 1814.

11. *Independent Chronicle,* July 4 and 7, 1815.

12. *Aurora*, July 3, 1812.

13. *Aurora*, July 2, 1812.

14. *Aurora*, July 3 and 4, 1812; Reese D. James, *Old Drury of Philadelphia* (New York, 1968), 19.

15. *Aurora*, July 7, 1812.

16. *Aurora*, July 7, 1813.

17. *Aurora*, June 30, 1814.

18. *Aurora*, July 1, 4, and 6, 1814.

19. *Charleston Courier*, June 26 and July 7, 1812.

20. Watts, *The Republic Reborn*, 282.

21. My brief of the reshaping of American politics after the War of 1812 is based upon James M. Banner, *To the Hartford Convention: The Federalists and the Origins of Party Politics in Massachusetts, 1789–1815* (New York, 1970); David Hackett Fischer, *The Revolution of American Conservatism* (New York, 1965): Paul Goodman, *The Democratic-Republicans of Massachusetts: Politics in a Young Republic* (Cambridge, Mass., 1964); Drew R. McCoy, *The Elusive Republic: Political Economy in Jeffersonian America* (New York, 1980), 209–59. Quote is from Goodman, *Democratic-Republicans*, 202.

22. *Aurora*, July 8, 1818.

23. *Aurora*, July 1, 1814.

24. Nicholas B. Wainwright, "The Diary of Samuel Breck," *Pennsylvania Magazine of History and Biography* 102 (1978): 476.

25. *Aurora*, July 6, 1815.

26. *Aurora*, July 7, 1815. Unfortunately, the writer did not elaborate what he thought those meanings were.

27. *Columbian Centinel*, July 1, 1815.

28. *Boston Gazette*, July 3, 1815.

29. *Columbian Centinel*, July 1, 1815; *Independent Chronicle*, July 3, 1815.

30. *Independent Chronicle*, July 6, 1815.

31. *Columbian Centinel*, July 5, 1815.

32. *Columbian Centinel*, July 6, 1816.

33. *Independent Chronicle*, July 6, 1816. While conciliatory in tone, the writer's appeal is an encapsulation of the message contained in Washington's Farewell Address—a quasi-Federalist manifesto now apparently suitable for print in a republican newspaper.

34. *Independent Chronicle*, July 8, 1816.

35. Robert E. Moody, ed., *The Papers of Leverett Saltonstall, 1816–1845* (Boston, 1978), 1:59.

36. Goodman, *The Democratic-Republicans*, 201.

37. *Boston Gazette,* July 3, 1817.

38. *Independent Chronicle,* July 8, 1817.

39. *Independent Chronicle,* July 8, 1817.

40. William Tudor, *Letters on the Eastern States* (Boston, 1821), 373–74.

41. *Prominent Features of a Northern Tour* (Charleston, S.C., 1822), 6.

42. *Boston Gazette,* July 10, 1815.

43. *Southern Patriot,* July 3, 1815.

44. Watts, *The Republic Reborn,* 284, 289.

45. *Southern Patriot,* July 5, 1815.

46. Watts, *The Republic Reborn,* 289.

47. *Southern Patriot,* July 3, 1815, and July 3, 1816.

48. Philip F. Detweiler, "The Changing Reputation of the Declaration of Independence: The First Fifty Years," *William and Mary Quarterly* 19 (October 1962): 571–74.

49. *Aurora,* July 6, 1818.

50. *Aurora,* July 8, 1819.

51. Wood, *The Rising Glory of America,* 2.

52. For contemporary comparisons of Jackson and Washington, see John William Ward, *Andrew Jackson: Symbol for an Age* (1953; reprint, New York, 1978), 42, 44, 189.

53. *Gazette of the United States,* July 7, 1815.

54. L. H. Butterfield, ed., *Letters of Benjamin Rush* (Princeton, N.J., 1951), 2:1089–90.

55. Robert E. Moody, ed., *The Saltonstall Papers, 1607–1815* (Boston, 1974), 2:491.

56. *Niles' Weekly Register* 6:18, July 1, 1820.

57. *Aurora,* July 8, 1818; *Charleston Courier,* June 29, 1818.

58. *Charleston Courier,* July 7, 1823.

59. *Aurora,* July 4, 1817.

60. *Poulson's American Daily Advertiser,* July 4, 1821.

61. *Aurora,* July 4, 1823.

62. *Aurora,* July 5, 1824; July 4, 1823.

63. *Poulson's American Daily Advertiser,* July 4, 1821.

64. *Poulson's American Daily Advertiser,* July 4, 1822.

65. *Poulson's American Daily Advertiser,* July 9 and 4, 1822.

66. Susan G. Davis, *Parades and Power: Street Theater in Nineteenth-Century Philadelphia* (Berkeley and Los Angeles, 1986), 42.

67. *Aurora,* July 6 and 7, 1826.

68. Krimmel's painting shows how quickly an embarrassing American defeat became remembered instead as a moral victory in American popular culture. American captain James Lawrence's famous last words quickly became the Navy's rallying cry.

69. Wood, *The Rising Glory of America*, 1.

70. *Aurora*, July 9, 1819.

7

JUBILEE

1. Diary of Deborah Norris Logan, July 4, 1826, and biographical notes, Historical Society of Pennsylvania, Philadelphia (HSP).

2. Diary of Samuel Breck, July 4, 1826, HSP.

3. Diary of Deborah Norris Logan, July 8, 1826, HSP; Diary of Samuel Breck, July 9, 1826, HSP.

4. *Aurora*, July 8, 1826.

5. Michael Kammen, *A Season of Youth: The American Revolution and the. Historical Imagination* (New York, 1978), 44.

6. Barbara G. Myerhoff, "A Death in Due Time: Construction of Self and Culture in Ritual Drama," in *Rite, Drama, Festival, Spectacle: Rehearsals Toward a Theory of Cultural Performance*, ed. John J. MacAloon (Philadelphia, 1984), 149, 150.

7. David G. Hackett, "The Social Origins of Nationalism: Albany, New York, 1754– 1835," *Journal of Social History* 21, no. 4 (1987–88): 672.

8. Harriet H. Robinson, *Loom and Spindle or Life Among the Early Mill Girls* (Kailua, Hawaii, 1976), 48.

9. Susan G. Davis, *Parades and Power: Street Theater in Nineteenth-Century Philadelphia* (Berkeley and Los Angeles, 1986), 148–49. See also Terrence Tirowen His Posthumous Papers, HSP, for his poem describing a July 4 celebration in Philadelphia, in which a lampoon of female temperance workers features prominently.

10. Sean Wilentz, "Artisan Republican Festivals and the Rise of Class Conflict in New York City, 1788–1837," in *Working Class America: Essays on Labor, Community, and American Society*, ed. Michael H. Frisch and Daniel J. Wolkowitz (Urbana, Ill., 1983), 43–45; Davis, *Parades and Power*, 167; Kammen, *A Season of Youth*, 45.

11. Gary B. Nash, *Forging Freedom: The Formation of Philadelphia's Black Community, 1720–1840* (Cambridge, Mass., 1988), 212–45; Davis, *Parades and Power*, 46. See also Shane White's conclusions in his " 'It Was a Proud Day': African Americans, Festivals, and Parades in the North, 1741–1834," *Journal of American History* 81, no. 1 (June 1994): 13–50.

12. Kammen, *A Season of Youth*, 45, 54.

13. Frederick Marryat, *A Diary in America With Remarks on its Institutions*, ed. S. W. Jackman (New York, 1962), 57, 58.

14. Nicholas B. Wainwright, *A Philadelphia Perspective: The Diary of Sidney George Fisher Coming from the Years 1834–1871* (Philadelphia, 1967), 224.

15. Lewis O. Sawm, *The Popular Mood of Pre–Civil War America* (Westport, Conn., 1980), 148.

16. George C. Rogers Jr., *Charleston in the Age of the Pinckneys* (Norman, Okla., 1969), 135–45.

17. *Charleston Gazette,* July 4, 1821, and July 4, 1823.

18. *Charleston Courier,* July 29, 1818; *Charleston Mercury,* July 28, 1823.

19. Alexander Garden, *Anecdotes of the Revolutionary War* (Charleston, S.C., 1822); Rogers, *Charleston in the Age of the Pinckneys,* 150–51.

20. *Charleston Mercury,* June 28, 1825, and July 4, 1826. Massachusetts people were doing much the same thing; the Charleston promoters of a Fort Moultrie monument pointed to the recently completed obelisk at Bunker Hill for example.

21. *Southern Patriot,* July 5, 1817; Charles Fraser, *An Oration, delivered in St. Michael's Church, before the Inhabitants of Charleston, on the 4th of July, 1808, in Commemoration of American Independence* (Charleston, S.C., 1808), 4.

22. James H. Kettner, *The Development of American Citizenship, 1608–1870* (Chapel Hill, N.C., 1978), 3.

23. Mark D. Kaplanoff, "How Federalist was South Carolina in 1787–1788?" in *The Meaning of South Carolina History: Essays in Honor of George C. Rogers, Jr.,* ed. David R. Chestnutt and Clyde N. Wilson (Columbia, S.C., 1991), 67–103.

24. The term "cultural fiction" is borrowed from Peter C. Mancall's review of *The Middle Ground: Indians, Empires, and Republics in the Great Lakes Region, 1650–1815,* by Richard White, *American Historical Review* 95, no. 5 (December 1992): 1588.

25. *Charleston Courier,* June 29, 1818.

26. A. V. Huff Jr., "The Eagle and the Vulture: Changing Attitudes Toward Nationalism in Fourth of July Orations Delivered in Charleston, 1788–1860," *South Atlantic Quarterly,* 73, no. 1 (Winter 1974): 10–22; Kammen, *A Season of Youth,* 54–55.

27. James Epstein, "Understanding the Cap of Liberty: Symbolic Practice and Social Conflict in Early Nineteenth-Century England," *Past and Present* 122 (February 1989): 77.

28. John J. MacAloon, introduction to his *Rite, Drama, Festival, Spectacle,* 1.

29. On the "failure" of rituals see Clifford Geertz, "Ritual and Social Change: A Javanese Example," *American Anthropologist* 59, no. 1 (February 1957): 34. As Nina Silber demonstrates, the "reconciliation" of North and South after the Civil War is now part of the mythos of American history. Silber, *The Romance of Reunion: Northerners and the South, 1865–1900* (Chapel Hill, N.C., 1993).

BIBLIOGRAPHY

PRIMARY SOURCES

Manuscript

Boston. Massachusetts Historical Society
        Cushing-Orne Papers
        C. E. French Papers
        Jacob Norton Papers
        Otis Papers
        Robert Treat Paine Papers
        Pierce Papers
        Diary of Elizabeth Cranch
        Diary of Nathan Webb
        Memoirs of John Pierce

Charleston. South Carolina Historical Society
        Ralph Izard Family Letters, Cheves-Middleton Papers

Philadelphia. Historical Society of Pennsylvania
        Clifford Papers
        Pemberton Papers
        Wayne Papers
        Terrence Tirowen His Posthumous Papers
        Diary of Samuel Breck

Diary of John Frisker
Diary of Rebecca Guest
Diary of Deborah Norris Logan
Diary of George Nelson
Diary of Thomas F. Pleasant
Diary of Nathaniel R. Snowden
Diary of William Wood Thackera
Records of Old Swedes Church (Gloria Dei): Burial
    Records, 1750–1831.

Philadelphia. Library of the American Philosophical Society
Diary of Charles Willson Peale

Newspapers

Boston
Boston Gazette
Columbian Centinel
Evening Gazette and General Advertiser
Independent Chronicle

Philadelphia
Aurora General Advertiser
Constitutional Diary
Daily Advertiser
Gazette of the United States
Independent Gazetteer
Niles' Weekly Register
Pennsylvania Evening Post
Pennsylvania Gazette
Pennsylvania Ledger
Pennsylvania Packet
Philadelphia Minerva
Porcupine's Gazette
Poulson's American Daily Advertiser
Universal Gazette

Charleston
Charleston Courier
Charleston Mercury
City Gazette
Columbian Herald
Gazette of the State of South Carolina
South Carolina Gazette and General Advertiser
South Carolina State Gazette
Southern Patriot
State Gazette of South Carolina

Printed Works

Biddle, Charles. *The Autobiography of Charles Biddle, Vice-President of the Supreme Executive Council of Pennsylvania.* Philadelphia: E. Claxton, 1853.

"Boyle's Journal of Occurrences in Boston, 1759–1778," *New England Historical and Genealogical Register* 85 (1931): 117–33.

Burke, John. *Bunker-Hill; or the Death of General Warren. An Historic Tragedy in Five Acts.* New York: T. Greenleaf, 1797.

Butterfield, L. H., ed. *Letters of Benjamin Rush.* 2 vols. Princeton: Princeton University Press, 1951.

By-Laws and Orders of the Town of Boston. Boston: Manning and Loring, 1801.

Cordozo, J. N. *Reminiscences of Charleston.* Charleston: Joseph Walker, 1866.

Chestnutt, David R., et al., eds. *The Papers of Henry Laurens.* Vol. 13. Columbia: University of South Carolina Press, 1968–92.

Crane, Elaine Forman, ed. *The Diary of Elizabeth Drinker.* 3 vols. Boston: Northeastern University Press, 1991.

Davis, John. *Travels of Four Years and a Half in the United States of America, During 1798, 1799, 1800, 1801, and 1802.* New York: Henry Holt, 1909.

Derounian, Kathryn Zabelle, ed. *The Journal and Occasional Writings of Sarah Wister.* Cranbury, N.J.: Associated University Presses, 1987.

"Diary of Edward Hooker, 1805–1808." *Annual Report of the American Historical Association for the year 1896,* 842–929. Washington, D.C.: GPO, 1897.

"Diary of Grace Growden Galloway." *Pennsylvania Magazine of History and Biography* 55 (1931): 32–94.

Duane, William, ed. *Extracts from the Diary of Christopher Marshall, Kept in Philadelphia and Lancaster During the American Revolution, 1774–1781.* Albany, N.Y.: Joel Mansell, 1877.

Dwight, Timothy. *Travels in New England and New York.* 4 vols. Reprint, Cambridge: Belknap Press of Harvard University Press, 1969.

Fraser, Charles. *An Oration, delivered in St. Michael's Church, before the Inhabitants of Charleston, on the 4th of July, 1808, in Commemoration of American Independence.* Charleston, S.C.: J. Hoff, 1808.

"A Frenchman Visits Charleston, 1817." *South Carolina Historical and Genealogical Magazine* 49, no. 3 (July 1948): 131–54.

Gray, Thomas. *A Sermon Delivered in Boston before the African Society on the Fourteenth Day of July, 1818, the anniversary of the Abolition of the Slave Trade.* Boston: Parmenter and Norton, 1818.

Green, Ashbel. *The Life of Ashbel Green.* New York: Robert Carter and Bros., 1849.

Hall, Prince. *A Charge, Delivered to the African Lodge at Menotomy.* Boston: Benjamin Edes, 1797.

Harrison, Eliza Cope, ed. *Philadelphia Merchant: The Diary of Thomas P. Cope, 1800–1851.* South Bend, Ind.: Gateway Edition, 1978.

[Hopkinson, Francis]. *An Account of the Grand Federal Procession, Philadelphia, July 4, 1788. To which is Added, a Letter on the Same Subject.* Philadelphia: M. Carey, 1788.

Janson, Charles William. *The Stranger in America, 1793–1806.* New York: Press of the Pioneers, 1935.

Johnson, Elmer Douglas, trans. "A Frenchman Visits Charleston in 1777." *South Carolina Historical and Genealogical Magazine* 52, no. 2 (April 1951): 88–92.

Jones, George Fenwick. "The Siege of Charleston as Experienced by a Hessian Officer." *South Carolina Historical Magazine* 88, no. 2 (April 1987): 63–75.

Marryat, Frederick. *A Diary in America With Remarks on its Institutions.* Edited by S. W. Jackman. New York: Knopf, 1962.

Martin, Julien Dwight. "The Letters of Charles Caleb Cotton, 1798–1802." *South Carolina Historical and Genealogical Magazine* 51, no. 3 (July 1950): 132–44; 51, no. 4 (October 1950): 216–28; 52, no. 1 (January 1951): 17–25.

Mohl, Raymond A., ed. " 'The Grand Fabric of Republicanism': A Scotsman Describes South Carolina." *South Carolina Historical Magazine* 71, no. 3 (July 1970): 170–88.

Moody, Robert E. *The Saltonstall Papers, 1607–1815.* 2 vols. Boston: Massachusetts Historical Society, 1974.

——, ed. *The Papers of Leverett Saltonstall, 1816–1845.* 3 vols. Boston: Massachusetts Historical Society, 1978.

Moreau de St. Mery's American Journey. Translated and edited by Kenneth Roberts and Anna B. Roberts. New York: Doubleday, 1947.

Moultrie, William. *Memoirs of the American Revolution.* 2 vols. New York: Arno, 1968.

Ordinances of the City Council of Charleston, in the State of South Carolina, Passed between the 24th Day of September, 1804, and the 1st Day of September, 1807. Charleston, S.C.: G. M. Bounetheau, 1807.

Ordinances of the City Council of Charleston, in the State of South Carolina, Passed since the Incorporation of the City. Charleston, S.C.: W. P. Young, 1802.

Ordinances of the City Council of Charleston, in the State of South Carolina, Passed since the 28th of October, 1801. Charleston, S.C.: W. P. Young, 1804.

Prominent Features of a Northern Tour. Charleston, S.C.: C. C. Sebring, 1822.

Ramsey, David. *An Oration, delivered on the Anniversary of American Independence, July 4, 1794, in St. Michael's Church, to the Inhabitants of Charleston, South Carolina.* London: J. Ridgway, 1795.

Reports of the Records Commissioners of the City of Boston. 39 vols. Boston, 1876–1909.

Roberts, Kenneth, and Anna B. Roberts, eds. and trans. *Moreau de St. Mery's American Journey.* New York: Doubleday, 1947.

Robinson, Harriet H. *Loom and Spindle or Life Among the Early Mill Girls.* Kailua, Hawaii: Press Pacifica, 1976.

Rutledge, Henry M. *An Oration delivered in St. Philip's Church, before the Inhabitants of Charleston, South Carolina on Wednesday, the 4th of July, 1804, in Commemoration of American Independence.* Charleston, S.C.: W. P. Young, 1804.

Schoepf, Johann David. *Travels in the Confederation.* Translated by Alfred J. Morrison. 1911. Reprint. New York: Ben Franklin, 1968.

Scudder, H. E., ed. *Recollections of Samuel Breck, with Passages from his Note-Books, 1771–1862.* Philadelphia: Porter and Coates, 1877.

Sherril, Charles H., ed. *French Memoirs of Eighteenth-Century America.* 1915. Reprint, Freeport, N.Y.: Books for Libraries, 1971.

Smith, Billy G., and Susan E. Clepp. "The Records of Gloria Dei Church: Burials, 1800–1804." *Pennsylvania History* 53 (1986): 56–79.

Smith, William. *An Oration in St. Phillip's Church, before the Inhabitants of Charleston, South Carolina, on the Fourth of July, 1796, in Commemoration of American Independence.* Charleston, S.C.: W. P. Young, 1796.

Tudor, William. *Letters on the Eastern States.* 2d ed. Boston: Wells and Lilly, 1821.

Wainwright, Nicholas B. "The Diary of Samuel Breck." *Pennsylvania Magazine of History and Biography* 102 (1978): 469–508; 103 (1979): 85–113, 222–25, 356–82, 497–527.

——. *A Philadelphia Perspective: The Diary of Sidney George Fisher Coming from the Years 1834–1871.* Philadelphia: Historical Society of Pennsylvania, 1967.

Wells, Louisa Susannah. *The Journal of a Voyage from Charleston, S.C. to London Undertaken During the American Revolution by a Daughter of an Eminent American Loyalist in the Year 1778 and Written from Memory Only.* New York: New York Historical Society, 1906.

SECONDARY SOURCES

Abraham, Roger, and Richard Bauman. "Ranges of Festive Behavior." In *The Reversible World,* edited by Barbara Babcock, 193–208. Ithaca: Cornell University Press, 1977.

Albanese, Catherine L. *Sons of the Fathers: The Civil Religion of the American Revolution.* Philadelphia: Temple University Press, 1976.

Alexander, John K. "The Fort Wilson Incident of 1779: A Case Study of the Revolutionary Crowd." *William and Mary Quarterly,* 3d ser., 31 (1974): 589–612.

Albert, Peter, and Ronald Hoffman, eds. *Arms and Independence: The Military Character of the American Revolution.* Charlottesville: University Press of Virginia, 1984.

Ames, William. *The Marrow of Theology.* Boston: Pilgrim Press, 1968.

Anderson, Benedict. *Imagined Communities: Reflections on the Origin and Spread of Nationalism.* London: Verso, 1983.

Andrews, James R., and Ritter, Kurt W. *The American Ideology: Reflections of the Revolution in American Rhetoric.* Falls Church, Va.: Speech Communication Association, 1978.

Appleby, Joyce. *Capitalism and a New Social Order: The Republican Vision of the 1790s.* New York: New York University Press, 1984.

Baltzell, E. Digby. *Puritan Boston and Quaker Philadelphia: Two Protestant Ethics and the Spirit of Class Authority and Leadership.* New York: Free Press, 1979.

Banner, James M., Jr. *To the Hartford Convention: The Federalists and the Origins of Party Politics in Massachusetts, 1789–1815.* New York: Knopf, 1970.

Beals, Ralph, and Harry Hoijer. *An Introduction to Anthropology.* New York: Macmillan, 1956.

Boissevain, Jeremy. *Saints and Fireworks: Religion and Politics in Rural Malta.* New York: Humanities, 1965.

Boorstin, Daniel J. *The Americans: The National Experience.* New York: Random House, 1965.

Bushman, Richard L. *King and People in Provincial Massachusetts.* Chapel Hill: University of North Carolina Press, 1985.

Bynum, Caroline Walker. "Women's Stories, Women's Symbols: A Critique of Victor Turner's Theory of Liminality." In *Fragmentation and Redemption: Essays on Gender and the Human Body in Medieval Religion,* by Caroline Walker Bynum, 27–51. New York: Zone Books, 1991.

Cannadine, David. "The Context, Performance, and Meaning of Ritual: The British Monarchy and the 'Invention of Tradition.'" In *The Invention of Tradition,* edited by Eric Hobsbawm and Terrence Ranger, 101–64. Cambridge: Cambridge University Press, 1983.

Cohen, Lester H. *The Revolutionary Histories: Contemporary Narratives of the American Revolution.* Ithaca: Cornell University Press, 1980.

Cohn, William H. "Popular Culture and Social History." *Journal of Popular Culture* 11, no. 1 (Summer 1977): 167 / 28–179 / 41.

Coser, Lewis A. *The Functions of Social Conflict.* Glencoe, Ill.: Free Press of Glencoe, 1964.

Cress, Lawrence Delbert. *Citizens in Arms: The Army and Militia in American Society to the War of 1812.* Chapel Hill: University of North Carolina Press, 1982.

Cressy, David. *Bonfires and Bells: National Memory and the Protestant Calendar in Elizabethan and Stuart England.* Berkeley and Los Angeles: University of California Press, 1989.

Curti, Merle. *The Roots of American Loyalty.* New York: Atheneum, 1946.

Da Matta, Roberto. "Constraint and Licence: A Preliminary Study of Two Brazilian National Rituals." In *Secular Ritual,* edited by Sally Moore and Barbara G. Myerhoff, 244–64. Amsterdam: Van Gorcum, Assen, 1977.

Davis, Natalie Zemon. *Society and Culture in Early Modern France.* Stanford: Stanford University Press, 1975.

Davis, Susan G. *Parades and Power: Street Theatre in Nineteenth-Century Philadelphia.* Berkeley and Los Angeles: University of California Press, 1986.

Detweiler, Philip F. "The Changing Reputation of the Declaration of Independence: The First Fifty Years." *William and Mary Quarterly* 19 (October 1962): 557–74.

Earle, Alice Morse. *Customs and Fashions in Old New England.* New York: Scribner, 1899.

Eberlein, Harold D., and Hubbard, Cortlandt V. "The American 'Vauxhall' of the Federalist Era." *Pennsylvania Magazine of History and Biography* 68 (1944): 150–74.

Epstein, James. "Understanding the Cap of Liberty: Symbolic Practice and Social Conflict in Early Nineteenth-Century England." *Past and Present* 122 (February 1989): 75–118.

Farley, M. Foster. "Mighty Monarch of the South: Yellow Fever in Charleston and Savannah." *Georgia Review* 27 (1973): 56–70.

Feeley-Harnik, Gillian. *The Lord's Table: Eucharist and Passover in Early Christianity.* Philadelphia: University of Pennsylvania Press, 1981.

Feldberg, Michael. "The Crowd in Philadelphia History: A Comparative Perspective." *Labor History* 15, no. 3 (Summer 1974): 323–66.

Firth, Raymond. *Symbols: Public and Private.* Ithaca: Cornell University Press, 1973.

Fischer, David Hackett. *The Revolution of American Conservatism.* New York: Harper and Row, 1965.

Foner, Philip S., ed. *The Democratic-Republican Societies, 1790–1800: A Documentary Sourcebook of Constitutions, Declarations, Addresses, Resolutions, and Toasts.* Westport, Conn.: Greenwood, 1976.

Friedrich, Paul. "Revolutionary Politics and Communal Ritual." In *Political Anthropology,* edited by Marc J. Swartz, Victor Turner, and Arthur Tuden, 191–220. Chicago: Aldine, 1966.

Gabriel, Ralph Henry. *The Course of American Democratic Thought.* 3d ed. New York: Greenwood, 1986.

Garden, Alexander. *Anecdotes of the Revolutionary War.* Charleston, S.C.: A. E. Miller, 1822.

Geertz, Clifford. "Centers, Kings, and Charisma: Reflections on the Symbolics of Power." In *Culture and its Creators: Essays in Honor of Edward Shils,* edited by Joseph Ben-David and Terry Nichols Clark, 151–72. Chicago: University of Chicago Press, 1977.

——. "Deep Play: Notes on The Balinese Cockfight." In *Myth, Symbol, and Culture,* edited by Clifford Geertz, 1–29. New York: Norton, 1971.

——. "Ritual and Social Change: A Javanese Example." *American Anthropologist* 59, no. 1 (February 1957): 32–54.

Glassberg, David. "Patriotism from the Ground Up." *Reviews in American History* 21, no. 1 (March 1993): 1–7.

Goodman, Paul. *The Democratic-Republicans of Massachusetts: Politics in a Young Republic.* Cambridge: Harvard University Press, 1964.

Green, Fletcher M. "Listen to the Eagle Scream: One Hundred Years of the Fourth of July in North Carolina." In *Democracy in the Old South and Other Essays,* edited by J. Isaac Copeland, 111–56. Nashville: Vanderbilt University Press, 1969.

Griffith, James. "We Call It 'Tucson Eat Yourself': The Role of Food at a Constructed Festival." In *"We Gather Together": Food and Festival in American Life,* edited by Theodore C. Humphrey and Lin T. Humphrey, 219–33. Ann Arbor: UMI Research Press, 1988.

Grimes, Ronald. *Beginnings in Ritual Studies.* Lanham, Md.: University Press of America, 1982.

——. *Symbol and Conquest: Public Ritual and Drama in Santa Fe, New Mexico.* Ithaca: Cornell University Press, 1976.

Hackett, David G. "The Social Origins of Nationalism: Albany, New York, 1754–1835." *Journal of Social History* 21, no. 4 (1987–88): 659–81.

Hall, John A. "Nefarious Wretches, Insidious Villains, and Evil-Minded Persons: Urban Crime in Charleston's *City Gazette,* in 1788." *South Carolina Historical Magazine* 88, no. 3 (July 1987): 151–68.

Handler, Richard. *Nationalism and the Politics of Culture in Quebec.* Madison: University of Wisconsin Press, 1988.

Hay, Robert P. "The Liberty Tree: A Symbol for American Patriots." *Quarterly Journal of Speech* 55 (1969): 414–24.

Hellmann, John. *American Myth and the Legacy of Vietnam.* New York: Columbia University Press, 1986.

Higginbotham, Don. "The Early American Way of War: Reconaissance and Appraisal." *William and Mary Quarterly* 44, no. 2 (April 1987): 230–73.

Hill, Christopher. *Society and Puritanism in Pre-Revolutionary England.* New York: Schocken Books, 1964.

Hobsbawm, Eric. "Introduction: Inventing Traditions." In *The Invention of Tradition,* edited by Eric Hobsbawm and Terrence Ranger, 1–14. Cambridge: Cambridge University Press, 1983.

Hoerder, Dirk. *Crowd Action in Revolutionary Massachusetts, 1765–1780.* New York: Academic Press, 1977.

Howe, John R., Jr. "Republican Thought and the Political Violence of the 1790s." *American Quarterly* 19 (1967): 147–65.

Huff, A. V., Jr. "The Eagle and the Vulture: Changing Attitudes Toward Nationalism in Fourth of July Orations Delivered in Charleston, 1788–1860." *South Atlantic Quarterly* 73, no. 1 (Winter 1974): 10–22.

Hunt, Lynn. *Politics, Culture, and Class in the French Revolution.* Berkeley and Los Angeles: University of California Press, 1984.

Isaac, Rhys. *The Transformation of Virginia, 1740–1790.* Published for the Institute of Early American History and Culture, Williamsburg, Virginia. Chapel Hill: University of North Carolina Press, 1982.

James, Reese D. *Old Drury of Philadelphia.* New York: Greenwood, 1968.

Jordan, Cynthia S. " 'Old Words' in 'New Circumstances': Language and Leadership in Post-Revolutionary America." *American Quarterly* (1988): 491–513.

Kammen, Michael. *A Season of Youth: The American Revolution and the Historical Imagination.* New York: Knopf, 1978.

Kaplanoff, Mark D. "How Federalist was South Carolina in 1787–1788?" In *The Meaning of South Carolina History: Essays in Honor of George C. Rogers, Jr.,* edited by David R. Chestnutt and Clyde N. Wilson, 67–103. Columbia: University of South Carolina Press, 1991.

Kettner, James H. *The Development of American Citizenship, 1608–1870.* Chapel Hill: University of North Carolina Press, 1978.

Klein, Rachel N. *Unification of a Slate State: The Rise of the Planter Class in the South Carolina Backcountry, 1760–1808.* Chapel Hill: University of North Carolina Press, 1990.

Kohn, Hans. *American Nationalism: An Interpretive Essay.* New York: Macmillan, 1957.

———. *The Idea of Nationalism: A Study in its Origins and Background.* New York: Macmillan, 1944.

Lawson, Cedric. "Patriotism in Carmine: 162 Years of July 4th Oratory." *Quarterly Journal of Speech* 26 (February 1940): 12–25.

Leach, Edmund R. *Political Systems of Highland Burma.* Cambridge: Harvard University Press, 1954.

Lentz, Richard. *Symbols, the News Magazines, and Martin Luther King.* Baton Rouge: Louisiana State University Press, 1990.

Link, Eugene Perry. *The Democratic-Republican Societies, 1790–1800.* New York: Columbia University Press, 1942.

MacAloon, John J., ed. *Rite, Drama, Festival, Spectacle: Rehearsals toward a Theory of Culture.* Philadelphia: Institute for the Study of Human Issues, 1984.

Mancall, Peter C. Review of *The Middle Ground: Indians, Empires, and Republics in the Great Lakes Region, 1650–1815,* by Richard White. *American Historical Review* 95, no. 5 (December 1992): 1588.

Marley, M. Foster. "Mighty Monarch of the South: Yellow Fever in Charleston and Savannah." *Georgia Review* 27 (1973): 56–70.

McCoy, Drew R. *The Elusive Republic: Political Economy in Jeffersonian America*. New York: Norton, 1980.

Merritt, Richard L. *Symbols of American Community, 1735–1775*. New Haven: Yale University Press, 1966.

Miller, Richard G. *Philadelphia—The Federalist City: A Study of Urban Politics, 1789–1801*. Port Washington, N.Y.: Kennikat, 1976.

Monaghan, Frank. *John Jay, Defender of Liberty*. New York: Bobbs-Merrill, 1935.

Moore, Sally F., and Barbara G. Myerhoff, eds. *Secular Ritual*. Amsterdam: Van Gorcum, Assen, 1977.

Murrin, John M. "A Roof without Walls: The Dilemma of American National Identity." In *Beyond Confederation: Origins of the Constitution and American National Identity*, edited by Richard Beeman, Stephen Botein, and Edward C. Carter II, 333–48. Chapel Hill: University of North Carolina Press, 1987.

Myerhoff, Barbara G. "A Death in Due Time: Construction of Self and Culture in Ritual Drama." In *Rite, Drama, Festival, Spectacle: Rehearsals Toward a Theory of Cultural Performance*, edited by John J. MacAloon, 149–78. Philadelphia: Institute for the Study of Human Issues, 1984.

———. "We Don't Wrap Herring in a Printed Page: Fusion, Fictions and Continuities." In *Secular Ritual*, edited by Sally F. Moore and Barbara G. Myerhoff, 199–224. Amsterdam: Van Gorcum, Assen, 1977.

Nadelhaft, Jerome. *The Disorders of War: The Revolution in South Carolina*. Orono: University of Maine Press, 1981.

Nash, Gary B. *Forging Freedom: The Formation of Philadelphia's Black Community, 1720–1840*. Cambridge: Harvard University Press, 1988.

———. *The Urban Crucible: The Northern Seaports and the Origins of the American Revolution*. Cambridge: Harvard University Press, 1986.

"Nefarious Wretches, Insidious Villains, and Evil-Minded Persons: Urban Crime in Charleston's *City Gazette*, in 1788." *South Carolina Historical Magazine* 88, no. 3 (July 1987): 151–68.

Phillips, Ulrich B. "The South Carolina Federalists." *American Historical Review* 14, no. 3 (April 1909): 529–43; 14, no. 4 (July 1909): 731–43.

Plescia, Joseph. *The Oath and Perjury in Ancient Greece*. Tallahassee, Fla.: Florida State University Press, 1970.

Pollock, Thomas Clark. *The Philadelphia Theatre in the Eighteenth Century*. Philadelphia: University of Pennsylvania Press, 1933.

Porter, Susan L. *With an Air Debonair: Musical Theater in America, 1785–1815*. Washington, D.C.: Smithsonian Institution Press, 1991.

Proctor, David E. *Enacting Political Culture: Rhetorical Transformations of Liberty Weekend 1986*. New York: Praeger, 1991.

Pythian-Adams, Charles. "Ceremony and the Citizen: The Communal Year at Coventry, 1450–1550." In *Crisis and Order in English Towns 1500–1700: Essays in Urban History*, edited by Peter Clark and Paul Slack, 57–85. London: Routledge and Kegan Paul, 1972.

Ritter, Kurt W., and James R. Andrews. *The American Ideology: Reflections of the Revolution in American Rhetoric*. Falls Church, Va.: Speech Communication Association, 1978.

Rogers, George C., Jr. *Charleston in the Age of the Pinckneys*. Norman: University of Oklahoma Press, 1969.

———. *Evolution of a Federalist: William Loughton Smith of Charleston, 1758–1812*. Columbia: University of South Carolina Press, 1962.

Ross, Marjorie Drake. *The Book of Boston: The Federal Period, 1775 to 1837*. New York: Hastings House, 1961.

Rosswurm, Steven. *Arms, Country, and Class: The Philadelphia Militia and the "Lower Sort" During the American Revolution*. New Brunswick: Rutgers University Press, 1987.

——. "The Philadelphia Militia, 1775–1783: Active Duty and Active Radicalism." In *Arms and Independence: The Military Character of the American Revolution*, edited by Ronald Hoffman and Peter J. Albert, 75–118. Charlottesville, N.C.: University Press of Virginia, 1984.

Roth, Rodris. "Tea-Drinking in Eighteenth-Century America: Its Etiquette and Equipage." In *Material Life in America, 1600–1860*, edited by Robert Blair St. George, 439–62. Boston: Northeastern University Press, 1988.

Royster, Charles. *A Revolutionary People at War: The Continental Army and American Character, 1775–1783*. New York: Norton, 1979.

Ryan, Mary P. *Women in Public: Between Banners and Ballots, 1825–1880*. Baltimore: Johns Hopkins University Press, 1990.

Santayana, George. *The Sense of Beauty, Being the Outlines of Aesthetic Theory*. New York: Modern Library, 1955.

Sawm, Lewis O. *The Popular Mood of Pre–Civil War America*. Westport, Conn.: Greenwood, 1980.

Schlesinger, Arthur. "Liberty Tree: A Genealogy." *New England Quarterly* 26 (December 1952): 435–58.

Schwartz, Barry. *George Washington: The Making of an American Symbol*. New York: Free Press, 1987.

Senese, Donald J. "The Free Negro and the South Carolina Courts, 1790–1860." *South Carolina Historical and Geneological Magazine* 68 (July 1967): 140–53.

Shaw, Peter. *American Patriots and the Rituals of Revolution*. Cambridge: Harvard University Press, 1981.

Silber, Nina. *The Romance of Reunion: Northerners and the South, 1865–1900*. Chapel Hill: University of North Carolina Press, 1993.

Smith, Barbara Clark. *After the Revolution: The Smithsonian History of Everyday Life in the Eighteenth Century*. New York: Pantheon, 1985.

Smith, Billy G. *"The Lower Sort": Philadelphia's Laboring People, 1750–1800*. Ithaca: Cornell University Press, 1990.

Sprogle, Howard O. *The Philadelphia Police, Past and Present*. Philadelphia: n.p., 1887.

Stansell, Christine. *City of Women: Sex and Class in New York, 1789–1860*. New York: Knopf, 1986.

Stauffer, Michael. "Volunteer or Uniform Companies in the Antebellum Militia: A Checklist of Independent Companies, 1790–1899." *South Carolina Historical Magazine* 88, no. 2 (April 1987): 108–16.

Sydnor, Charles Sackett. *American Revolutionaries in the Making: Political Practice in Washington's Virginia*. New York: Free Press, 1965 (originally published 1952).

Thomas, Keith. *Religion and the Decline of Magic*. New York: Scribner, 1971.

Turner, Victor. "Liminality and the Performative Genres." In *Rite, Drama, Festival, Spectacle: Rehearsals Toward a Theory of Cultural Performance*, edited by John J. MacAloon, 19–41. Philadelphia: Institute for the Study of Human Issues, 1984.

——. *The Ritual Process: Structure and Anti-Structure*. Chicago: Aldine, 1969.

Tyler, Moses Coit. *Literary History of the American Revolution*. 2 vols. New York: Putnam, 1897.

Walsh, Richard. *Charleston's Sons of Liberty: A Study of the Artisans, 1763–1789*. Columbia: University of South Carolina Press, 1968.

Ward, John William. *Andrew Jackson: Symbol for an Age*. 1953. Reprint New York: Oxford University Press, 1978.

Warner, Sam Bass, Jr. *The Private City: Philadelphia in Three Periods of its Growth*. Philadelphia: University of Pennsylvania Press, 1968.

Warren, Charles. "Fourth of July Myths." *William and Mary Quarterly* 2, no. 3 (July 1945): 237–72.

Watts, Stephen. *The Republic Reborn: War and the Making of Liberal America, 1790–1820.* Baltimore: Johns Hopkins University Press, 1987.

Weigley, Russell Frank. *Philadelphia: A 300-Year History.* New York: Norton, 1982.

White, Shane. " 'It Was a Proud Day': African Americans, Festivals, and Parades in the North, 1741–1834." *Journal of American History* 81, no. 1 (June 1994): 13–50.

Whitehall, Walter Muir. *Boston: A Topographical History.* Cambridge: Belknap Press of Harvard University Press, 1979.

Wilentz, Sean. "Artisan Republican Festivals and the Rise of Class Conflict in New York City, 1788–1837." In *Working-Class America: Essays on Labor, Community, and American Society,* edited by Michael H. Frisch and Daniel J. Walkowitz, 37–77. Urbana: University of Illinois Press, 1983.

——. *Chants Democratic: New York City and the Rise of the American Working Class.* New York: Oxford University Press, 1984.

——, ed. *Rites of Power: Ritual and Politics Since the Middle Ages.* Philadelphia: University of Pennsylvania Press, 1985.

Williams, George W. *Saint Michael's, Charleston, 1751–1951.* Columbia: University of South Carolina Press, 1951.

Wills, Gary. *Under God: Religion and American Politics.* New York: Simon and Schuster, 1990.

Wood, Gordon. *The Creation of the American Republic, 1776–1787.* Chapel Hill: University of North Carolina Press, 1969.

——. "Interests and Disinterestedness in the Making of the Constitution." In *Beyond Confederation: Origins of the Constitution and American National Identity,* edited by Richard Beeman, Stephen Botein, and Edward C. Carter II, 69–109. Chapel Hill: University of North Carolina Press, 1987.

——. *The Rising Glory of America, 1760–1820.* New York: George Braziller, 1971.

Wood, Peter. *Black Majority: Negroes in Colonial South Carolina from 1670 through the Stono Rebellion.* New York: Knopf, 1974.

Zarefsky, David. *President Johnson's War on Poverty: Rhetoric and History.* Tuscaloosa: University of Alabama Press, 1986.

INDEX

Population: black, in cities, 142, 144, 146;
growth in cities, 118
Preble, Edward, 175
Processions and Independence Day, 2, 6,
15, 30, 35, 37, 45, 46–47, 48, 61, 64, 67,
70–87, 98–99, 106, 107, 119, 136, 158,
164, 166, 167, 170, 171, 197, 202; and
artisans, 71, 72, 74, 75, 76, 79, 81, 83–
84, 98, 166, 242 n.1
Proctor, David, 4, 69
Protest, political, on Independence Day,
88, 97–98, 144, 170–71, 192–94

Quakers, and Independence Day
celebrations, 23, 24, 114, 118, 137, 234
n.31
Queenstown, battle of, 193
Quincey, Josiah (orator), 49, 157

Ramsay, David (orator), 27
Read, William, 118
Reconcilliation, political, on
Independence Day, 196, 197, 199
Reed, William, 69
Republican Blues (Philadelphia), 137–
39
Republicanism, 8, 89, 182, 184, 199
Republican Legion (Philadelphia), 140,
170, 179
Republican motherhood, 135–36, 140
Republicans, 8, 11, 88–106, 112, 117, 119,
155–88, 191–99
Revere, Paul, 119
Rights of Man, 90
"Rising generation," and Independence
Day, 48, 56–57, 112–13, 166, 167, 190,
206, 215–17
Rite of passage, 23, 27, 227; and
Independence Day, 28–30, 31, 54, 95
Ritter, Kurt, 5
Ritual, 4–5, 183, 224; defined, 12–13, 232
nn.35, 36; adaptation of old, 16, 20, 41,
65; and ambiguity, 86–87; ceremonial,
16; as communication, 28, 70, 84, 226;
as contested performance, 83–87; "de-
structuring," 183; and political culture,
4–5, 6–7, 11, 12, 70, 225; and social
function, 7, 10, 54, 56–57, 86–87, 184–
85, 226; "structuring," 12, 16, 52, 67,
188
Rogers, William (orator), 37

Rush, Benjamin, 34, 78, 79, 81, 82, 83, 85,
86, 94, 118, 135, 208
Rutledge, Henry M. (orator), 31, 191

Sabbath, Independence Day as, 43, 50,
110–11
St. Mery, Moreau de, 110
Saltonstall, Leverett, 155, 189, 202, 208
Schoepf, Johann, 64
Seider, Christopher, 59
Serapis (ship), 75
Shaw, Peter, 17, 113
Sign, 105, 175; defined, 101
Signal, 105; defined, 101
Signs, language of, 57, 85, 86, 104, 175,
206, 222
Slaves and slavery, 39, 94, 116, 222;
relation to Independence Day, 145–53
Smith, Sol, 143
Smith, William Laughton (orator), 49
Snowden, Nathaniel, 81, 117, 121
Society of the Cincinnati, Independence
Day and, 37, 61, 74, 159, 197
Sons of St. George (Philadelphia), 176
Stono Rebellion, 147
Street theater, 73. *See also* Independence
Day activities, theatrical
presentations
Strong, Caleb, 193, 195
Sullivan, James, 165
Sullivan's Island, battle of. *See* Fort
Moultrie, battle of
Symbol, 87, 101, 102, 105–6, 175; defined,
12, 231 n.34; architecture as, 74, 78–79;
eagle as, 78; George Washington as,
34, 92, 97, 158, 162, 176, 195, 207; ma-
nipulation of, 162–63; rising sun as, 71,
78; ship as, 71, 75–76, 79, 85, 166, 167,
168; words as, 12, 182, 200, 231 n.31

Thackera, William Wood, 137
Theatrical presentations. *See*
Independence Day activities
Toasts. *See* Independence Day activities
"Tories," and Independence Day, 23, 24,
26, 38–39, 184, 185, 234 nn.29, 31
Trade associations, and Independence
Day, 115–16, 221
Tradition, invented, 11
Tudor, William, 203–4
Turner, Victor, 54, 65, 66, 235 n.48